B-trees for BASIC

by Raymond Robertson

Library Of Congress Catalog Card Number: 91-50841

10 9 8 7 6 5 4 3 2 1

FOREWARD

Why read this book?

Time is one of the most valuable assets we have. You might very well ask "Why should I spend my time to learn what is in this book?"

This is one of those questions that is best answered by another question: "Why should a person go through math classes and learn how to divide, multiply and do other arithmetic operations when for very little money they can buy a calculator and simply punch buttons?"

The answer in both cases is the same. When you learn how something works fundamentally, you have complete control over it and you will never be lost when it comes to using anything based on that concept. People who do not have fundamental knowledge of what they are doing will spend their lives trying to remember which magic buttons they are supposed to punch in order to get the answers to their questions.

The uninformed leader

Unfortunately, there are businesses full of these people, with the leader of the office simply being the person that remembers the most menu commands. This gives rise to the observation that "In the land of the blind giants, the one-eyed midget is king." The uninformed who have responsible positions in business are doomed to waste enormous amounts of *time and money* dragging others down a blind path to uncertain destinations.

Fortunately, the people who read and understand books like the one in your hands will be replacing these people. In this case, you will not only learn database concepts; you will also be able to create, from scratch, your own database. You will know where every byte is and what it does.

If you intend to do any database work, the B-tree is unquestionably at the heart and soul of almost every major database you will encounter. In fact the code for the B-tree system you will analyze in this book, called "TeachBase", is a self-contained database system.

Software available

The B-tree system and all other programs listed and analyzed and in this book are available from the publisher on floppy. If you wish to send for the software it will save you a considerable amount of typing, and possible errors. Also available from the publisher is a program called BASIC-base, which is a much more advanced version of TeachBase. If you like TeachBase, it is highly recommended that you get BASIC-base as it will allow you to make your own custom database in a shorter amount of time. It also contains additional programs such as a program that allows you to jump into the middle of the B-tree at any point and start listing elements on the tree. We are sure you will find it more than worth the expense. You can write or call the publisher for more information, and there is also a discount coupon at the back of this book.

As a final note, TeachBase was developed using Microsoft's Quick BASIC. It can run in the interpreted mode without any changes on the MAC, MSDOS and UNIX operating systems (we used SCO Xenix for a test). It will not work with "GW BASIC" because of limitations in the language (although you could adapt it to work). We have also compiled the program to make sure it compiles on the different systems. In short, we have gone out of our way to make sure this is as "system independent" a program as possible.

Contact (you may order by phone or mail):

BALDAR
P.O. Box 4340
Berkeley, CA 94704 USA
Tel. (800) 367-0930 or (510) 841-2474
FAX: (510) 841-2695

Table Of Contents

Section I
Introduction

Section II
Defining & Constructing A B-tree

Section III
Using The Teachbase B-tree System

Section IV
Changing The B-tree System

Section V
Appendices

SECTION I

Introduction

1

Overview

VOCABULARY

We assume that the reader of this book understands the fundamental vocabulary of the BASIC language (commands like GOTO, RUN, etc.).

This publication is for people who understand BASIC terms and are now interested in getting information out to disk and back in the quickest and most orderly manner possible, even if the information is being sent to the disk in a disorganized manner.

the mailing list

As an example, you may want to input a large number of addresses at random and then want them printed out immediately in alphabetical order (without having to sort the addresses into order). Then you may want them printed out, again without having to wait for any sorting, in telephone code order, and then in some other order (for example, ordered according to a special ID code you input). You may also want to look up and edit an address in this disorganized list using what is scientifically one of the fastest possible lookup procedures available to programmers.

If this is your situation, then this is the book for you. There is no scientifically better solution available for the above problems than the one we present in this book, and *we present you not only with the theory but with the programs as well.*

ORGANIZATION OF BOOK

This is a practical, user-oriented book designed not only to give you a thorough understanding of the B-tree, but also to give you all the code in a working B-tree system.

working B-tree system

We need to name the working B-tree system that we are giving you in this book, so we will refer to it as the "TeachBase" system. We feel that the best way to approach the task before us is as follows:

1) *Section one:* This chapter where we will give you very general introduction.

2) *Section two:* We will then familiarize you with the B-tree structure by going through, with many diagrams, the logical steps in each of the major programs needed to run a B-tree (addition of items to the B-tree, deletion, search and listing).

3) *Section Three:* We will then analyze, line by line, the B-tree system presented in this book (the program is listed in appendix C).

4) *Section four:* We will then discuss the theory behind the B-tree, and show how to change the B-tree system presented in this book to meet your specific needs.

About Appendix A

BASIC file concepts in Appendix A

Because many books on the BASIC language do not devote a great deal of coverage to fundamental file opening and closing statements, we have furnished Appendix A, which explains all the "file concepts" the reader will need in understanding this book. This is for those of you who want to review the definitions of some of the fundamental BASIC terms pertinent to this book, such as how to open a file. If you are very experienced, you might want to skip the appendix and read on.

THE BIG PICTURE

B-tree name

A B-tree is a highly-organized method of storing data. Simply stated, a B-tree is a random access file with a record number, called a pointer, in each record that tells you what record to go to next in order to list all the records in the file in order. Discovered in 1970 by Rudolf

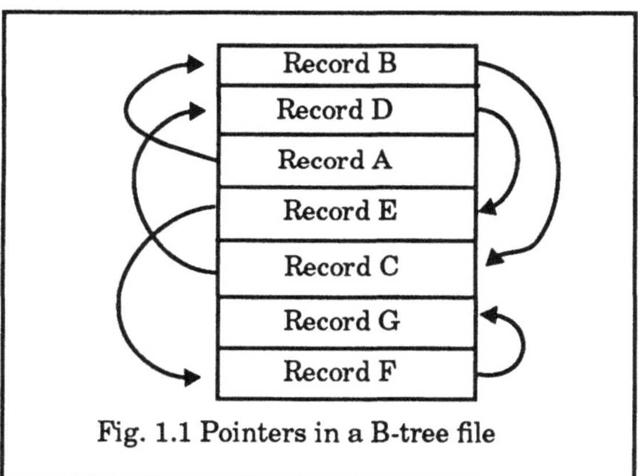

Fig. 1.1 Pointers in a B-tree file

Bayer (and independently discovered by Kaufman), this data structure takes its name from the first letter of Bayer, and the fact that you can best illustrate the relationship of the pointers by comparing them graphically to an upside-down tree. The upside-down tree analogy is so helpful in discussing the B-tree that major BASIC items (such as records) are assigned names like roots, branches, and leaves. The data stored in a B-tree can be accessed with amazing speed for additions, deletions, modifications, and other database management tasks.

Random addresses

The very big picture of how a B-tree is used is really very simple. Let's suppose you want to make a mailing list. You create a random access file called "people", and start inputting your addresses. Let's say the address names are in random order; thus the names are entered into your file in random order, creating a disorganized file of names.

Number of probes to find an address

At a later date you decide to retrieve a name. Now you are faced with the problem of locating your name in a giant disorganized file. One way of locating your name is to read every name from the start of the file until you find your desired name. This is obviously not a good method because if you have 100,000 names you would, on average, have to read through 50,000 names before you find the name you are looking for.

Another methodology is to first sort your file into alphabetical order, and then use some kind of probing method to find the desired name. This is faster, but it means that you would have to alphabetically sort your file every single time you got ready to search for a name. And you would still be faced with the problem of "How do I find a name if all I have is the phone number?" The B-tree is designed to solve these problems. Let's discuss a little further how a B-tree is used.

Keywords & Outside files:

The most common way to use a B-tree is to create a block of data which we call a keyword. This keyword is the same length for every entry because we are using a random access file, and random access file records have a fixed length. For data that is of variable length, such as pictures, sound, or memos, we can devise some sort of

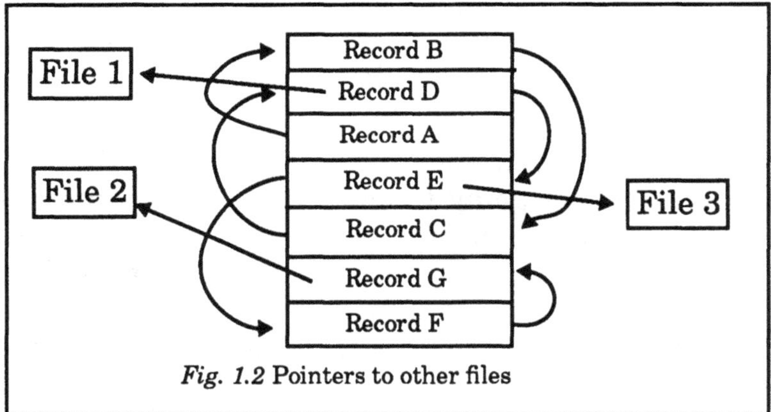

Fig. 1.2 Pointers to other files

pointer that points to a sequential file or another random access file where the "variable length" data related to this keyword is located. This method is very common. Note that a B-tree record would then have a pointer to the next B-tree record in order and a pointer, if desired, to an outside file.

Other B-trees:

The keywords that we have entered into our B-tree file are kept in order by pointers. To do this the program inspects the first characters of the keyword and then attaches to the keyword the appropriate pointer. Suppose, however, that we decide that we also want to keep the B-tree file in order according to characters 5 through 9 instead of the first characters. What do we do then? The solution is simple. We make another B-tree whose keywords simply have characters 5 through 9 and each keyword has a pointer telling it where it came from in the main file. You can have as many of these as you desire but, of course each time you make one you have more "overhead" or things you have to do each time you have action in the database. You can also write your program so you only have to type the keyword in once even though you make several B-trees from it.

Example:

Suppose you are ready to start a mailing list. You want

alpha & phone order

to keep the list in alphabetical order (by address), in phone code order, in zip code order and you want to be able to enter the list information at random.

First you would open your main file (call it "Btree1"), into which you are going to enter all your list information (which could be quite extensive) in random order. You have decided on a keyword which is 160 bytes long and you have decided to subdivide that keyword into five, 32 byte segments for the four lines of the address plus one line that has the zip code + phone. Any excess space will be filled with blanks. The first five bytes of the last 32 byte segment is for the zip code and the remaining 27 bytes are for the phone number.

You then open another random access file called "Btree2" which is going to keep track of your main list in zip code order. Each keyword in Btree2 will be 5 bytes for the keyword (which is the zip code) plus a pointer telling us what record we came from in Btree1.

Then you open a third random access file called "Btree3" which will keep track of your main list in telephone number order. Each keyword will be the 27 character phone number plus a pointer telling us where you came from in Btree1.

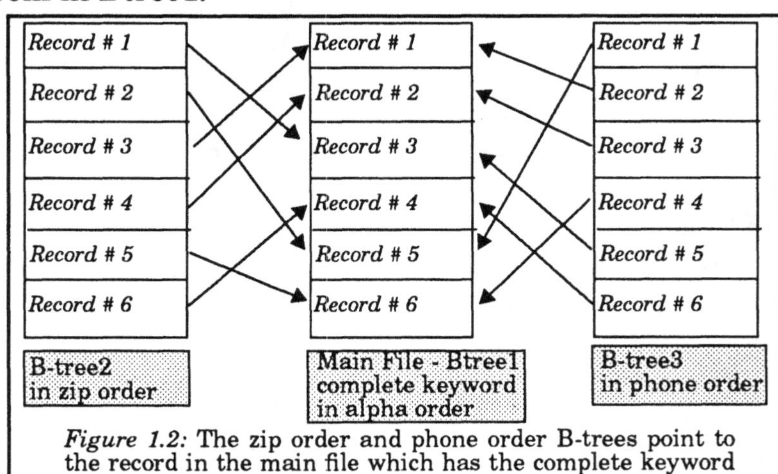

Figure 1.2: The zip order and phone order B-trees point to the record in the main file which has the complete keyword and is in alpha order.

The idea is simple. Every time you enter a keyword in the main file (Btree1) you put the zip code on Btree2 and the phone number on Btree3 and give each of them a pointer so they know where the main record is.

With the above scheme you can ask to see a address by simply typing in the zip code or typing the phone number or the address itself. Note that if you desired the records in the main file could also point to other variable length files such as pictures, etc.

This all sounds very simple, and you might say, "Why should I use a B-tree when I could probably just search through a random access file one record at a time and find my address?"

Here is the answer: The random keywords you gave the B-tree program were stored in the B-tree file in a way that is designed mathematically to allow the quickest possible retrieval. How quick is quick? Consider, for example, that you have two million addresses in your main file. How many records, on average, would you have to look at in order to find your address? If they are in random order, you would have to look at half the file, on average, or one million records (unless the address is not in the file and then it is the whole two million).

How quick is quick?

Now let's ask the question: How many records in a typical B-tree file do you have to look at in order to find your address record number or determine if the address exists? It depends on how the B-tree is designed but a common answer is: *never more than 7 (seven) records.* That's looking at seven records versus looking at a million: a considerable difference! In addition to all this, the B-trees are always in order so that you can immediately read out the entire main file one entry after another, whenever you wish, in zip code order, telephone code order or alphabetically. This is what is known as keeping your list in order in **real time** (i.e. no sorting necessary before you read the list out).

Other methods:

Immediate access to data

Technically, there are other methods for doing what the B-tree does. However, for a file of randomly-ordered items the B-tree is the professional's method of choice, by a very wide margin, for keeping large amounts of data in order. This is particularly true if your data is maintained dynamically; that is, if you constantly add or delete items and want the data maintained for immediate access after insertion or deletion. Appendix B is devoted to discussing some other methods that compete with the B-tree for those of you that want a more technical discussion.

SECTION II

Defining and Constructing a B-tree

2

Defining and Constructing a B-tree

B-TREE VOCABULARY

Before learning how to use a B-tree file, one must first understand how the B-tree is structured. In the next few chapters we will show that structure by following some of the algorithms that allow B-trees to fulfill their useful, everyday tasks. First, however, let's define some terms.

keyword definition
element definition
pointer definition

Let's say that the data that you want to put on the B-tree is called the "**keyword**". All keywords have the same length (number of characters). As a definition, let's say that an **element** is defined as our keyword plus any "pointers" associated with the keyword. A **pointer** is defined as either a record number or the file name of a foreign file. In short, the pointer is used to tell you where to go to next.

In our earlier discussion, each element in btree1 consisted of a keyword (the address) plus an element pointer that would point to the next record in the B-tree file. This, however, does not always have to be the case. The other B-trees (btree2 and btree3) had a keyword, a pointer that pointed to the main file, and then their element pointer.

Simplest B-tree

In theory, the simplest B-tree does not have any auxiliary B-trees or any foreign files to point to. For example, perhaps all you want to do is enter, at random, a large number of prices or bar code numbers from merchandise. You want to constantly keep these numbers in numerical order. In other words, you want to keep the list sorted in real time, which, as we stated in chapter one, means the list is instantly sorted as soon as you enter an item: you never have to stop and sort the file into order.

definition real time

We will use this simple example of a B-tree for our discussion and analysis. Thus, from now on you will not hear about pointing to other files, because it makes the illustrations unbearably cluttered, but remember that it is possible to incorporate this feature with no difficulty at all. Don't worry; the TeachBase program we give you toward the end of this book will allow you to point to other files.

"tree" analogy

We mentioned earlier that to better understand the relationship between the records in a B-tree file, people like to illustrate or diagram the records in a manner that looks like an upside-down tree. If you look at the top of

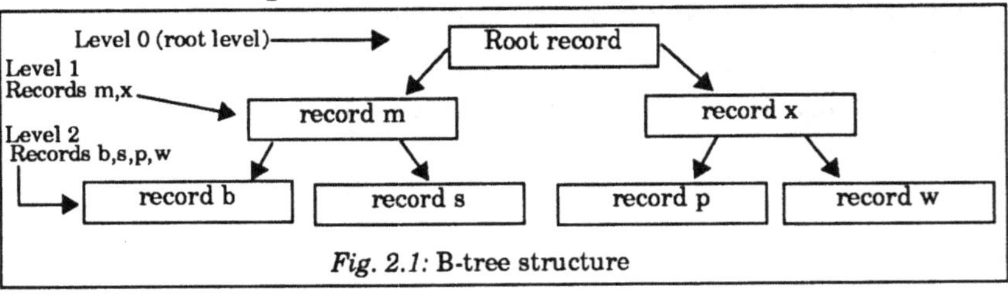

Fig. 2.1: B-tree structure

the diagram, which would be the root of the "tree", the record that occupies that position is indeed called the root. There can be only one root record. You should also note that it is convenient to refer to the "level" on which a record is located. The root record is the only record that can occupy level zero.

One other item we should bring up at this point is that each record in a B-tree might (and usually does) contain more than one element. So several keywords can fit in one B-tree record. We will now define each record in a B-tree file as a **page**. For every page, or record, in the B-tree there is one **page pointer** that is located at its end. This is used to transfer you to the next page, in order, that has keywords that are higher than the ones on your current page. I know all this new jargon sounds strange and confusing right now, but this is all part of the standard terminology used in discussing B-trees. Things will become understandable shortly. Just remember that a

page definition
page pointer definition

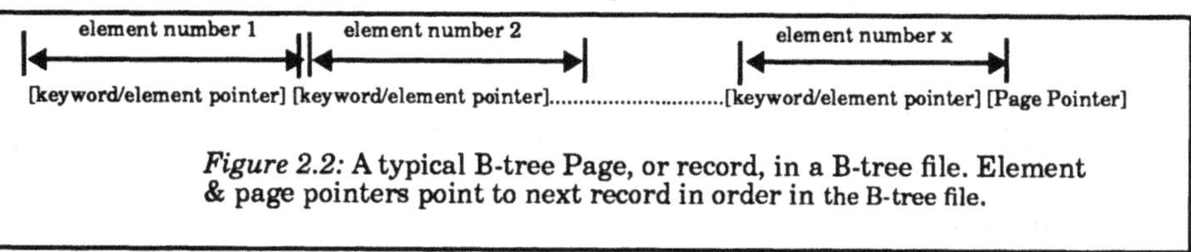

Figure 2.2: A typical B-tree Page, or record, in a B-tree file. Element & page pointers point to next record in order in the B-tree file.

record in a B-tree file is called a page, each page can contain several elements, and each element consists of a keyword plus a pointer. Of course, how many elements there are per page is determined by you, the programmer.

Another term is used to discuss how large the B-tree record is. The user defines what is called the **order**[1] of the B-tree. The order of a B-tree can be any number

Order: definition

1. There are a few terms in database literature that are defined differently. Order is one of them. The original definition is the one that we are using. Since then, it has also become popular to define order as the maximum number of descendants any page may have.

greater than 1. It is the minimum number of elements any non-root page *must* contain. Also, the maximum number of elements any page may contain is defined as twice the order. The root page is the only exception to this rule, since it may contain as little as one element.

SHORT REVIEW OF TERMS

Let's do a short review of some of the major points we have covered.

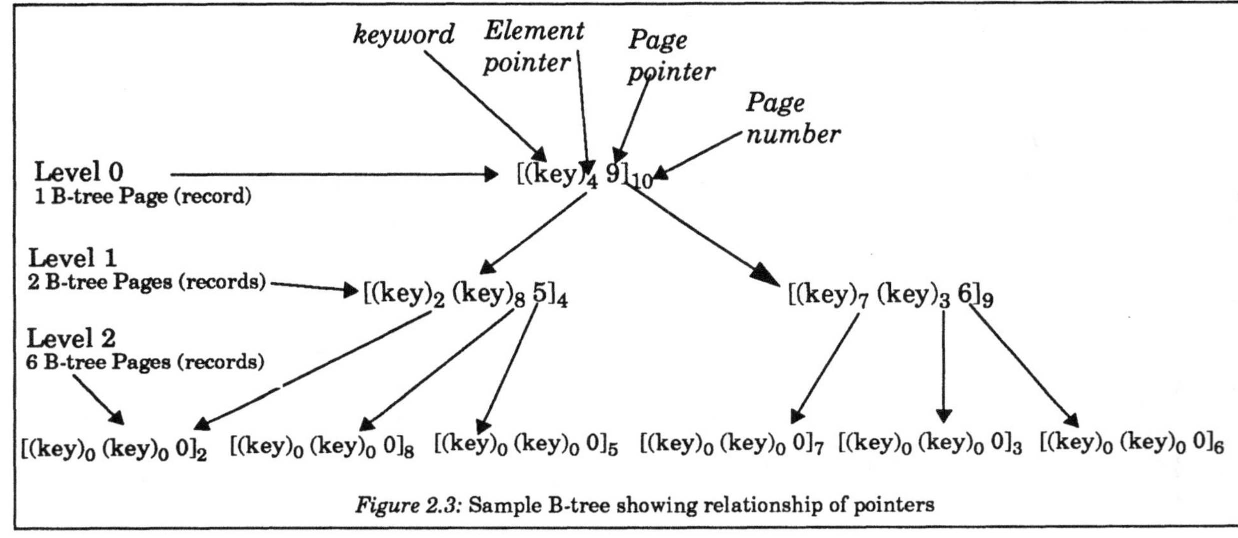

Figure 2.3: Sample B-tree showing relationship of pointers

A B-tree file is a random access file. The records in the B-tree file have a particular relationship, which we will be detailing in this book. A record in a B-tree file is called a page. Within each page there exist one or more elements.

summation of terminology

An element consists of a keyword plus an element pointer. The number of characters in the keyword is defined by the user at the creation of the B-tree. All elements have the same number of characters.

Since the number of elements on a B-tree page is twice the order, the length of the B-tree page is determined by the "ORDER" assigned by the programmer at the creation of the B-tree. The length of each page will be the order multiplied by the element length, plus the length of the page pointer at the end of the record. At the end of the page is one and only one page pointer. A pointer, in our simple B-tree, is simply the page number of another page in the B-tree. All pointer numbers are stored in a page using the BASIC short integer (MKI$& CVI) format, so they are all the same length.

no keywords

In Figure 2.3, we say "key" where the actual keyword would be. The square brackets represent pages. Outside the square brackets, to the lower right, is the page number for the page. We write the element pointer, which comes right after the keyword, as a subscript to the lower right of each keyword in the diagram, and the page pointer as the last number inside the page brackets.

Figure 2.3 is designed to show the locations of all the pointers. As you can see, pointers are of two varieties. There are element pointers, and *one* page pointer. Both of these pointers point to a page on the next lower level.

USING THE B-TREE

Let's suppose we have a B-tree already constructed. What do we want to do with the B-tree? Let's make a list of the main functions we want:

(1) Search and find any desired element on the B-tree.

Potential uses for a B-Tree

(2) List, in order, all the elements on the B-tree.

(3) Put a new element on the B-tree.

(4) Delete an element from the B-tree.

Note we are using the phrase "on the B-tree" but we really mean "in the B-tree file". Programmers become used to thinking of the file's tree-like structure and therefore speak of putting something "on the tree", when they really mean adding an element (keyword + element pointer) to a page (record) in the B-tree file.

In order to accomplish the above four tasks, we obviously need to write a program to execute them. Before we can write a program, however, we need to understand exactly how a B-tree works. We'll begin this analysis of a B-tree's workings by discussing how a keyword is searched for on a B-tree.

3

Searching a B-tree

Algorithm about to be discussed:
(1) Search and find any desired element on the B-tree.
(2) List, in order, all the elements on the B-tree.
(3) Put a new element on the B-tree.
(4) Delete an element from the B-tree.

To simplify things, in the B-tree we are about to analyze, we will not be pointing to any external files. To further simplify things, let's say that our element consists of a keyword that is simply a positive integer number plus, of course, any element pointer demanded by the B-tree structure. Thus the purpose of our simple B-tree will be to keep all the numbers we input in order and allow immediate printout, look-up and deletion.

We will keep the size of the keyword a fixed length by storing the integer in BASIC's short integer (MKI$) format, which converts all positive integers from 0 to 32,000 into a two-character expression. We will do the same for any pointers.

Inspecting a B-tree after entries are made.
Let's look at the B-tree after it has a few numbers entered. Because there are a lot of entries, we will graphically illustrate only the keywords (which are simply integer numbers), and not the element and page pointers.

Since a B-tree is just a file of several pages (records), there is no harm in our diagramming the pages in whatever manner we wish. We wish to illustrate what is in our B-tree file by listing the pages in the previously mentioned "upside-down tree" arrangement, as depicted in Figure 3.1:

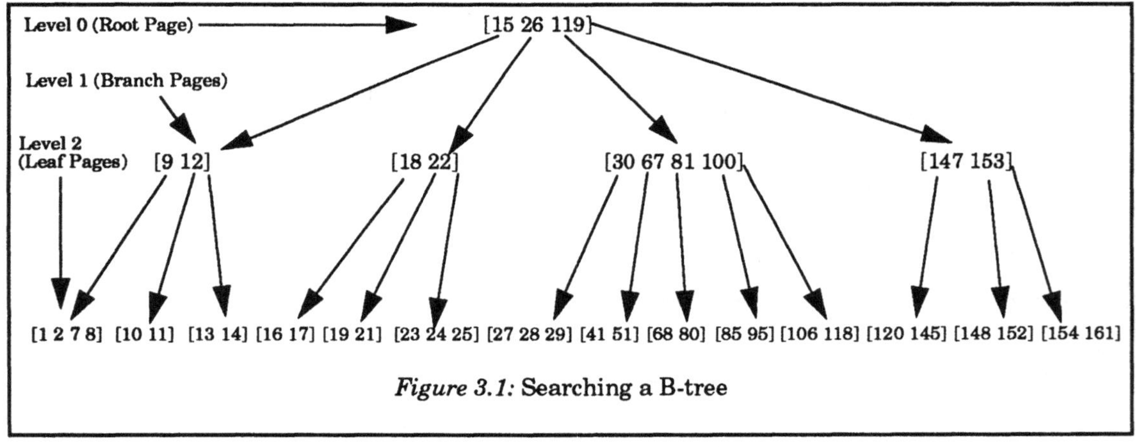

Figure 3.1: Searching a B-tree

Now let's inspect Figure 3.1. We'll describe the B-tree, defining terms as we go, and then review what we have seen.

root definition

Fig. 3.1 is a three-level B-tree whose keywords are 45 integers in the range 1 through 161. The top level, or **root,** consists of a single page, the root page, having three keywords on it: 15, 26, and 119. The bottom, or **leaf**, level consists of 14 pages. In any tree, the levels

definition leaf

between the root level and the leaf level are called **branch levels**, and the pages on these levels are called **branch pages** (also sometimes called "node" pages). Like the root page (unless the root page is the only page on the tree), branch pages are created with element pointers and page pointers, which point to pages on the level below.

branch levels
branch pages

pointers

Notice that the keywords, which are integers, are arranged left to right on the pages in ascending order. Keep in mind that except for the pages on the lowest level, every integer is associated with an **element pointer** which points to a page on the next lower level. Further note that all the elements on the page pointed to are *less than* the element that pointed to that page. At the end of each page there is a **page pointer** pointing to a page on the next level, all of whose elements are *greater than* any element on the page with the pointer. The pointer associated with each element, by definition, is called an element pointer. Each element has only one element pointer. The pointer on the end of each branch page is defined as the page pointer for that page. Each branch page has only one page pointer.

element pointer

page pointer

Short summary

I think you are getting the idea. Every element on a branch page has an element pointer, which points to a page whose elements are all *less than* the value of the element doing the pointing. The page pointer, at the end of the page, does the opposite. It points to a page whose elements all have a value *higher than* any element on the page. This arrangement of pointers makes searching possible and quite easy.

How does this arrangement of pointers make searching possible? Let's say we want to search for a certain keyword. We start with the root page (you always start searching with the root page). To search any page for a

start search

given keyword, we inspect each element on the page (going left to right or lowest value to highest value) until we either find our sought-for keyword, or failing to find it:

(1) Come to an element whose keyword is greater than the sought-for keyword, or

(2) Determine, after reading all the elements, that the sought-for keyword is larger than any on the page being searched.

following branch element pointer

If we are not at the bottom level, what happens? In example (1), where we find a keyword larger than our keyword, we do the following: go to the page indicated by the element pointer associated with this first keyword that is larger than our sought-for keyword. Then we start doing a search of that page. We continue this until we get to the bottom (or leaf) level of the B-tree.

Following branch page pointer

In example (2), where our keyword is larger than any on the page, we go to the page indicated by the page pointer associated with that page, and continue the search there.

leaf level & end of search

If either of these two cases occur, *and* we are on the bottom level, we know that the sought-for keyword is not on the tree because there are no pointers on the leaf level, and we have run out of elements (actually, there are pointers, but the values are all set to zero because there is nowhere to point to).

Search example:

search example

Suppose we want to find the element 68 in Figure 3.1. We start searching on the root page. 68 is greater than 15 and 26, so we proceed past them to 119. 68 is less than 119, so we follow 119's pointer and search the page to which it points. On that page, we read past 30 and 67 and go to the page pointed to by 81; there we find 68. If, however, we had been searching for 69, we would have known it was absent after finding an 80 on the leaf page.

other B-trees

If you want to be extremely technical, a B-tree does not have to be a search tree (a numerically, alphabetically or otherwise ordered B-tree), but we are not interested in B-trees that are not search B-trees. A search B-tree can be in either ascending or descending order. Since a B-tree in descending order is simply the opposite of an ascending B-tree, we describe only the ascending B-tree. Figure 3.2 is a flow chart of the search through a B-tree for a keyword.

finding root page

The pointer structure that makes searching a B-tree systematic and efficient also makes it possible to easily read the tree in ascending or descending order. We will see this in the next chapter.

As a programming concern, also note that the page number of the root page is subject to change, as new roots are formed and the tree grows in height (we will see this later when we learn how B-trees are formed). This creates a problem when we quit the program and close the B-tree file, because we lose everything in memory, including the location of the root page. To solve this problem, we sacrifice the first record in the B-tree file and use it to store a pointer that tells us where the root page is.

In database literature, and in the rest of this book, you will frequently find terms from the field of geneology used. Suppose you are looking at a family tree. Select any person on the tree. This person is obviously the child of the persons above them, their parents. You also can say that all persons above this child are the child's ancestors. Expect to see these terms child, parent and ancestor used. e.g. the element pointer of one element points to that element's child, etc.

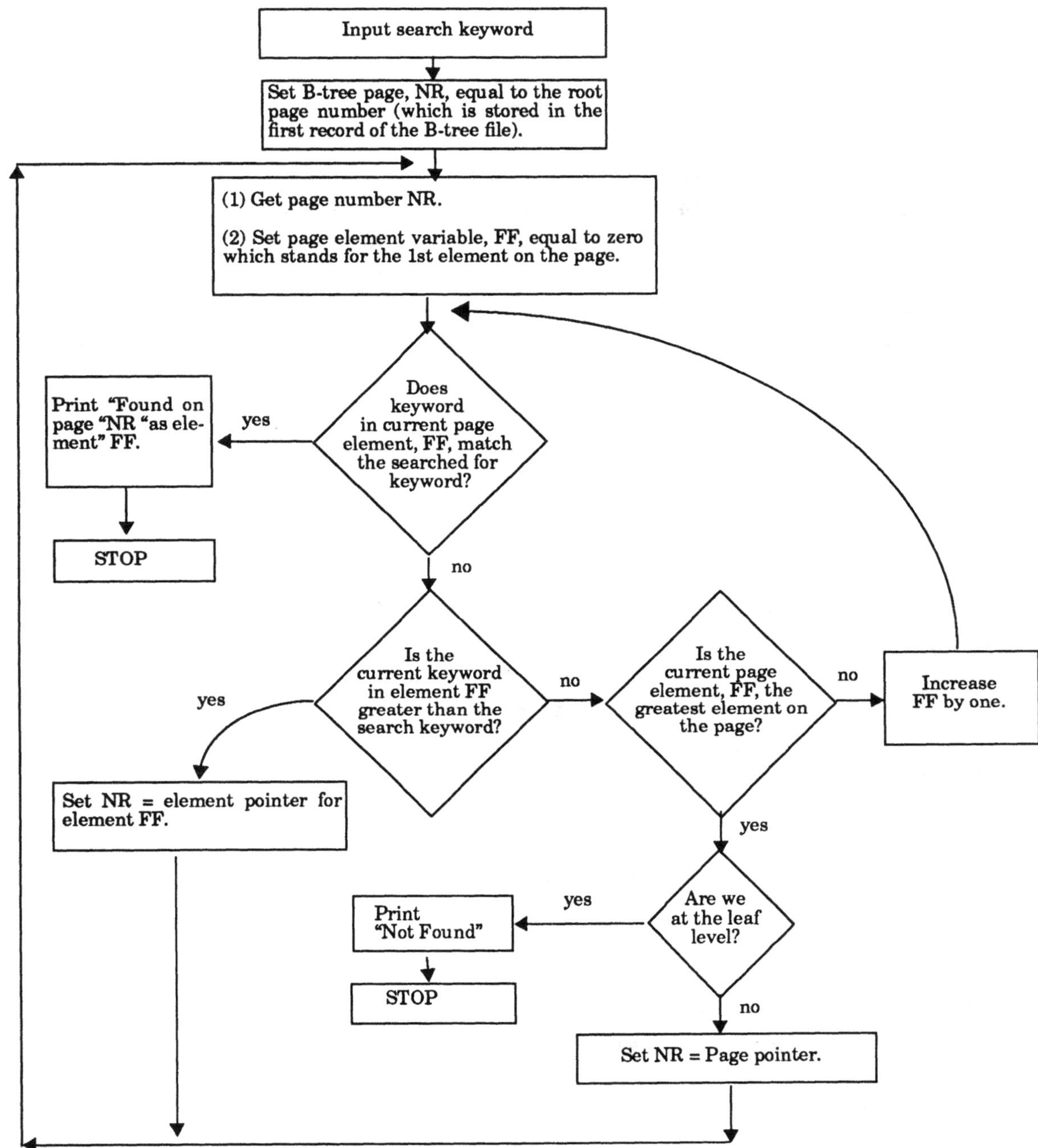

Figure3.2. Searching for a keyword.

4

Listing Elements on a B-tree

Algorithm about to be discussed:
(1) Search and find any desired element on the B-tree.
(2) List, in order, all the elements on the B-tree.
(3) Put a new element on the B-tree.
(4) Delete a element from the B-tree.

LISTING THE B-TREE

(Listing the elements on the B-tree)

Listing-definition

Listing a B-tree means reading its elements in ascending order. We accomplish this task by a simple algorithm. Note that the B-tree just described has its pointers arranged so that the page with the smallest elements is furthest left, on the lowest level. It is reached by starting at the root page and following the *element* pointers from the first element on each page to a page on the next-lowest level. Thus, when we reach the lowest level, we find the page where

dropping to the lowest element

the smallest elements are stored. Similarly, we reach the page with the largest elements by starting at the root and following the *page* pointers of each page until we come to a page on the leaf level.

If we drop to the lowest keyword on the B-tree and then start reading keywords, we find that we can read all the keywords in keyword order, as diagrammed in Figure 4.1. By following the diagram arrows from the smallest to the largest keyword on the B-tree, we get a readout of tree keywords in ascending order. By following the diagram arrows backwards from the greatest to the smallest keyword on the tree, we get a readout of the tree keywords in descending order.

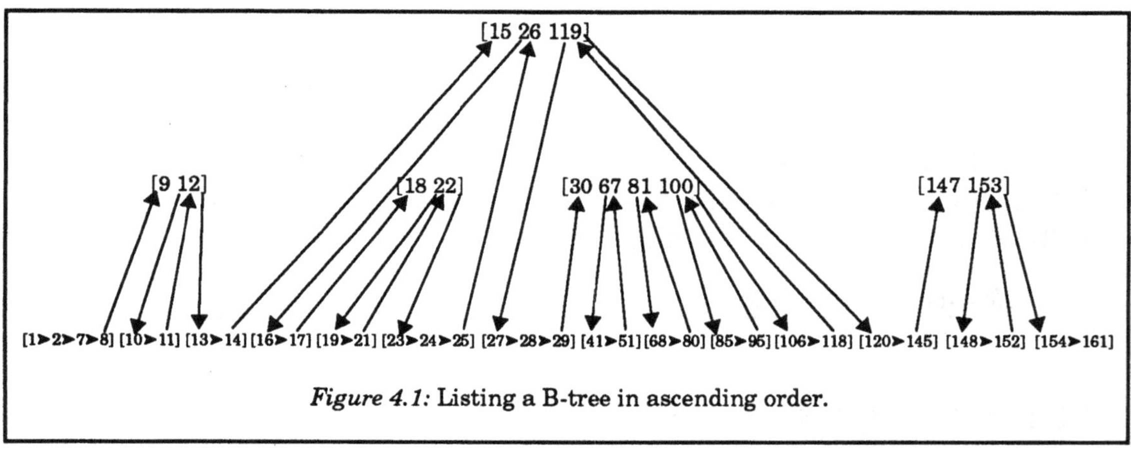

Figure 4.1: Listing a B-tree in ascending order.

reading elements

Figure 4.1 clearly depicts what the listing algorithm does. To get a readout in ascending order, we drop from the root to the lowest page and the lowest keyword on that page (the number 1). As shown by the small arrowheads, we readout all the keywords on this smallest leaf in sequential order and ascend to the page above it to readout the keyword that pointed to our leaf (the number 9). Then we follow the element pointer of the next keyword on the page (the number 12) to the leaf it points to. After reading that leaf, we again ascend, and this time there are no more elements. So we follow the page pointer. We repeat this process until we have read all the keywords in the leaf page pointed to by the page pointer (the number 14 is the last such keyword).

We call the process just described **ascending from a leaf**. Ascending from a leaf is no longer possible when we have just read a leaf pointed to by a page pointer. In this case, we **ascend from a branch**. In Figure 4.1 we can see that the root page is above our branch page, so we go to the root page and read the number 15. At this point we have read all the keywords below and including the number 15. We then move over to the next keyword (the number 26) and, following the element pointers starting with number 26's element pointer, we drop to the lowest keyword on the leaf page (the number 16). Then we repeat the above keyword reading procedure until we have read all the keywords below and including the number 26. We continue this until all the keywords are read.

ascending from a leaf

ascending from a branch.

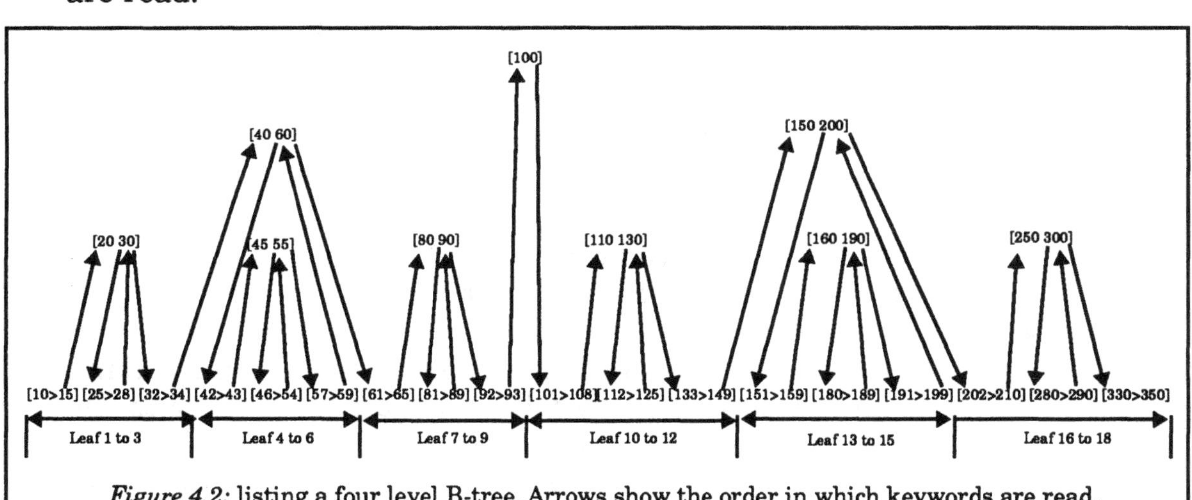

Figure 4.2: listing a four level B-tree. Arrows show the order in which keywords are read.

B-trees with many levels:

Suppose there is another branch level in our B-tree, as in Figure 4.2, and we have just finished reading the

child branch

number 34 on the third leaf. We are now in a place where we have read all the keywords on the third leaf and all the keywords on the lower branch (called the **child branch**) - in this case the pair [20 30] is the child branch of the pair [40 60]). We have also read those keywords pointed to by the page pointer of the child branch [20 30].

ancestor branch

dropping from an ancestor branch

We now must ascend to a higher branch level than [20 30]. Therefore, we must go to the branch above [20 30], called the **ancestor branch**, to read the keyword that pointed to the child branch (in this case the number 40). After reading that keyword, we take the element pointer of the next element in the page (in this case the number 60's element pointer) and descend all the way to leaf level to read the smallest unread leaf. To find that leaf, we drop from the ancestor branch to the next-lowest level (the pair [45 55]), and drop to the leaf level by following the element pointer on the first unread element (in this case 45). You can see how this process will work on as large a tree as you can grow.

ascend to ancestor

The concept is this: each time we drop down to the leaf page from an ancestor keyword, we read in ascending order all the pages lower than the ancestor keyword. After that, we read the ancestor keyword, then we move over in the page to the next pointer and repeat the process. When we ascend to an ancestor branch, if we find that all the keywords on this page have been read and that we have already followed the page pointer to the smallest unread leaf page, we need to ascend to another branch. Therefore, this ancestor becomes the child branch, and we repeat the process by ascending to the ancestor branch of this new child branch.

final reading

I am sure you get the idea. We keep repeating the ascending process until we find an ancestor branch with unread keywords or, if all the keywords have been read, one whose page pointer we have not yet followed to leaf level. This process continues until we find ourselves at the root page and know that the root page pointer has already been used. At that point we are done because all the keywords on the tree have been read.

MARKING POSITION ON BRANCH PAGES:

The Listing Variables (TV, NO And NR Arrays)

need for listing variables

You may say; "all this sounds fine, but how do we know what page to ascend to if all the pointers are going down?!" The simple solution is that when we drop to a leaf we keep track of what pages and what elements we have read with some variables.

For our discussion, we will use the variables that will appear in the TeachBase program you will get later in the book. There are three arrays and one array-indexing variable used to keep track of things:

ST variable

ST ≡ Stacking variable; it indicates the level under discussion.

NR(ST) variable

NR(ST) ≡ The page number at level ST that you passed through on your way down. Note that there can only be one page number at level ST that you pass through on your way down.

TV(ST) variable

TV(ST) ≡ The next element to be read in page NR(ST).

NO(ST) variable

NO(ST) ≡ The number of elements in page NR(ST).

Using the stacking variable.

root level means ST=0

As we read down to the leaf level (originally from the root page, and subsequently from each branch page) we use the stacking variable, **ST**. We start by setting ST=0 at the root level, and each time we drop to a new level, we increase ST by one. If we go back up a level, we decrease ST by one. Thus ST always tells us what level we are on. Also, each time we start at a branch that we

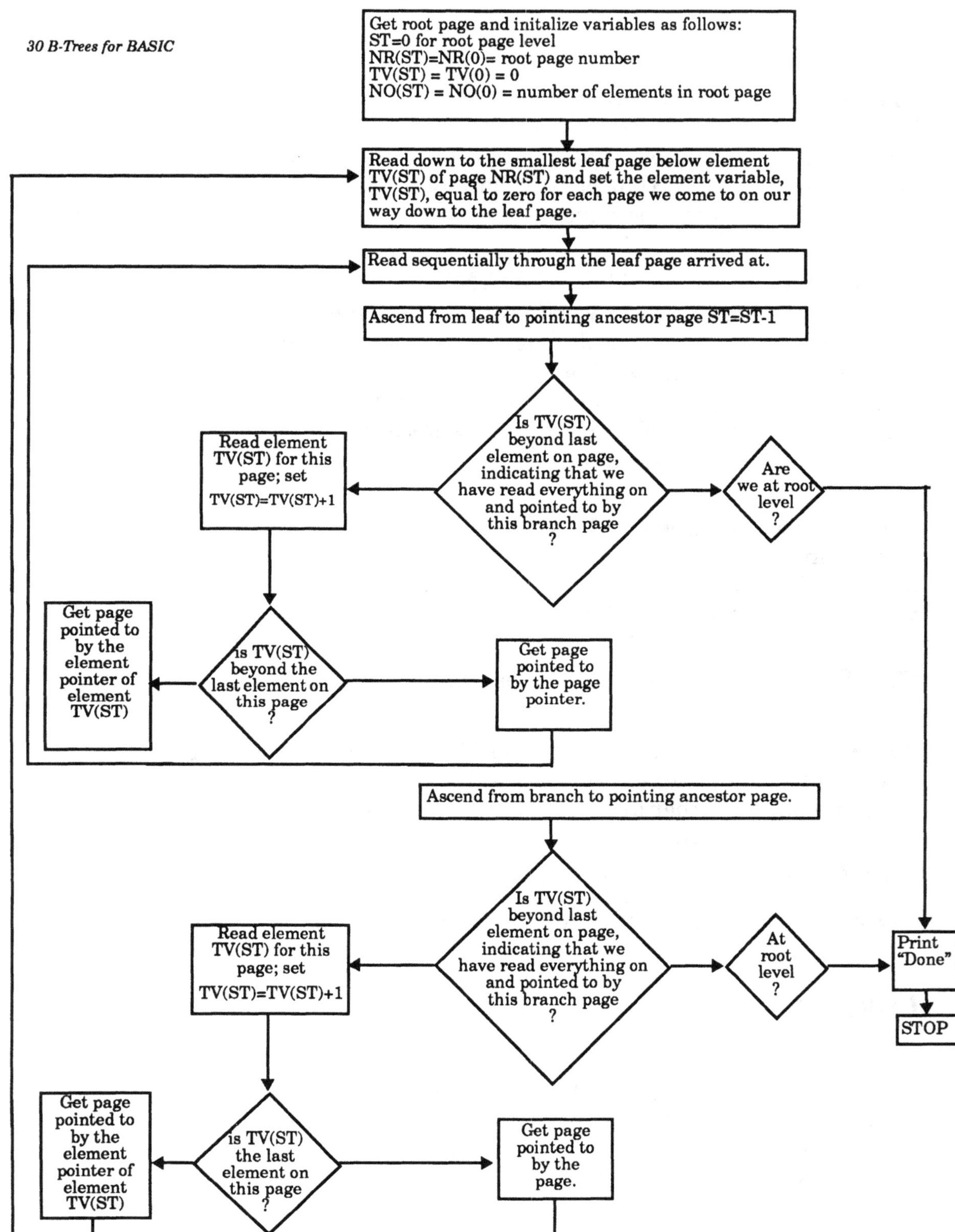

Figure 4.3: Listing a B-tree in ascending order.

are going to drop to the leaf level from, we assign NR(ST) the page number. Thus NR(0) will always equal the root page number and the other values of NR(ST) will change as we drop from different branch pages. This strategy allows us to save, for later backtracking, the trail we followed in reaching leaf level.

initalize NR(st)

NO(ST) is the element-counting variable. It tells us how many elements a page contains. Therefore, when we come to a page while descending to leaf level, we set NO(ST) equal to the number of elements that page contains.

initalize NO(st)

TV(ST) is used to tell us how far we have read into a page. It works in this manner: when we first come to a page while descending to leaf level, we set TV(ST) to zero. This indicates that on level ST we have not read any of the elements. When we first ascend to this page, we read the first element and its pointer and add one to TV(ST). This continues until we ascend and find that TV(ST)=NO(ST). When NO(ST)=TV(ST), we have obviously read all the pointers on the page: one for each element plus the page pointer (Remember that TV(ST) was first set equal to zero. When we get to NO(ST)=TV(ST) we have actually read n+1 elements, where n is the number of elements on the page). When NO(ST)=TV(ST) we must ascend to the next level above (if there is one) since we have read and followed all pointers on the page.

initalize TV(ST)

Using the variables in the ascending procedure.
The whole procedure of ascending, of course, occurs once you have read all elements on a leaf page. Once all the leaf elements are read the following occurs:

ascending procedure

1) We take our stacking variable ST and subtract one from it.
2) We then find our page number from NR(ST) and get the page. Note that there will only be one page for

NR(ST) because there is only one page on level ST that we descended through on our way down.

3) We then look at TV(ST), which tells us the next element to be read in the page. If TV(ST)=NO(ST) then we have read that entire page, plus the page pointer and we need to ascend to the next-highest page. We then go to Step 1 (above) to ascend to the level above. If NO(ST) does not equal TV(ST), then we read out the element TV(ST) and increase TV(ST) by one. If TV(ST) is not now equal to NO(ST), then we proceed to step 4 where we follow the element pointer of element TV(ST); otherwise we follow the page's page pointer.

4) We are now ready to descend to the leaf level again. Note that this means that we follow a trail different from the one by which we previously descended to leaf level. As we descend, adding one to ST each time we go down a level, we set TV(ST) equal to zero, NO(ST) equal to the elements on each new page, and NR(ST) equal to the page number. Note that although the levels below the page from which we descend are re-initializing TV(ST), NO(ST), and NR(ST), or the levels above the page from which we descend the values of TV(ST) and NO(ST) will be untouched.

Thus we can easily read the elements stored on a B-tree in ascending order. Moreover, using a stacking variable to mark our trail as we read down a B-tree allows us to search for a given element on the tree, and then read the rest of the elements sequentially from the found element onward.

search + listing possible

It is sometimes mistakenly believed that the B-tree structure allows for search, but not for subsequent listing of B-tree elements in order. *We must emphasize that this is not true.* Indeed, one can search for and find an element on a B-tree, and then list the tree in either direction from the found element.

5

Adding Elements to a B-tree

Algorithm about to be discussed:

(1) Search and find any desired element on the B-tree.
(2) List, in order, all the elements on the B-tree.
(3) Put a new element on the B-tree.
(4) Delete an element from the B-tree.

ADDING ELEMENTS TO A B-TREE

(Generating a B-tree of order 2)

We will now examine adding elements to a B-tree of Order 2 in a step-by-step manner. We choose Order 2 because it is the smallest order and easiest to diagram. Order 2 means that the fewest number of elements on a non-root page is 2 and the maximum number of elements on any page is 4.

Again, let's say that each keyword on the B-tree will simply be a positive integer number.

Step 1

$[(22)_0\ 0]_2$

Figure 5.1: Step 1

Refer to figure 2.3 for the convention we are using in our figure notation. We start the tree with a random number, 22, placed in the root page, which is page number two. We begin with page two, because we want to reserve page one for storing the record number of the current root page. We need this storage location because, as the growing tree acquires new pages, other pages become the root page at some stage in the tree's development. In order to access an element on the tree, we must always begin our search for the element at the root, so we must always know where the root is. Therefore, every time we form a new root, we store its page number on page one. For fast programming access, the best thing to do is to store the page number of the root in a variable in memory. As long as the program is running it remains available, but you must store it on disk in record 1 of the B-tree file when you decide to quit the program.

root page

Step 2

$[(12)_0\ (22)_0\ (27)_0\ (48)_0\ 0]_2$

Figure 5.2: Step 2

Here we have added the elements 12, 27, and 48 to the tree. They go to the root page, the only page in the tree, and are stored in numerical order. Since the tree is of order 2, any page can hold a maximum of four elements. Hence, page two is full, and the addition of another element forces the **splitting** of this root page to form another page as well as a new root page – which happens in step three.

full page

definition splitting

Step 3

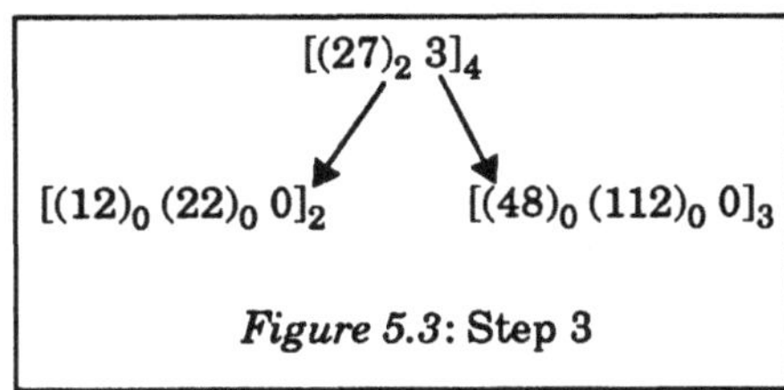

Figure 5.3: Step 3

We have added 112 to page two. Since page 2 was full, the addition of a new element has forced it to split and form a new page (page 3), with the middle element, 27, **lifted** to form a new root page (page 4).

page splitting

lifted definition

In general, for a tree of order N, the maximum on a page would be 2N elements. This means that when a B-tree page is full, it always contains an even number of elements. When the addition of an element leads to page splitting, the first N of the elements are retained on the original page, and the last N elements form the new page. The odd middle element is lifted onto the level above.

middle element

Thus, the addition of 112 to the full page has resulted in this page configuration: [(12) (22) (27) (48) (112)].

Since a page is allowed to hold a maximum of four elements, it splits to form a new root, page 4, consisting of the middle element 27. The first two remaining elements stay on page 2, and the last two go to the newly-formed page 3.

For a tree of order 2, this splitting operation results in the formation of a branch page, because we need pointers to lead from the branch to the pages below it. We need an element pointer associated with the element 27 to point to the page holding elements less than 27. We also need a page pointer associated with page 4 to point to the page holding elements greater than 27. These

create element pointers

pointers are written in our figures according to the convention we established with Figure 2.3, Chapter 2.

Step 4

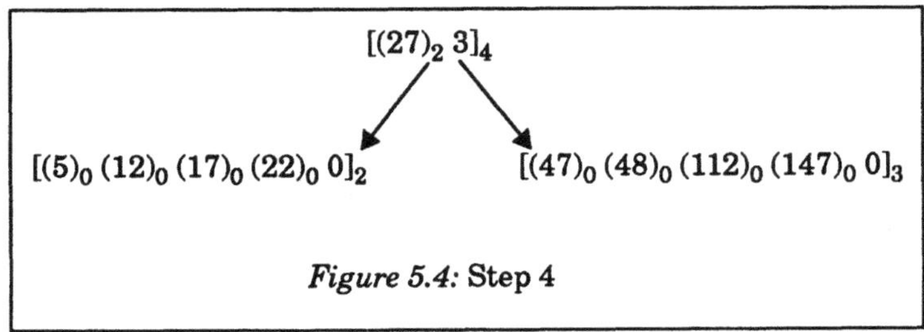

Figure 5.4: Step 4

always add elements to leaf page

Adding elements on a B-tree always takes place on a leaf page. In Figure 5.4 we have added the elements 47, 5, 17, and 147 to the tree. This has caused both page 2 and 3 to become full. The next element added to the tree will cause page splitting because it will be put into one of these leaf pages. It is very important to understand how all elements added to a tree must go to a leaf page. Elements are added to a root or branch page only due to splitting of the lower page. To add the elements 47, 5, 17, and 147 to the tree, we start on the root page and compare the element to be added with each element on the page until either:

1) We find an element greater than the element to be added. In this case we know that the element to be added must go on the page pointed to by the greater element. We travel to the page pointed to by that element, and since it is a leaf page, we place the element to be added there; or

2) We come to the end of the page without finding an element greater than the one to be added. In this case, we know the element to be added is greater than any on the page and must go to the page pointed to by that page. We travel to the pointed-to page, and since it is a leaf page, we place the element to be added there.

Note that the addition of elements 5 and 17 requires procedure 1, and that the addition of elements 47 and 147 requires procedure 2. In either case, however, the new element always goes on a leaf page.

That any added element must go to a leaf page is illustrated in Step 5 when we add 24 to the tree. We might expect to put it on the root page in front of 27, but it goes to the leaf page, 2, which then splits.

Step 5

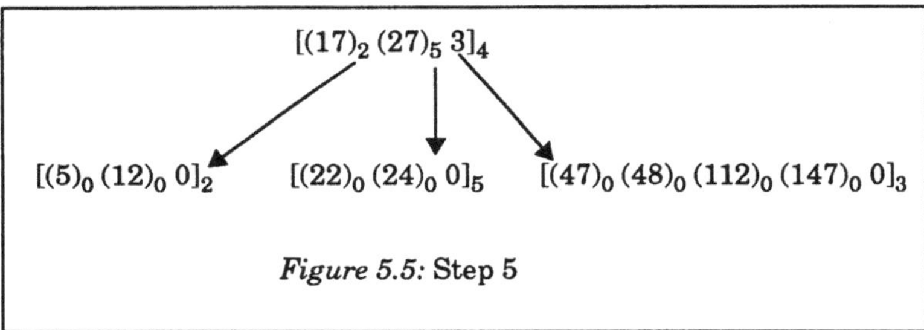

Figure 5.5: Step 5

Here the tree has been changed by the addition of the element 24. When adding 24, we start comparing on the root page. 24 is less than 27, so we follow the element pointer associated with element 27 to page 2. We place 24 at the end (where it belongs) of page 2 and, at this point, page 2 now looks like this: [(5) (12) (17) (22) (24)]

This causes page 2 to overflow, so that it splits to form page 5, which receives the elements 22 and 24. The elements 5 and 12 remain on page 2, and the middle element, 17, is lifted to the page above (root page 4), where it is placed in its proper position in front of element 27.

new page created

The creation of this new page requires some modifications in the pointer structure of the tree. Note that when 17 is lifted to the root page it is furnished with a pointer pointing to page 2, and that the pointer associated with 27 is changed to point to the newly created page (page 5).

Step 6

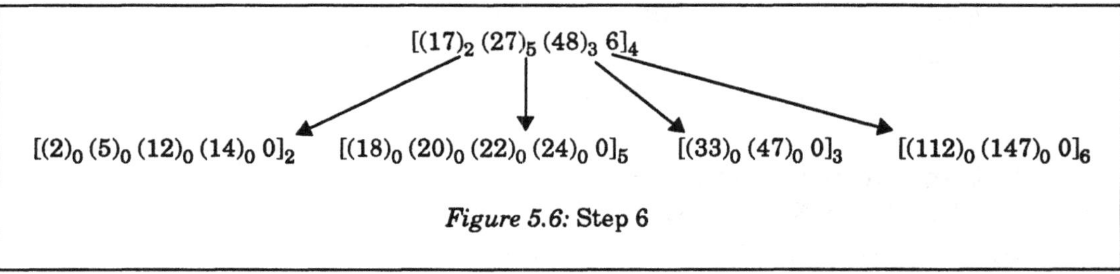

Figure 5.6: Step 6

simple addition = no splitting occurs

Here the tree has been modified by the addition of the elements 33, 14, 2, 18, and 20. The simple addition of the elements 14, 2, 18, and 20 requires no splitting. The elements 2 and 14 have been placed, after searching down from the root, in their proper positions on page 2. Likewise, the elements 18 and 20 have been placed in their proper positions on page 5. This has filled both of the pages to their capacity of four elements. The addition of element 33 to the filled page 3, however, has produced the following overflow: [(33) (47) (48) (112) (147)].

This overflow has resulted in the splitting of page 3 to form a new page (page 6). The elements 33 and 47 stay on page 3, while elements 112 and 147 go to the new page 6. The middle element, 48, is lifted to the root page, where it takes its place following 27. Note that the middle element has been furnished with a pointer indicating page 3, and that the pointer at the end of page 4 has been changed to point to the newly-created page 6.

Step 7

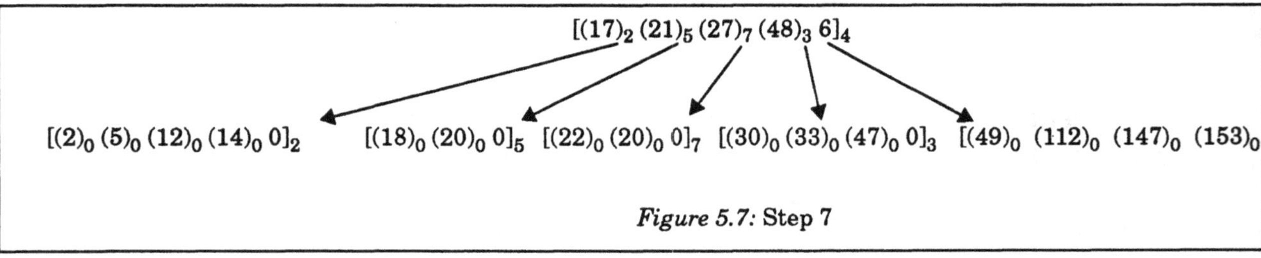

Figure 5.7: Step 7

We now add 153, 21, 30, and 49. The addition of 21 has

resulted in the splitting of page 5 to form a new page, 7. The pointer on 27 is changed to point to page 7, and the middle element, 21, has been furnished with a pointer to page 5 and lifted to the root page, which is now filled to its capacity.

Step 8

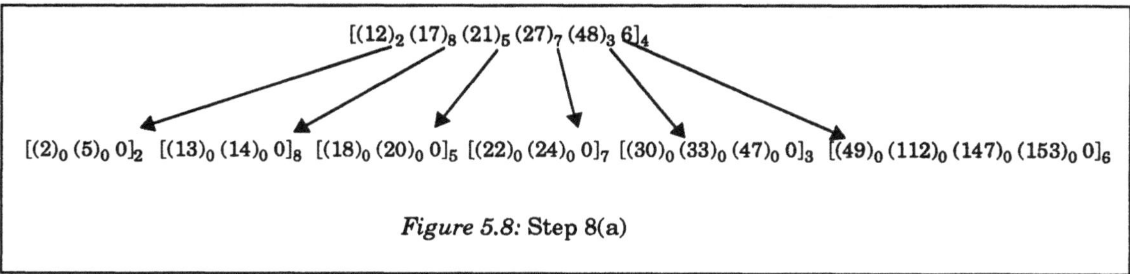

Figure 5.8: Step 8(a)

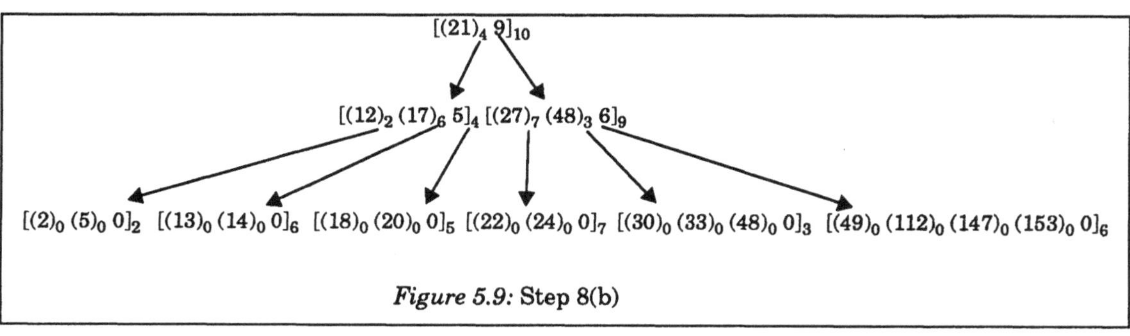

Figure 5.9: Step 8(b)

In Figure 5.8 and Figure 5.9 the addition of the element 13 to the tree has initiated a chain of splitting, leading to the root. First, 13 is added to the full page 2, which splits to form the new page, page 8. The middle element from the splitting process, 12, is furnished with a pointer pointing to the old page, page 2, and is lifted to page 4. The element 17 in page 4, which previously pointed to page 2, now points to this new page. This is the intermediate configuration represented in Figure 5.8.

Since page 4 is full, adding the element 12 causes it to split and form a new page (page 9), and to lift the overflowing middle element, 21, to form a new root page,

new root page

page 10. In the formation of this root, note that the element pointer associated with 21 points to the old page, page 4, while the page pointer associated with the new root page (page 10), points to the newly created page 9. Also note that when 21 was lifted from the overflowing page 4, its pointer stayed behind to act as the new page pointer associated with page 4. After the splitting, the page pointer that page 4 had before becomes the page pointer associated with the newly created page, page 9.

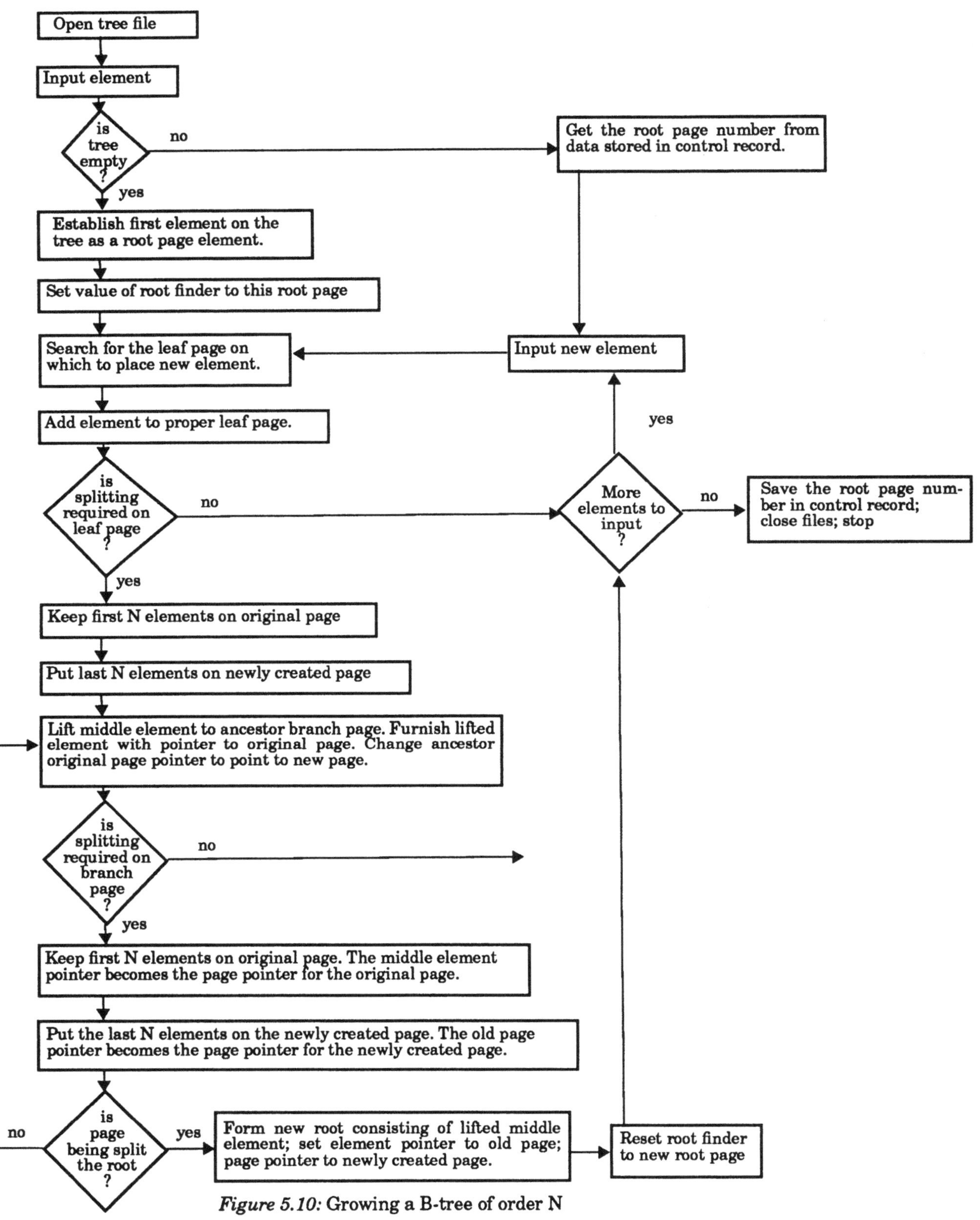

Figure 5.10: Growing a B-tree of order N

6

Deleting Elements from a B-tree

Algorithm about to be discussed:
(1) Search and find any desired element on the B-tree. *(2) List, in order, all the elements on the B-tree.* *(3) Put a new element on the B-tree.* *(4) Delete an element from the B-tree.*

DELETING ELEMENTS FROM A B-TREE

It would seem that deletion of elements from a B-tree is simply the reverse of addition. The deletion process, however, is somewhat more complex. In this chapter we'll describe how deletion occurs. The description may seem a little complicated, but we will follow it with an explicit example which will make the process clear.

THE DELETION PROCESS

Deleting leaf elements

Note that if you want to delete a leaf element, and the leaf has more than the tree order number of elements, the process is really simple. In this case, you simply delete an element from the leaf and are done. If the leaf has only the tree order number of elements, you delete the element but are not yet done, because the leaf is then too small. This condition of a too-small leaf will be dealt with shortly.

Deleting non-leaf elements

definition: deletion element

definition: immediate predecessor element

Let's say you have a B-tree and decide that you want to delete a non-leaf element. We define this as the **deletion element**. The way you delete a non-leaf element is to first find the element that immediately precedes it in value (let's define this as the **immediate predecessor** element). It is an interesting property of a B-tree that this immediately predecessor element is always found on the leaf page. You then replace (and hence delete) the deletion element with the immediate predecessor. This, of course, leaves two copies of the immediate predecessor element on the B-tree. So the last step is to delete the immediate predecessor element found on the leaf page.

I know this seems unusual but one of the interesting, and most critical, characteristics of the B-tree is that for any given element on the B-tree, the element with the highest value that is less than the value of the given element (the immediate predecessor element) is always located on a leaf page. The exact steps for finding an immediate predecessor element are: (1) Pick any non-leaf element on the B-tree. (2) Follow the element pointer to the page on the next level down. (3) From then on follow all the page pointers to a leaf page. (4) The immediate predecessor of the element you picked will be the last element on that leaf page.

The deletion procedure works as follows:

1) Select an element to be deleted (henceforth called the deletion element).

2) If the deletion element is a leaf page element, proceed with leaf element deletion as explained in the next section.

3) Otherwise, find your immediate predecessor element using the steps listed above.

4) Replace the deletion element with the immediate predecessor element.

5) Delete the immediate predecessor element from the leaf page, as explained in the next section.

This sounds quite simple. We can even make a flow chart for the process. It looks like this:

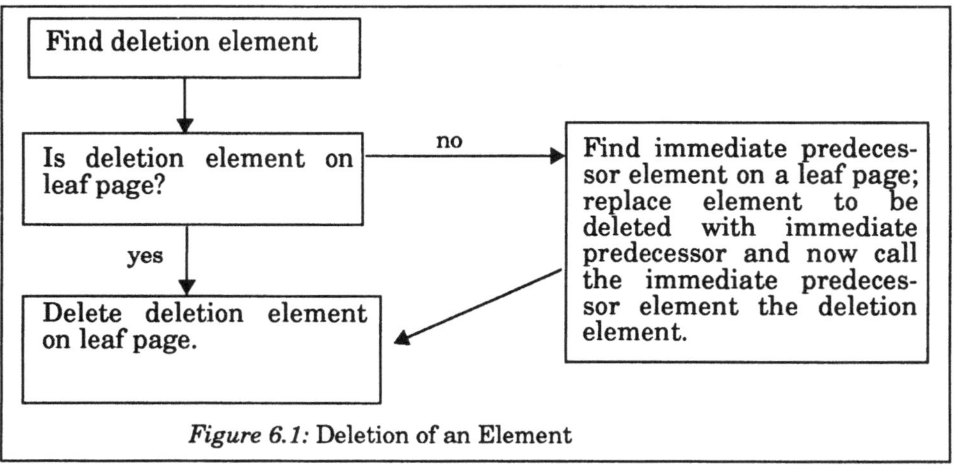

Figure 6.1: Deletion of an Element

BALANCING-AND-ABSORPTION

leaf-element deletion

As you have just seen, deletion of an element from a B-tree, even if it is not on a leaf page, always comes down to the deletion of a leaf element. Let's consider, then, leaf element deletion.

As previously mentioned, if the leaf page involved contains more than the order number of elements, we simply delete it and are finished. The process is more

balancing and absorption

complicated, however, if the leaf contains only the order number of elements, because each page must contain at least order elements. We resolve this difficulty by the processes of balancing and absorption, which we will now discuss.

We have gotten to this section on balancing and absorption because we have encountered the problem of a leaf page becoming too small.

You will find later that leaf pages are not the only pages that find themselves using the process of balancing-and-absorption. It is possible that a branch page may find itself with less than order elements in the deletion process, and it would have to undergo balancing-and-absorption as well. So this discussion of balancing-and-absorption is for both leaf pages and branch pages.

too-small page – definition

unbalanced – definition

As we know, the fewest number of elements allowed on a B-tree page is the order of the B-tree. If the order of the B-tree is N and the deletion of an element from a page leaves N-1 elements on the page, we will call this the **too-small page**; the B-tree is said to be **unbalanced** and does not conform to B-tree rules.

unbalanced condition

borrowing

absorption - definition

When removal of an element creates a too-small page, this unbalanced condition is corrected by borrowing one or more elements, if any are available, from an adjacent page on the same level. If the adjacent page is so small, however, that you cannot borrow elements from it without it becoming unbalanced, then the too-small page can be absorbed into the adjacent page and this process is defined as **absorption**. In the case of branch pages we have to be aware of the pointers on the ancestor level; this is particularly true if the elements are absorbed into adjacent pages.

When we borrow element(s) from an adjacent page, we

try to equalize the number of elements on the resulting two pages to give the B-tree a more balanced structure. For this reason we call the process of borrowing element(s) the **balancing** process.

definition: balancing

In summary, the process of deletion always starts at the leaf page and may simply involve the deletion of one element on the leaf page. If the B-tree becomes unbalanced, however, deletion may require page balancing or page absorption. If page absorption is involved, the page on the level above the leaf level becomes affected and, depending on its nature, perhaps even higher levels are affected due to the absorption of a pointing element from the level above. Thus, an absorption chain spreading all the way to the root is possible any time we delete an element from a B-tree.

absorption chain

In general, we can say that if removal of an element causes an unbalanced B-tree, we have to either borrow element(s) and balance the page or absorb the page. We may also say that this can occur on either a leaf page or a branch page. We can start to summarize a little by saying that in deletion we are dealing with varying degrees of complexity, depending on where your page is, and we have four possibilities:

If we are dealing with a leaf page:

1) leaf-balancing

2) leaf-absorption

If we are dealing with a branch page:

3) branch-balancing

4) branch-absorption

Lastly, we must take into account the readjustment of the page or element pointers that get moved in the deletion process.

relocating element & page ptrs

The page containing the element which you want to delete will be pointed to by either an element pointer or a page pointer. The procedure for relocating the element pointer and relocating the page pointer are different. In final summary, depending on how the B-tree becomes unbalanced you will wind up doing one of eight possible procedures:

If we are dealing with a leaf page:

1) element-pointer leaf-balancing

2) page-pointer leaf-balancing

3) element-pointer leaf-absorption

4) page-pointer leaf-absorption

If we are dealing with a branch page:

5) element-pointer branch-balancing

6) page-pointer branch-balancing

7) element-pointer branch-absorption

8) page-pointer branch-absorption

deletion versus addition algorithms

It is not quite as difficult as it sounds, because once you understand the logic behind the process it is evident what needs to be done. However, whether absorbing or balancing, the deletion algorithm is obviously more complex than the addition algorithm and takes a little more time to understand and appreciate.

Perhaps the clearest way to describe the rules involved in the deletion process is to give an example that uses all the techniques. We will do that now.

DELETING FROM A B-TREE OF ORDER 2

We now illustrate and explain B-tree deletion in a step-by-step fashion. First, consider Figure 6.2. It is a diagram representing a B-tree. This is the tree of order 2 that we grew previously. Now, proceeding one step at a

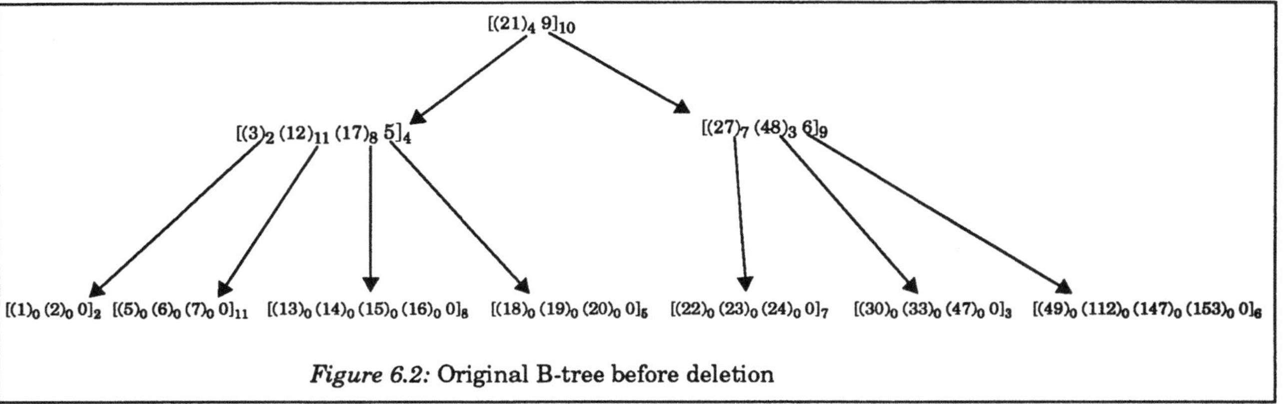

Figure 6.2: Original B-tree before deletion

time, we are going to delete elements from this tree until it consists of a single page.

deleting elements from a B-tree step-by-step

Step 1

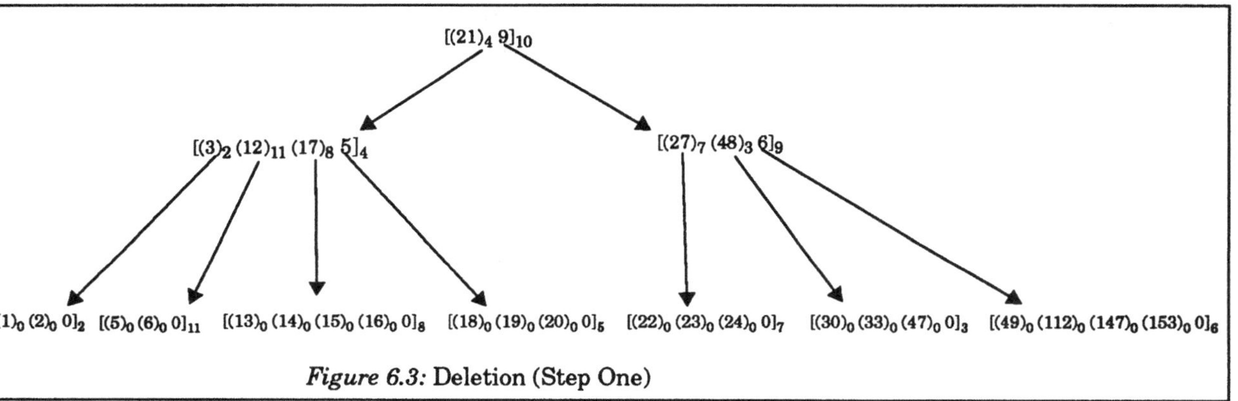

Figure 6.3: Deletion (Step One)

In the first step, we have asked the computer to delete element 7 from page 11; this is shown in Figure 6.3. The following two conditions are true for the element 7: (1) it was on a leaf page, page 11; and (2) Page 11, having three elements, could have an element deleted without having fewer elements than the order of the tree after deletion. This, then, is the simplest of all possible cases of tree deletion. We can simply remove 7 from page 11 and be done with the deletion of that element; the B-tree requires no further modification. We refer to this type of deletion as **simple leaf deletion**.

simple leaf deletion: example

Step 2

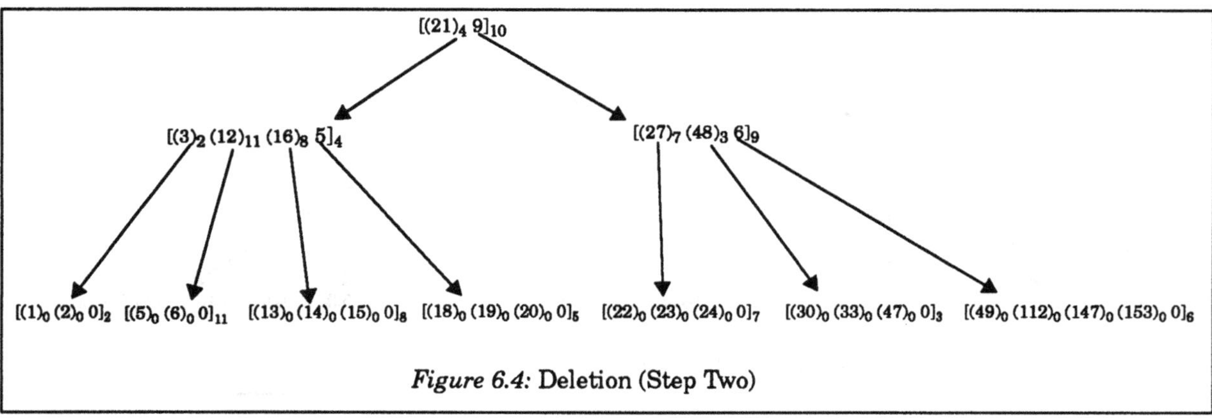

Figure 6.4: Deletion (Step Two)

remove duplicate element

In Figure 6.4 we have removed the element 17 from the tree. Element 17 was on a branch page, page 4, so we are deleting a non-leaf element. We cannot simply remove 17 without eliminating the essential pointer indicating page 8, so we replace 17 with the element immediately below it in value, 16. When we replace 17 with 16, we provide 16 with the pointer 17 used to have, and the pointer structure of the tree remains unchanged. The leaf page (page 8) from which 16 came then has the element 16 deleted from it.

How branch deletion translates to leaf deletion is also shown in the next step, in which we delete 21 from the top of the tree on the root page.

Step 3

In Figure 6.5, we have deleted 21, which was found on the root page (page 10). Following the procedure (outlined earlier) for finding the immediate predecessor element, we follow the element pointer to page 4, and then the page pointer to page 5 to find the immediate predecessor element (always on a leaf page). We get that element (element 20) and write it over the element to be deleted (element 21). Then, we perform a leaf element deletion on the immediate predecessor. In this case we perform a simple leaf deletion to remove the element 20

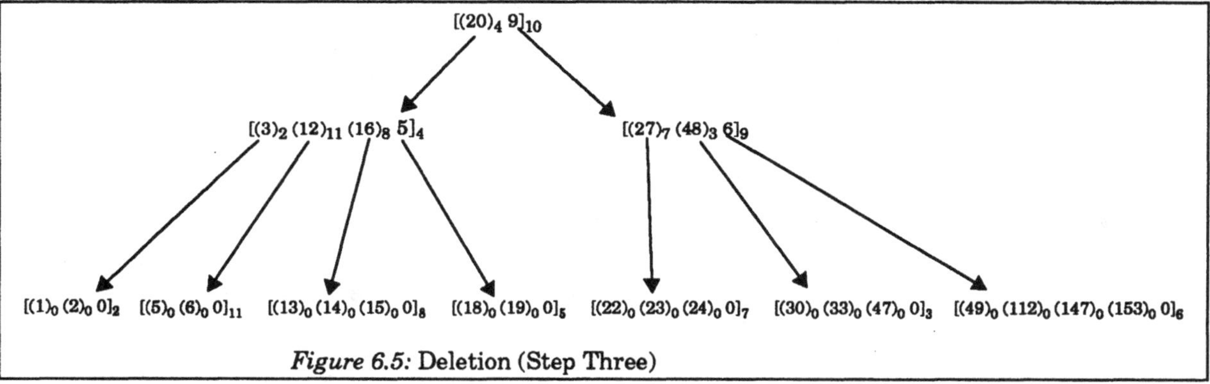

Figure 6.5: Deletion (Step Three)

from page 5.

Until now we have dealt with simple leaf deletion, because we have deleted from pages holding three or more elements. When an element must be deleted from a leaf page holding only two elements, we can no longer rely on simple leaf deletion. Rather, we must use one of the two types of non-simple leaf deletion: balancing or absorption. The first of these, leaf deletion with balancing, is illustrated in Step 4.

Step 4

In Figure 6.6 we have deleted element 6 from page 11. Since page 11 had only two elements in it, 5 and 6, the deletion of element 6 threatens to reduce page 11 to less than the minimum of two elements. In order to avoid this, we take one of two options.

leaf deletion with balancing

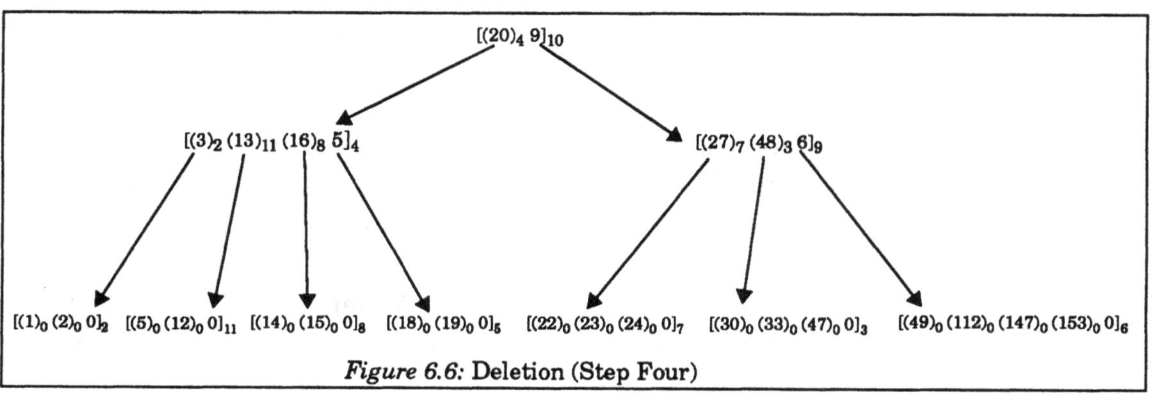

Figure 6.6: Deletion (Step Four)

1) *Balancing:* We find out how many elements are on one of the two pages adjacent to the too-small page. Which of these pages we check depends on the type of pointer pointing to the too-small page. If it is an element pointer, we check the adjacent page on the right; if it is a page pointer, we check the adjacent page to the left. We call the page we choose the **appropriate adjacent page**. If the appropriate adjacent page contains N+1 or more elements, we will borrow one or more elements from it.

appropriate adjacent page

2) *Absorption:* If the appropriate page contains only N elements, we eliminate the too-small page by absorbing it into the appropriate adjacent page.

In this particular case, page 11 is pointed to by an element pointer on page 4, so we check the adjacent page on the right. Since the adjacent page on the right, page 8, contains three elements, we may borrow.

balance definition

borrowing for balance

When we say **balance** we mean that we want to finish the borrowing procedure with an equal number of elements on the two pages involved in the borrowing. To balance our pages as we borrow elements, we divide equally the total number of elements contained on the borrowing page and the lending page. This is so that after the borrowing they will be distributed as equally as possible on these two pages. Of course, perfect equality is possible only if the total number of elements on the two pages is an even number. With an odd number, we make the arbitrary choice that the lending page will retain the extra element.

The borrowing method used for balancing depends on whether the too-small page is pointed to by an element or page pointer.

1) *Element pointer borrowing:* When the too-small page is pointed to by an element pointer, we add the point-

ing element on the ancestor page to the end of it. Then, we remove the first element in the right adjacent page and put it in the place formerly occupied by that ancestor element. If another element will be borrowed, we repeat this process until all the borrowing has been completed. *element pointer borrowing*

2) *Page pointer borrowing:* When the too-small page is pointed to by a page pointer, we proceed in a similar manner. We take the last element on the ancestor page and place it at the beginning of the too-small page. We then remove the last element of the left adjacent page and write it onto the place formerly occupied by that ancestor element. Then, if another element is to be borrowed, we repeat the process until all the borrowing has been completed.

We have just described the general algorithm for balancing a leaf page. This balancing takes place when deletion from a leaf page results in a page of less than minimum size, and when at least one element is available for borrowing. This algorithm, applied to the specific case of deleting element 6 from page 11, works as follows. We first note that since page 11 is pointed to by an element pointer, we borrow from the adjacent page on the right, and we borrow one element only. We first delete 6 from page 11. We then add 12 to the end of page 11, since 12 is the element on the ancestor page that actually points to page 11. Next, we replace 12 on the ancestor page with 13, the first element from the right adjacent page (page 8). Finally, we remove element 13 from page 8. *balancing a leaf page*

Step 5

In Figure 6.7 we have removed 48 from branch page 9. This operation begins by replacing the element to be deleted with the immediate predecessor element, which is always found on a leaf page. Then, to avoid duplicates, we remove the immediate predecessor from the leaf page. This removal is merely the removal of an element from a leaf page, or simple leaf deletion, so we simply take 47, the immediate predecessor element, off page 3

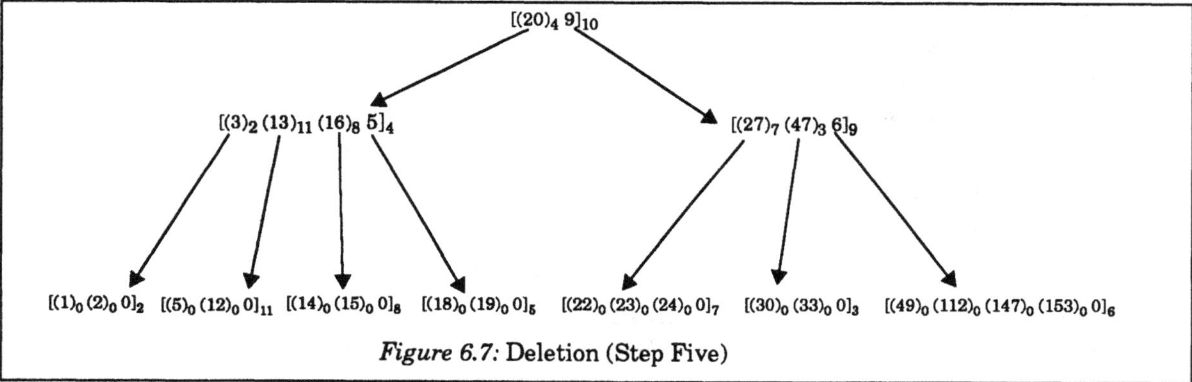

Figure 6.7: Deletion (Step Five)

and put it in element 48's place. We ended this procedure with the simple leaf deletion of 47 from page 3.

leaf balancing

If we now wish to remove 47 from the tree, we will again use leaf deletion on page 3. However, since page 3 has only two elements, this will not be simple leaf deletion. Page 6 has extra elements, so we employ leaf-balancing. We demonstrate this in Step 6, when we will, in fact, delete 47 from the tree.

Step 6

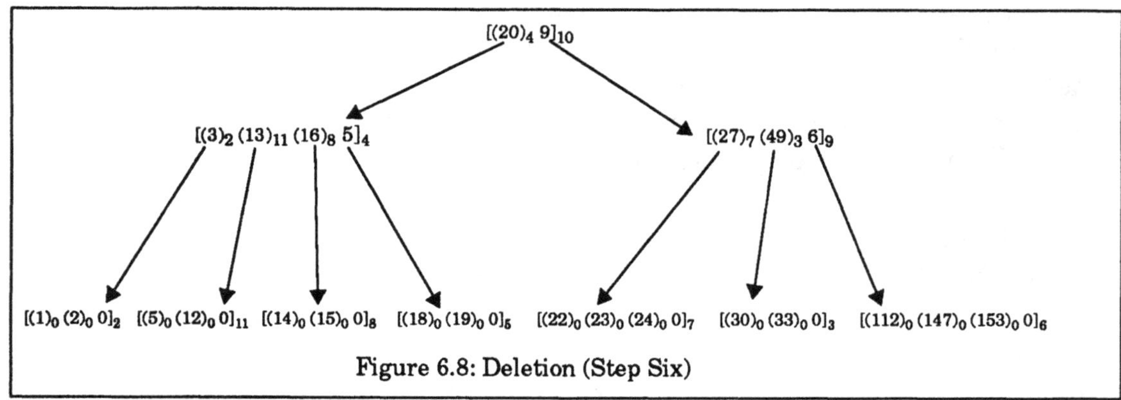

Figure 6.8: Deletion (Step Six)

Deleting 47 results first in its replacement by 33, and then in the leaf deletion of 33 from page 3. Element 49 is borrowed from page 6, so that 33 goes from page 9 back down to page 3, and 49 takes the place briefly occupied by 33 on page 9. Note that if another element were borrowed from page 6, it would take the place of 49, and 49 would go down to page 3.

Step 7

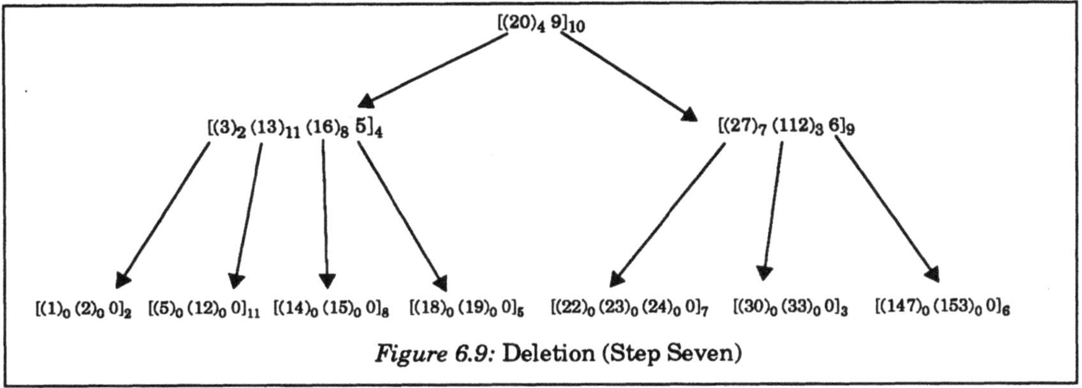

Figure 6.9: Deletion (Step Seven)

In Step 7 we have removed 49 from page 9. This requires the replacing of the branch element, 49, with the leaf element, 112, and then simple leaf deletion to get rid of the excess 112 on page 6.

Step 8

In Step 8 we will remove 33 from the tree. The deletion of 33, since it takes place in two distinct stages (one on the leaf level and the other on the branch level) is illustrated in two parts. We now discuss these two stages.

Step 8, Stage One

Element 33 was a leaf element on page 3, a page that contained only two elements. Furthermore, page 6, from which page 3 should borrow, also contained only two elements. Therefore, we must use leaf deletion with absorption.

leaf deletion with absorption

As mentioned earlier, we have two kinds of leaf deletion with absorption to choose from. The method chosen depends on whether the page from which an element must be removed is pointed to by a page pointer or by an

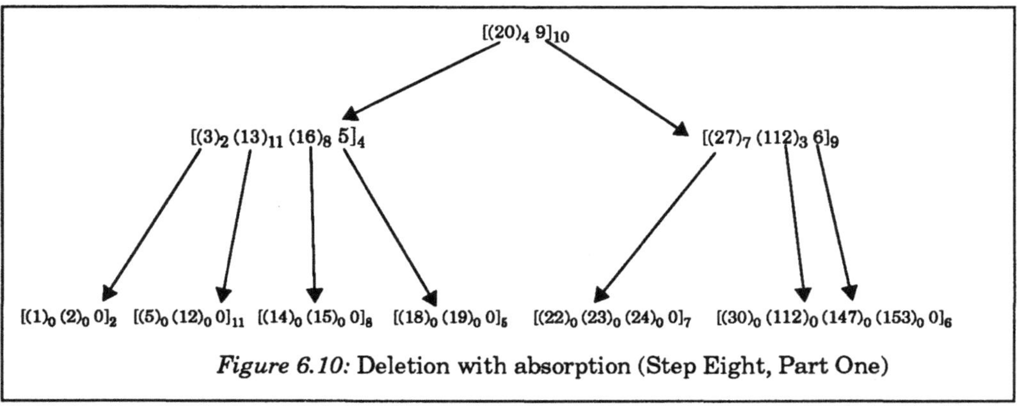

Figure 6.10: Deletion with absorption (Step Eight, Part One)

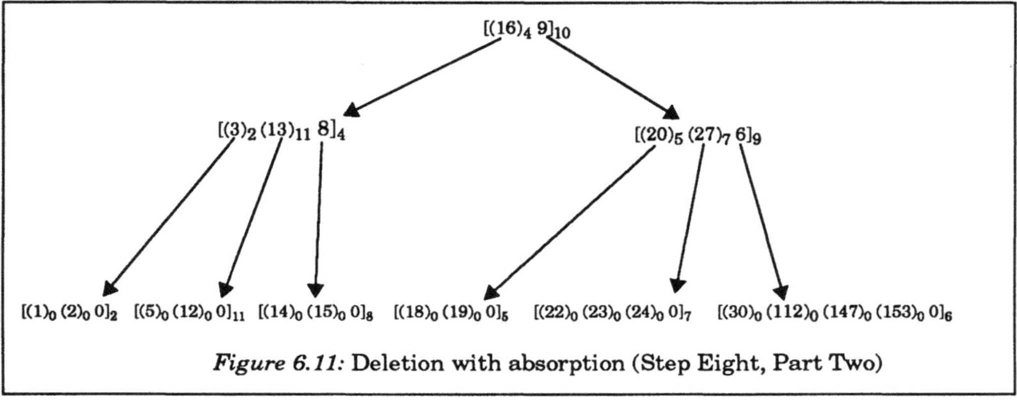

Figure 6.11: Deletion with absorption (Step Eight, Part Two)

page-pointer leaf-absorption

element-pointer leaf-absorption

element pointer. If the page is pointed to by a page pointer, we use **page-pointer leaf-absorption**. The other method is **element-pointer leaf-absorption**.

element-pointer leaf-deletion described

absorbing page definition

Our case is element-pointer leaf-absorption. In element-pointer leaf-absorption, the too-small page is absorbed into its right adjacent page. During this process, the element on the ancestor page that pointed to the too-small page is also absorbed into the right adjacent page. This resulting page containing both of the former pages and the pointing ancestor page element is called the **absorbing page**. The absorbing page is configured as follows: first, in their former order, are the elements of the too-small page; second, the pointing ancestor page element; and third, the elements of the right adjacent page, also in their former order.

Thus in step 8 we have a case of element-pointer leaf-absorption. The too-small page that was wiped out by absorption was page 3. It was pointed to by element 112 on the ancestor page, which is page 9. Page 3's right adjacent page was page 6. Figure 6.10, which depicts the tree's configuration at the end of the first stage, shows the final configuration of the absorbing page, page 6. It now contains the ancestor page pointing element, 112. 112 is still present in its old location on page 9. It must be deleted from page 9 in order to complete the change in the B-tree initiated by the deletion of 33.

element-page leaf-deletion with absorption

Before we explain part two of step 8, the process of getting rid of 112 from branch page 9, it would be best to first explain what would have happened if we had needed to use page-pointer leaf-absorption in stage one. The reason we want to digress and explain this is that once we have discussed both page pointer and element pointer absorption, we can make up a chart showing *all* the non-simple deletion methods.

In page-pointer leaf-absorption, the too-small page is pointed to by the page pointer on its ancestor page. In this case, the too-small page absorbs the left adjacent page, which is always the page pointed to by the last element on the ancestor page. This last element on the ancestor page is also absorbed into the too-small page. Thus, in page-pointer leaf-absorption, the left adjacent page is completely wiped out, and the too-small page becomes configured as follows: first, there are all the elements of the left-adjacent page; second is the last element on the pointing ancestor page; and third, all the elements of the too-small page. Once the absorbing page is finally configured, we must remove the pointing element from the ancestor page.

page pointer leaf absorption: a step-by-step explanation

Note that if we had deleted 147 or 153 instead of 33, we would have needed to use page-pointer leaf-absorption

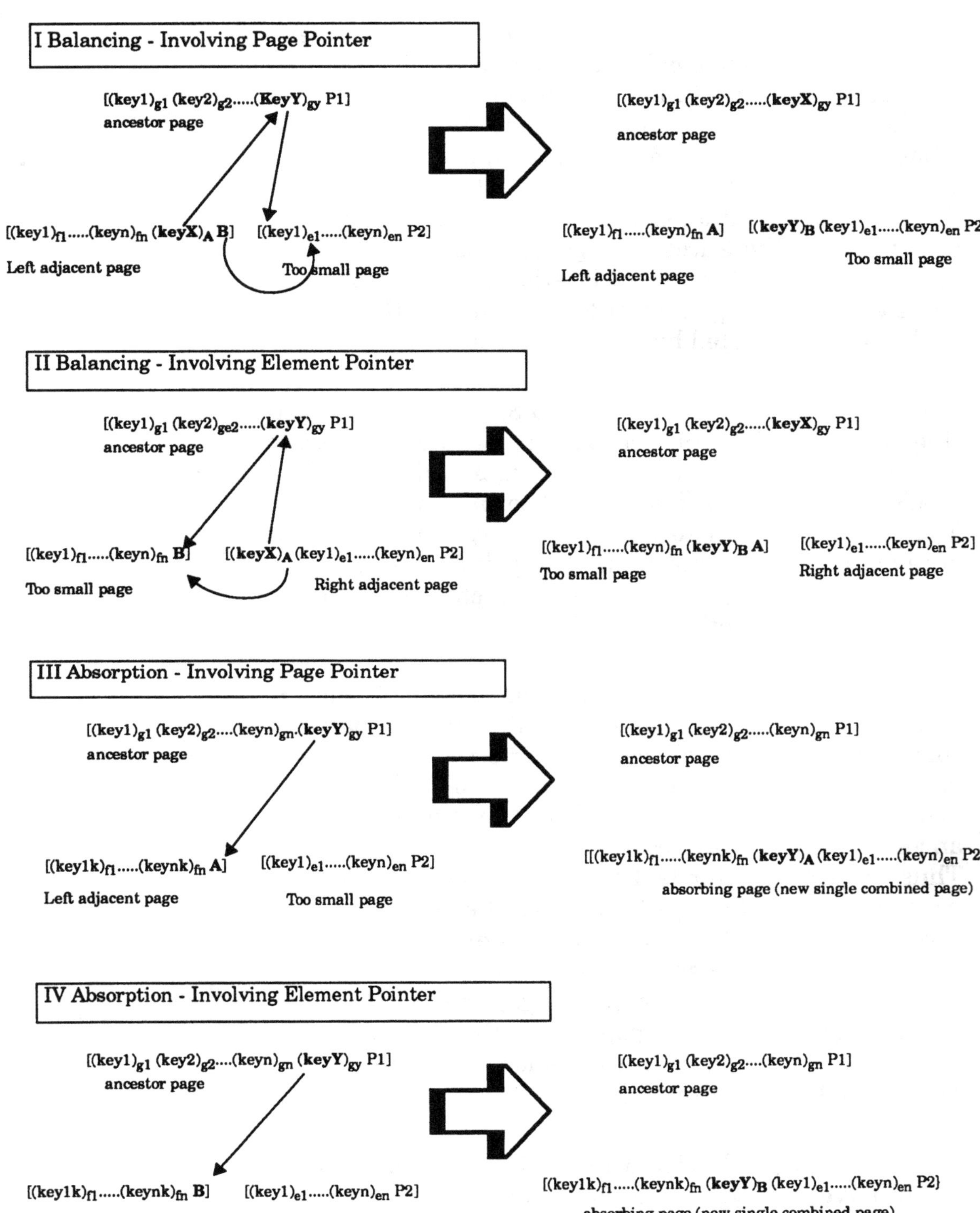

Figure 6.12: Branch pages Balancing & Absorbing

instead of element-pointer leaf-absorption.

deletion from branch page

Naturally, after every case of absorption we must delete the element on the ancestor page that pointed to the page wiped out by the absorption process. This is depicted in Figure 6.11, which shows the deletion of the element 112 from the branch page 9.

Summary

We can now make up a chart showing all the non-simple deletion methods. As we have already mentioned, there are eight kinds of non-simple deletion on leaf pages:

If we are dealing with a leaf page:

1) element-pointer leaf-balancing

2) page-pointer leaf-balancing

3) element-pointer leaf-absorption

4) page-pointer leaf-absorption

If we are dealing with a branch page:

5) element-pointer branch-balancing

6) page-pointer branch-balancing

7) element-pointer branch-absorption

8) page-pointer branch-absorption

branch page and leaf page algorithms: similarities and differences

Note that a particular branch-page algorithm is identical to the corresponding leaf-page algorithm in terms of left or right adjacent page, ancestor element and page pointers, and so forth. The only difference between a leaf page deletion algorithm and its corresponding branch page algorithm is that branch page deletion algorithms require the transfer of pointers during the balancing and absorption algorithms to preserve the tree structure and ordering throughout the deletion process. Thus, page pointers become element pointers in the absorption algorithms; in the balancing algorithms page pointers become element pointers, while element pointers become page pointers.

Figures 6.12 i-iv illustrate the four possible algorithms for branch pages– two for balancing and two for absorption. Note that when balancing, we demonstrate the transfer of pointers for the borrowing of only a single element. This procedure is repeated as frequently as required for the number of elements used in borrowing. We now summarize briefly the four cases depicted in Figure 6.12.

page-pointer branch page balancing.

i) *Page-pointer branch-balancing:* Here, when the ancestor-page-pointing-element is appended to the beginning of the too-small page, it must be given the proper pointer to keep the tree structure and order intact. The proper pointer is the page-pointer on the left-adjacent page. The old page-pointer on the left-adjacent page is then replaced by the pointer from the last element in the left-adjacent page. This element has been sent up to replace the element on the ancestor page, which was in turn sent to the too-small page. Note that although the value of the pointing element on the ancestor page is changed, the page pointed to remains unchanged.

element-pointer branch-page balancing

ii) *Element-pointer branch-balancing:* Here the element-pointer on the first element of the right-adjacent page becomes the new page-pointer for the too-small page, and the old page-pointer becomes the pointer for the element from the ancestor page. This element is brought down to, and placed at the end of, the too-small page. The place formerly occupied by the pointing element from the ancestor page is taken by the first element of the right adjacent page. Again, note that the value of the pointing element on the ancestor page is changed, but the pointer remains unchanged.

page-pointer branch-page absorption

iii) *Page-pointer branch-absorption:* Here the last element on the pointing ancestor page is appended to the beginning of the too-small page, and is furnished with the pointer that was formerly the page-pointer for the left-adjacent page-pointer.

iv) Element-pointer branch-absorption: Here the element on the ancestor page that points to the too-small page is appended to the beginning of the right adjacent page, and is furnished with the pointer that was formerly the page-pointer for the too-small page.

element-pointer branch-page absorption

Step 8, Stage Two

Returning to the specific case depicted in Figure 6.11, we note that this is page-pointer branch-balancing associated with the removal of 112 from page 9. Figure 6.11 is the configuration after this process is finished. Observe that 20 is appended to the beginning of page 9 and that it points to page 5. Page 5 had previously been pointed to by the page-pointer on page 4, the left-adjacent lending page. The page-pointer for page 4 now points to page 8, which is the page formerly pointed to by 16, the element which was raised to the ancestor page, page 10.

figure 26b

Step 9

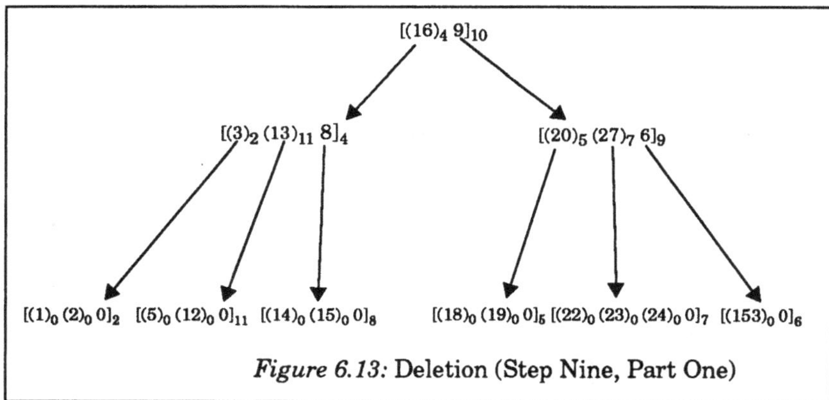

Figure 6.13: Deletion (Step Nine, Part One)

In Step 9, we deleted 30, 112, and 147 from page 6. The first pair of these deletions are simple leaf page deletions. The third, the deletion of element 147, requires leaf balancing. Note that since the too-small page is pointed to by a page pointer, this is the leaf-level version of the branch level case explained in Step 8. Therefore,

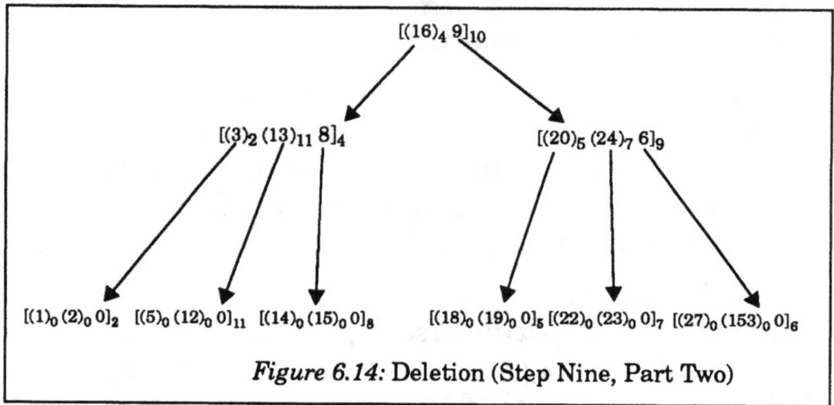

Figure 6.14: Deletion (Step Nine, Part Two)

in this case it is only necessary to note that the too-small page was page 6, the left-adjacent page was page 7, and the ancestor page was page 9. Figure 6.13 depicts the intermediate stage after the leaf deletion. Figure 6.14 depicts the final configuration after the balancing with page 7.

Note that any further deletion from the tree results in leaf absorption, which in turn will lead to branch absorption. This is illustrated in Step 10 with the removal of element 1.

Step 10

deleting number 1

The first stage in removing the element 1 from page 2 is depicted in Figure 6.15. It involves the element-pointer leaf-absorption explained in Step 8. This absorption has resulted in the loss of the too-small page, which is page 2. Note that the ancestor page was page 4, and that the right-adjacent page was page 11. The too-small page is absorbed into page 11.

Any case of absorption results in the removal of an element from the ancestor branch page which, by means of either a page or leaf pointer, pointed to the too-small page. However, when element 3 is sent to page 11 we have a too-small page in page 4. We cannot borrow from page 9, so we must do element-pointer branch-absorp-

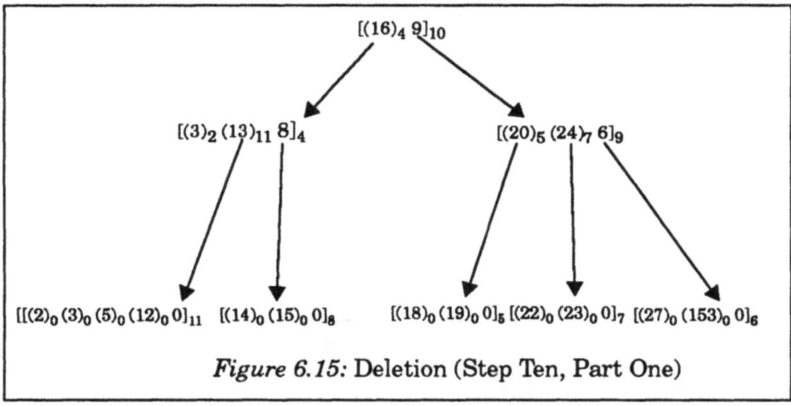

Figure 6.15: Deletion (Step Ten, Part One)

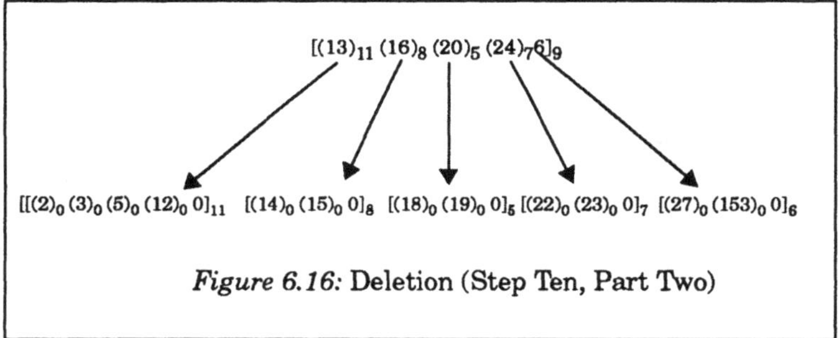

Figure 6.16: Deletion (Step Ten, Part Two)

tion. This situation is depicted in Figure 6.15, which shows the result of element-pointer branch-absorption, after page 4 has been absorbed into page 9. The ancestor page was page 10, the too-small page was page 4, and the right adjacent page was page 9.

t.ransfer of pointers

In summary, the absorption of page 4 into page 9 results from the transfer of 3 down to page 11. This in turn causes 16 to be transferred down to page 9. Since page 10, the page from which 16 was transferred, is the root page, the removal of 16 obviously causes no further modification--balancing or absorption--at higher levels in the B-tree because there are no higher levels.

Step 11

In Figure 6.17 we deleted element 153 from page 6. This is page-pointer leaf-absorption: the ancestor page being page 9, the too-small page being page 6, and the left-

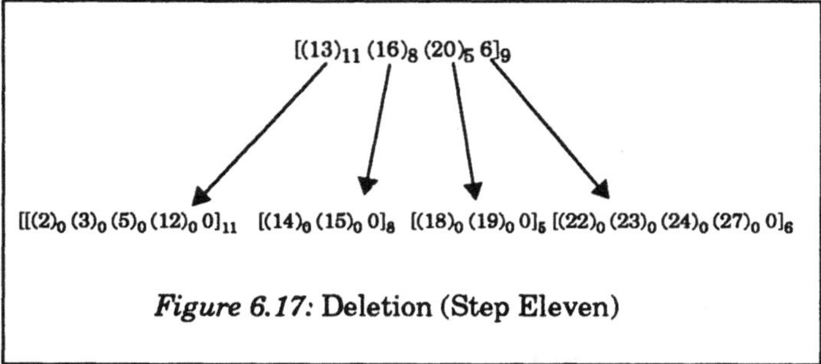

Figure 6.17: Deletion (Step Eleven)

adjacent page, page 7, being absorbed into the too-small page. The root-page element, 24, is transferred down to the too-small page, page 6.

Step 12

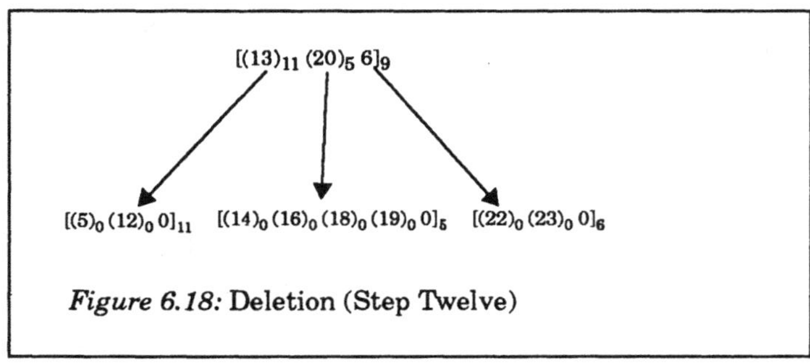

Figure 6.18: Deletion (Step Twelve)

In Figure 6.18 we have deleted elements 2 and 3 from page 11, and elements 24 and 27 from page 6. This is simple leaf deletion. We have also deleted element 15 from page 8 by means of element-pointer leaf absorption. The pointing element is element 16 on the ancestor page 9, the too-small page is page 8, and the right-adjacent page is page 5. The root-page element, 16, is transferred down to page 5 in the absorption process.

Step 13

In Step 13 (Figure 6.19), we show the simple leaf deletion of 14 and 16 from page 4.

Step 14

In Figure 6.20, with the removal of element 5 from page

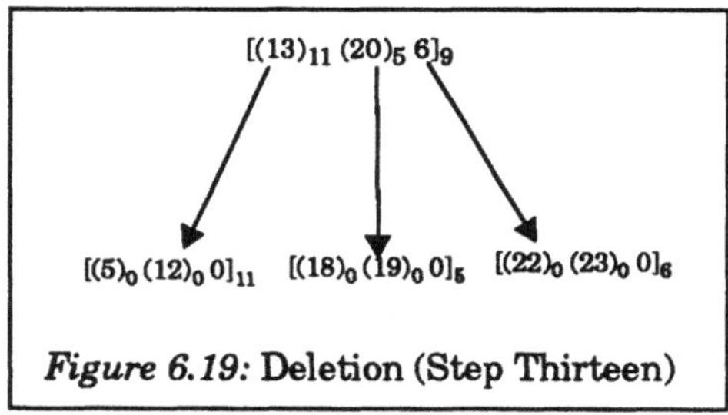

Figure 6.19: Deletion (Step Thirteen)

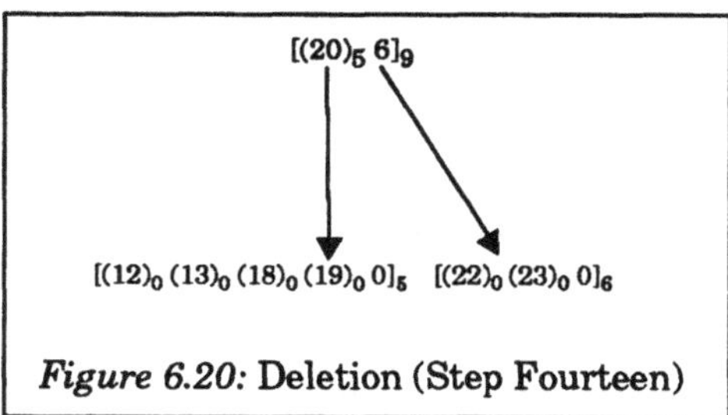

Figure 6.20: Deletion (Step Fourteen)

11, we have element-pointer leaf-absorption. The pointing element is 13 on ancestor page 9; the too-small page is page 11; and the right adjacent page is page 5. The root-page element, 13, is transferred down to page 5 in the absorption process.

Step 15

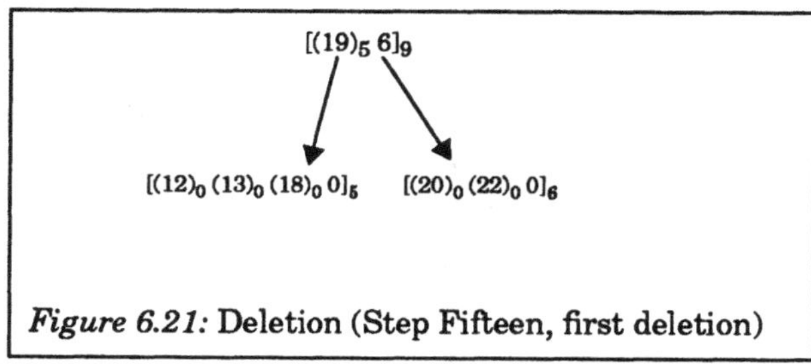

Figure 6.21: Deletion (Step Fifteen, first deletion)

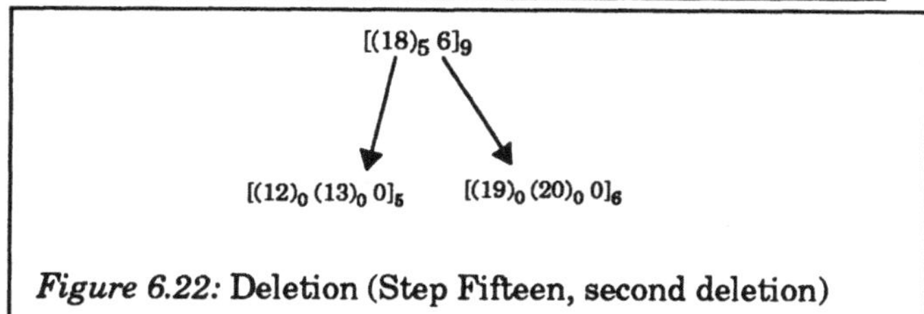

Figure 6.22: Deletion (Step Fifteen, second deletion)

In Step 15, the removal first of 23, and then of 22, from page 6 resulted in successive cases of page-pointer leaf balancing. In both cases, the too-small page was page 6, the left-adjacent page was page 5, and the ancestor page was 9.

Note that any further deletion of elements from the tree will bring about the collapse of the tree into a single root-page. This is what happens in the next step.

Step 16

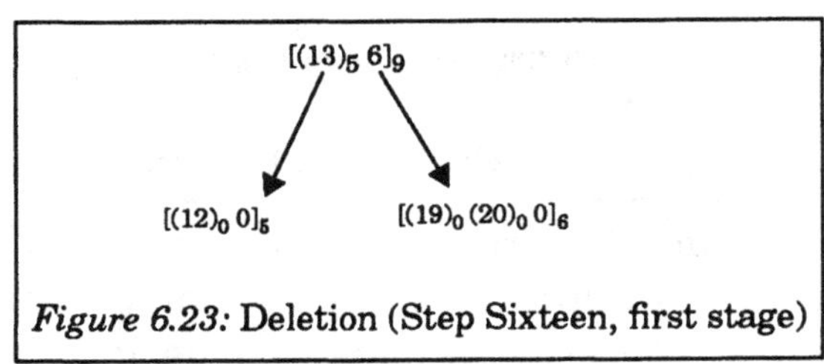

Figure 6.23: Deletion (Step Sixteen, first stage)

In step 16, we remove element 18. When we remove the root element 18, we must replace the deleted root with the appropriate leaf element (13) and absorb the too-small page, 5, into page 6. This is element-pointer leaf-absorption; the too-small page is page 5, the right-adjacent page is page 6, and the ancestor page is page 9. This absorption process results, of course, in the exhaustion of the ancestor root-page, page 9, when its sole element (13) is transferred down to the right-adjacent page, page 6. We are now left with a B-tree consisting of a single page. Any further deletion will, of course, be simple leaf deletion.

$[(12)_0\ (13)_0\ (19)_0\ (20)_0\ 0]_6$

Figure 6.24: Deletion (Step Sixteen, second stage)

SUMMARY OF B-TREE DELETION ALGORITHM

There are two kinds of deletion: deletion from a leaf

page and deletion from a branch page. Deletion from a branch page is achieved by first replacing the element to be deleted with the greatest element below it and then removing that lesser element from the tree (which is always found on the leaf level).

leaf & branch page deletion

There are three major ways to delete an element from a leaf page:

leaf page deletion

(1) Simple leaf-page deletion, in which the page in question can spare an element and still contain N or more elements, where N is the order of the tree.

(2) Leaf-balancing. In this case, the page on which the deletion occurs becomes too small and so borrows elements from whichever one of the adjacent pages on the same level is appropriate.

(3) Leaf-absorption, in which the page in question is too small but is unable to borrow from an adjacent page.

We find out if borrowing is possible by determining whether or not the appropriate adjacent page (on the right or on the left) contains more than N elements. If this is the case, borrowing is possible.

How do we determine which of the adjacent pages to check for borrowing? If the too-small page is pointed to by a page-pointer, we check the left-adjacent page; if it is pointed to by an element-pointer, we check the right-adjacent page.

If borrowing is possible, the elements of the too-small page and the appropriate adjacent page are divided so that the number of elements in the too-small page and the appropriate adjacent page are as evenly balanced as possible.

If borrowing is not possible, and if the too-small page

was pointed to from the ancestor page by an element pointer, the too-small page as well as the pointing element on the ancestor page are absorbed into the right adjacent page. The too-small page is then deleted. If the too-small page was pointed to by the ancestor page's page pointer, the left adjacent page as well as the last element on the ancestor page are absorbed into the too-small page, and the left adjacent page is deleted.

branch -level deletion

Since leaf-absorption results in the loss of an element on the ancestor branch-level page, we must deal with branch level deletion. This parallels the leaf-level method. If the ancestor page has at least N elements after the removal, then we are finished. If not, then we try to borrow, using the same criterion as was used for the leaf-level method. If borrowing is not possible, then, as described above, we must absorb a page. Branch balancing and absorption are exactly like leaf balancing and absorption, except that pointers must be passed between elements and pages to maintain the structure of the tree.

The flow chart in Figure 6.25 details the deletion algorithm just discussed.

From Figure 6.25, it is clear that B-tree deletion is a more complex process than addition, and you should plan to spend a little more time understanding and implementing it.

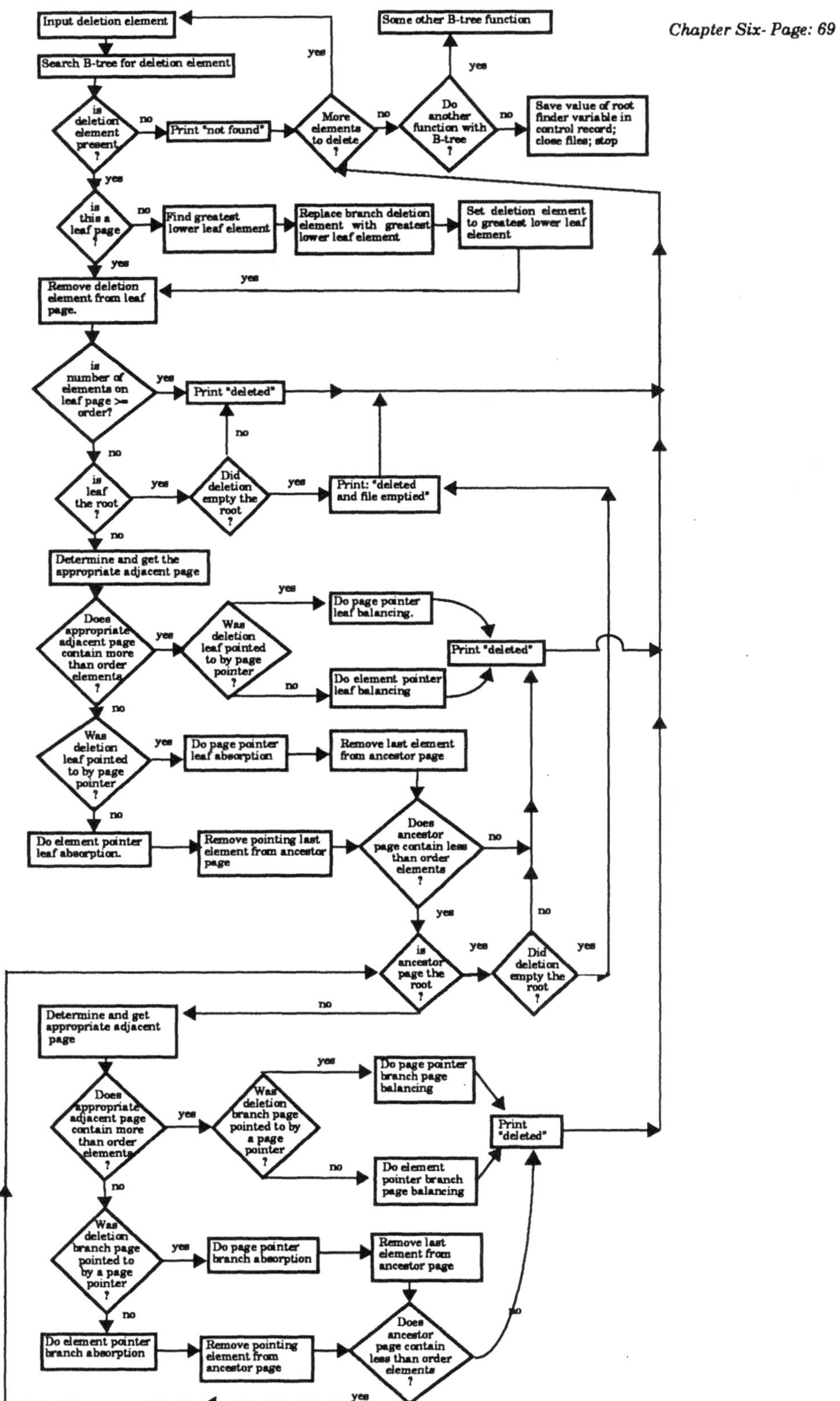

Figure 6.25: Flow chart for deletion from a B-tree

SECTION III

Using the TeachBase B-tree System

7

Overview of the TeachBase B-tree System

In Section II we discussed, in depth, the mechanics of how the B-tree works. Now we will put into practice what we have learned by looking at a B-tree system. This chapter will give you a overview of the items that will be in our B-tree system that you have not yet been exposed to. Then, in the next chapter, we will have a very thorough line-by-line analysis of the TeachBase B-tree system. A complete listing of the TeachBase B-tree system is in Appendix C.

The storage file

Early in this book we pointed out to you that any keyword that you put on a B-tree could have a pointer added to it so that the key word "pointed to" or was "connected to" a record in an outside file. We promised you that when we began creating our B-tree system we would make sure that it had this feature. Therefore, we are going to create a random access file that is separate from our B-tree file and we will call it the "storage" file. Every time you enter a keyword into the B-tree system,

storage pointer

the keyword not only goes into the B-tree file, but we will make a copy of the keyword and stick it in the storage file as well. We will then attach a short integer (MKI$) pointer to your keyword to keep track of the keyword in the storage file. So our storage file will consist of records that are just a few bytes longer than our keyword (the extra few bytes will be explained shortly) and each keyword on the B-tree will have a unique record in the storage file which will be pointed to by a "storage pointer" that comes after the keyword. Our whole element, then, will be keyword + storage pointer + element pointer.

Put keyword in storage file

Of course, you could send any data you want to the storage file. We are simply using the keyword because it is handy and it allows us to automatically send something to storage without having to ask you to keyboard data in. You can, of course, change the code to allow you to input anything you like.

When it comes time to readout the B-tree, the program is designed to take the storage pointer for each keyword, get whatever is in the storage file record corresponding to our keyword, and display it.

Thus our TeachBase program will be controlling the contents of a storage file with a B-tree. We need to point out that this is just one method of using a B-tree (see Chapter One) and we use it because it tends to exercise all the features of a B-tree.

The deletion problem

other programs needed to run a B-tree

In a database system where you are adding and deleting elements all the time, there are bound to be some times, as we recall from our "balancing and absorption" procedures, where B-tree records are deleted. You have to ask yourself the question "What happens to these records in actual practice?" If you have no plan of action, then your

B-tree will develop "holes" or "gaps" of dead records in it. Since we are now going to seriously design a B-tree system, we have to address this problem.

One way to handle this problem is to periodically regenerate the B-tree, with just the "current records", thus eliminating the space where the dead records were. We use a better method, however, by creating a list of all dead records. Then, the next time an entry is to be made into the B-tree, you use one of these dead records. In other words, you recycle the dead records. We have created two routines for this. One is an allocation routine, where we assign or allocate a dead record to the next new entry to be made. The other routine is called the deallocation routine, where we take a record that has just been killed and put it on the recycle list. We will discuss this allocation/deallocation procedure in more detail later in this chapter.

recycling dead records: allocation and deallocation

Utility programs

In addition to the four main programs and the allocation/deallocation routines, the TeachBase system has some "utility" programs that allow us to inspect and analyze how the B-tree is developing. The utility programs are:

1) **Show B-tree structure:** Graphically shows the existing B-tree structure.
2) **Show storage file deallocation list.** Lists all "dead" storage file record numbers stored in the storage file deallocation list waiting to be recycled.
3) **Show B-tree deallocation list.** Just like the storage file deallocation list, except this routine lists all the record numbers in the B-tree deallocation list.
4) **Save pointers and quit.** The quit program saves all variables we have in memory that point to the root page and the start of each deallocation list, so you

Update control record to disk frequently

know where they are located when you start up next time. Actually, every time the root changes or a record is added to or taken off a deallocation list this information should be written to the control record immediately, so that in case of power interruption it is not lost.

Menu Commands

We know that once a person starts inputting a long list of keywords they prefer not to be bothered with unnecessary menu commands. The same is true for deleting a lot of keywords. Therefore, the TeachBase system starts by asking you what the next keyword is you want to enter. Once entered, it asks for the next keyword, etc.

You can end this cycle by simply typing an asterisk(*) followed by a two letter code that will take you to any of the other programs.

TO MOVE FROM PROGRAM TO PROGRAM

Command	Moves You To The Program
*lc	list storage file in order (lexical listing)
*lr	list storage file in reverse order
*in	install (add) a keyword to B-tree
*de	delete a keyword
*se	search for a keyword
*ut	show B-tree structure
*as	show storage file allocation list
*at	show B-tree allocation list
*qu	quit program

ASCII definition

You probably noticed that the listing command says "lexical listing" and you might be wondering what that is. In the back of almost any programming book is a listing of ASCII character codes. ASCII stands for American Standard Code for Information Interchange and it is recognized by everyone in the computer industry. If you look at the listing, you will note that there is an order to the listings: numbers come first, then capital letters and then small letters, etc. This is called the **lexical** listing of characters, and our B-tree is kept in this order. You will note that everything is in numerical and alphabetical order with the exception that the entire alphabet in lower-case characters comes after the uppercase characters. You need to be aware of this because you would otherwise wonder why the keyword "Xapple" came before the keyword "apple".

Definition lexical

Duplicate Entries

We also have to answer the question of whether or not you can put duplicate entries on the B-tree (i.e. enter an identical item more than once). We decided to allow duplicate entries, but have the system keep track of how many times a duplicate entry is made. You can easily change this if you want. How to change the TeachBase system is covered in Chapter 10. To keep track of duplicate entries, we field the storage file records with two field variables:

keeping track of duplicate entries

1) **WD$** will be our first field and will contain your message which, in this case, will be our keyword.
2) **MN$** will be our second field. It will be a two-byte number, in MKI$ format, that will tell how many times this keyword has been entered into the B-tree system.

Fielding of B-tree and storage records

It is probably a good idea, at this time, to diagram for you how our B-tree and storage file records are fielded. The only item that will be in the diagrams that we have not mentioned yet is at the end of each B-tree record. We want to have a 2 byte "element counter" which will instantly tell us how many elements are in the B-tree record.

Element counter

Our B-tree records, then, are fielded as follows:

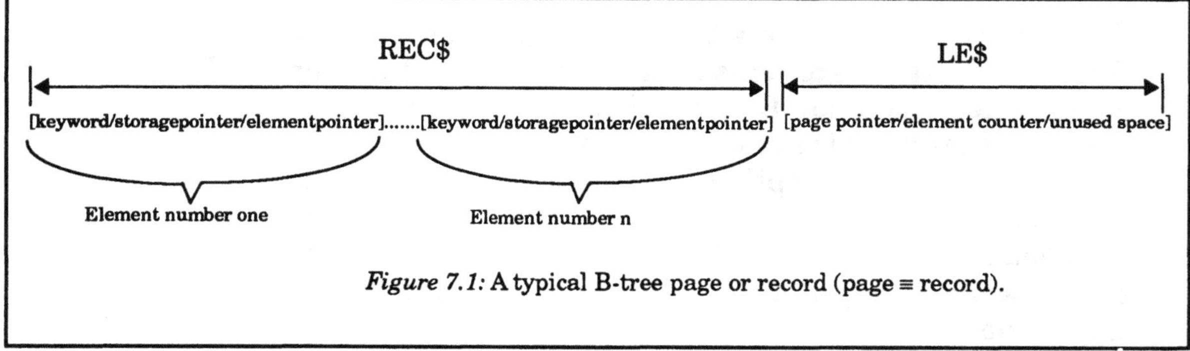

Figure 7.1: A typical B-tree page or record (page ≡ record).

Our storage file records are fielded as follows:

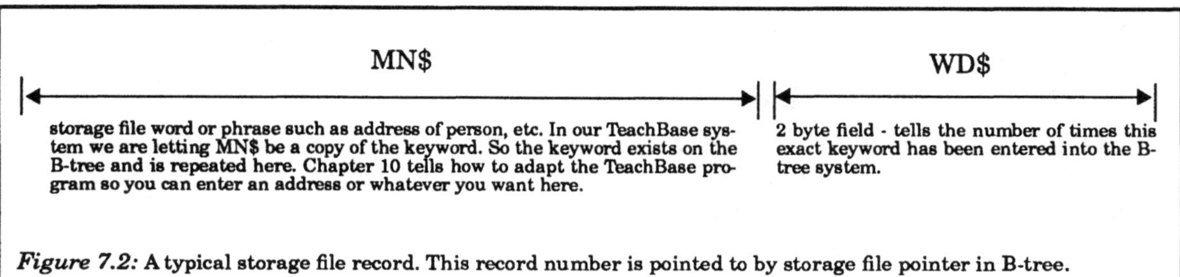

Figure 7.2: A typical storage file record. This record number is pointed to by storage file pointer in B-tree.

The Allocation/Deallocation Procedure

Now it is time for us to give you a more in-depth idea of how the allocation/deallocation procedure works. It is actually a fairly simple idea. In the course of everyday business, we are constantly deleting records from the middle of our B-tree and storage file. The ideal thing for us to do is to recycle these deleted records. In other words, we re-use them the next time a new record is called for. If we do not re-use the deleted records, we will have a file with a lot of "dead" records in it. The only other solution would be to constantly regenerate or somehow collapse the entire B-tree and storage file every time we have deletions in the middle of the file. This is not a good solution because of the time involved.

B-trees, after all, are supposed to save us time.

allocation / deallocation procedure

The allocation/deallocation solution is as follows: The first record of the B-tree file is reserved for special counters. The B-tree record is fielded into two parts which we call **REC$** and **LE$**. In normal usage, REC$ will contain all the elements and LE$ will contain the page pointer and element counter but in the first record, we will use the first two bytes of REC$ to store the record number of the root page and the second two bytes of REC$ to store the total number of words on the B-tree. We will use LE$ to help keep track of deleted records in the B-tree file and the storage file. We set it up like this:

Locate storage file dead records

The first two bytes of LE$ are used for the B-tree and the second two bytes are used for the storage file. They are both pointers that point to the most recent dead record. We store our record numbers in LE$ using the MKI$ format. We initiate things by setting both values to -1.

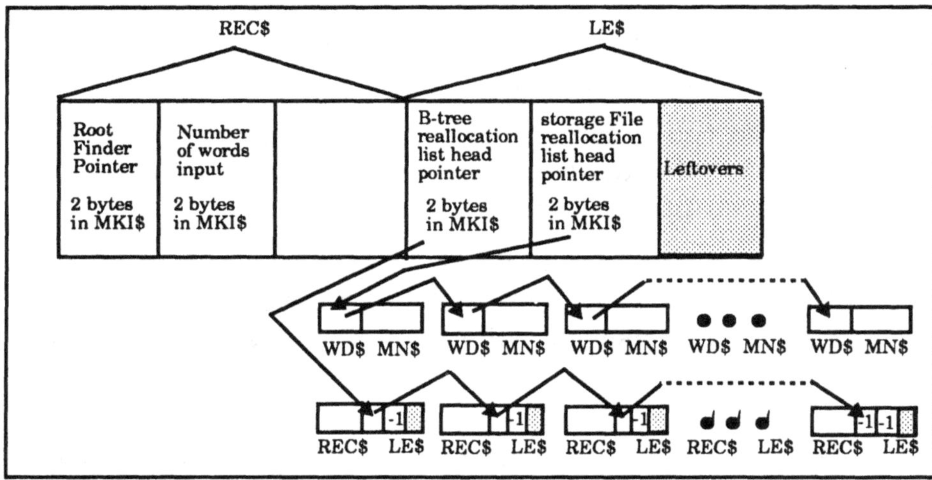

Figure 7.3: Control Record pointing to root and Reallocation List heads.

This means that if you go to LE$ and find a value of -1 in the first two bytes, you know that there are no B-tree records waiting to be re-used or re-allocated. Now let's say you are in the middle of a deletion and, because of absorption, you want to delete a B-tree record. We call this the deallocation of a B-tree record and the procedure goes as follows:

allocation procedure: step by step

1) Get the record number of the last deleted record from the first two bytes of LE$ in the control record.
2) Write that record number into the first two bytes of LE$ in the record you are now deleting.
3) Write the record number you are now deleting into the first two bytes of LE$ in the control record.

As you can see, this makes a "chain of deleted records" that can be easily used when we need a new record.

Allocate records

To re-use a record from the recycle list, we would simply do the opposite:

1) Get the record number of the last deleted record from the first two bytes of LE$ in the control record.
2) Retrieve that record deleted and read the first two bytes of LE$, which point to the next record in the chain of deleted records.
3) Write the record number of the next record in the chain of deleted records into the first two bytes of LE$ in the control record.

-1 means no deleted records

Note that when you find that -1 is the record number in LE$, there are no more deleted records waiting to be used. In this case you will create a new record at the end of the file.

What we have just described is the allocation/deallocation procedure for the B-tree file. It works exactly the same way for the storage file, except that the control record uses the third and fourth bytes of LE$ to point to the list head, and the record numbers of records in the list are stored in the first two bytes of WD$.

Order

The only other thing we should mention before analyzing our B-tree system is how we decide the ORDER of a B-tree page. In other words, how do we know how large we want our B-tree page to be? We devote an entire chapter, Chapter 9, to analyzing this problem and proving our conclusions. A summary is as follows:

Analyzing ORDER in Chapter 9

1) All you need to know in order to initialize the variables on our B-tree is the character length of your keyword.
2) You should try to make your page 512 bytes long. Determining the order, then, is trivial because you simply see how many times your keyword fits into 512 bytes, and remember the rule that two times the order is the maximum number of elements that can fit on a page (don't forget to leave room for the page and element pointers).
3) If your keyword is too big for the above procedure, make the order 2 and pick the smallest multiple of 512 bytes that you can for your page length.

Chapter 9 is devoted to a more rigorous treatment of the above conclusions and Chapter 10 is devoted to how you can change TeachBase to fit your needs.

Chapter 10 for how to change TeachBase

8

The TeachBase B-tree System Line-by-line

OVERVIEW

The following system of routines utilizes all the B-tree algorithms we have studied in this book. This system accepts keywords input from the keyboard and installs them on the B-tree. The keyword is then stored again. This time it is stored in a record in the storage file along with a 2-byte counter at the end of the record, which tells how many times the keyword has been entered.

Each time we input a keyword, the program searches the B-tree to see if it is already there. If it is, we get its record from the storage file and add one to the counter stored there. If it is not, a record in the storage file is allocated to it, and together with a storage file pointer it is installed as an element on a B-tree page.

TABLE OF GLOBAL VARIABLES

VARIABLE =	*DESCRIPTION*
ST =	Stacking variable; counter for the B-tree levels (i.e. ST=5 for level 5, etc.).
STACK =	Level counting variable; tells us the current level as we move up and down the tree; used to index several variables. It is the same as ST; some routines use STACK, others use ST.
NR(ST) =	The page number at level ST that you passed through on your way down. Note that there can only be one page number at level ST that you pass through on your way down.
NO(ST) =	The number of elements in page NR(ST).
RECLN =	Length of a record in the B-tree file.
LNG =	Length of a record in the keyword storage file.
T =	length of an element on a B-tree page (keyword + element pointer + storage pointer).
T0 =	Length of a keyword plus two bytes to include the keyword storage pointer for that keyword.
T1 =	Length of a keyword.
T2 =	Position within an element where the two-byte element pointer starts.
T3 =	Position within an element where the two-byte keyword storage pointer starts.
ORDER =	Order of the B-tree.
FULLPAGE =	Twice the order; the number of elements a full page contains.
BUF1 =	File number of the storage file, the keyword storage file.
BUF2 =	File number of the indexing file, the B-tree file.
ROOT =	Root finder variable holding the page number of the root page.
COUNT =	Total number, less deletions, of keywords input, including multiple entries of the same word.
TALLOC =	Record number of the list head for B-tree relocation list.
SALLOC =	Record number of the list head for the keyword storage allocation list.
NNW =	Record number of the record supplied by the B-tree allocation routine.
NNT =	Record number of the record supplied by the keyword storage file allocation routine.

Figure 8.1: The Global Variables

Note that we are allowing the same keyword to be entered on the B-tree as many times as desired. You could, of course, adapt the program to query the keyboarder and prevent duplicate entries.

preventing duplicates possible

GLOBAL VARIABLES:

There are certain variables that occur throughout all routines in the TeachBase system. They are listed in the chart on the opposite page along with their definitions.

ORGANIZATION OF CHAPTER 8

In Appendix C is a listing of the actual TeachBase B-tree system. In this chapter we will isolate and go through each of the routines contained in that B-tree system line by line. To make it easier to understand, we will list the lines of code on the left-hand-side page, and on the right-hand-side page we will describe what is happening.

The first lines of the program are used to initialize the variables used in the TeachBase system. This occurs in lines 100 through 1980. At line 1980 the program branches to line 5000, where the inputting of data begins. A thorough discussion of what the inputting code does, and how to modify it, occurs in Chapters 9 and 10.

We will cover the programs in the following order:

1) Input routine

2) Transversing (listing) a B-tree in ascending order

3) Transversing (listing) a B-tree in reverse order

4) Searching a B-tree

5) Allocation and de-allocation

6) B-tree structure's examination utility

7) B-tree generation

8) B-tree deletion

```
49585 '=================================================================
49587 '         input routine
49588 '==================================================================
49590 '---------- deletions ------------------
49600 GOSUB 65320: PRINT "To delete any existing keyword, type keyword
now;"
49605 PRINT"or use any * command to do other functions";
49610 INPUT WWW$: IF LEFT$(WWW$,1) = "*" THEN 49650
49612 K$ = STRING$(T1," ")
49614 MID$(K$,1) = WWW$
49616 GOTO 30110
49640 '---------- deal with commands -------------
49650 IF MID$(WWW$,2,2) = "lc" THEN 18800 'lexical listing
49655 IF MID$(WWW$,2,2)="at" THEN PRINT "Record number":GOTO 64000 'see
tree allocation list
49657 IF MID$(WWW$,2,2)="as" THEN PRINT "Record number":GOTO 65000 'see
word file allocation list
49660 IF MID$(WWW$,2,2) = "lr" THEN 60000 'list in reverse order
49675 IF MID$(WWW$,2,2) = "ut" THEN 22250 'see tree structure
49685 IF MID$(WWW$,2,2) = "in" THEN 50000 'install word
49688 IF MID$(WWW$,2,2) = "de" THEN 49600 'delete word
49690 IF MID$(WWW$,2,2) = "se" THEN 50200 'search for word
49695 IF MID$(WWW$,2,2) = "qu" THEN GOSUB 53000: PRINT "bye bye"
49698 END
49700 PRINT "Invalid command": GOTO 49600
```

INPUT ROUTINE

The input routine covers the lines 49600 to 52990. By input we mean that in these lines the computer will query you for inputting a keyword you want to delete from the B-tree, add to the B-tree, or search for. You can change from one mode to another mode, or request any one of a number of utilities, by simply typing an asterisk followed by the two-letter code for what you want to do. After completing a routine, such as listing, the program returns to the input routine in the deletion mode. This is an arbitrary choice; we had to send the user somewhere.

Lines 49600-49616

Here we are inputting a keyword we want to delete. A string of characters starting with an "*" is a command. If we input a string of characters starting with a "*", the program branches to the routine of lines 49650 to interpret the command. Otherwise, the program assumes a keyword has been input. The keywords are stored as the first part of each element and are T1 characters long. Therefore, to make the keyword input recognizable, we must left-set it into a field of T1 blanks. Here, the variable K$ is the keyword input, which is left-set in a field of T1 blanks. After the user inputs the keyword we branch to line 30110 to begin the deletion algorithm.

Lines 49650-49700

During any input routine — deletion, installation, or searching — one can indicate a command by letting "*" be the first character of the input string. All routines look at the first two characters following the "*" to see if they constitute a valid command. If a valid command is not received, we simply print "Invalid command" and branch to the deletion routine to try again. Otherwise, we make the appropriate branch depending on the command. The valid command letters are:.

```
50000 GOSUB 65320: PRINT "To install any keyword, type keyword now;"
50001 PRINT"or use any * command to do other functions";
50002 INPUT WWW$
50005 IF LEFT$(WWW$,1) = "*" THEN 49650
50010 word$ = STRING$(T1," ")
50020 MID$(word$,1) = WWW$
50100 GOTO 3100
50190 ' ---------- search procedure ----------------------
50200 GOSUB 65320: PRINT "To search for any keyword, type keyword now;"
50205 PRINT"or use any * command to do other functions";
50210 INPUT WWW$
50220 IF LEFT$(WWW$,1) = "*" THEN 49650
50230 W$ = STRING$(T1," ")
50240 MID$(W$,1) = WWW$
50250 GOTO 49520
50251 '
52990 '=================================================================
52994 '       up date control record
52998 '=================================================================
53000 LSET REC$ = MKI$(root) + MKI$(count)
53010 LSET LE$ = MKI$(TALLOC) + MKI$(SALLOC)
53050 PUT BUF2,1
53060 RETURN
```

Command	*Moves You To The Program*
*lc	list storage file in order (lexical listing)
*lr	list storage file in reverse order
*in	install (add) a key keyword to B-tree
*de	delete a key keyword
*se	search for a key word
*ut	show B-tree structure
*as	show storage file allocation list
*at	show B-tree allocation list
*qu	quit program

Figure 8.2: TeachBase commands.

Lines 50000-50100

Here we input a keyword we want to add to the B-tree system. The keyword is leftset into the variable WORD$, which consists of T1 blanks. Then WORD$ is sent to the installation routine (routine for installing a keyword on the B-tree) which starts at line 3100.

Lines 50200-50250

Here we input in the search mode. The keyword input goes into the variable W$, left-set into a field of T1 blanks. Then W$ is sent to the search routine of line 49520.

Lines 53000-53060

We are sent to these lines when we give the quit command. Here we update the control record and exit the program.

```
'==================================================================
18650 '       btree transversal - normal (left to right) order
18700
'==================================================================
18800 IF count = 0 THEN PRINT "No words in file": GOTO 49600
18850 PRINT "Total words in file: "; count
18860 PRINT "order";TAB(14) "storage word and number of times entered"
18900 ST = 0: E = 0
19100 NR(ST) = root
19300 '-------------- drop to bottom ----------------------------
19400 GET BUF2, NR%(ST%)
19500 NO%(ST%) = CVI ( MID$ (LE$,3,2)) : TV%(ST%) = 0: NR%(ST% + 1) =
CVI ( MID$ (REC$,T2 + T*TV(ST),2))
19600 IF NR%(ST% + 1) <> 0 THEN ST% = ST% + 1 : GOTO 19400
19700 ' ============== READ LEAF PAGE ===============================
19850 FOR I=0 TO NO(ST) - 1
19900 TRANSVERSE = I: GOSUB 21800
20000 NEXT I%
20100 IF NR(ST)=root THEN PRINT "DONE": GOTO 49600
```

LISTING THE CONTENTS OF THE B-TREE SYSTEM IN ASCENDING ORDER

Lines 18800 - 19100

If there are keywords in the B-tree file (COUNT is not zero) we set the level variable, ST, to zero; the keyword counter variable, E, to zero; and the record number variable, NR(ST), to ROOT.

Lines 19400-19600

Here we read our way down from page NR(ST) to the page on leaf level containing the smallest keywords less than the first keyword on page NR(ST). We get there by following the element pointers on the first element of the pages we come to. As we drop down, we record the number of elements for each page we come to, on the page, in the variable NO(ST). We also initialize to zero a variable, TV(ST), that tells how far we have read into this page. We set NR(ST+1), the record number of the next page in the search chain, to the pointer found in the first element on the page. If NR(ST+1) is zero we are at the leaf level and we have the page we have been looking for; therefore, we read that page in line 19850. Otherwise, we increase the level counter by one and return to line 19400 to continue the search on the next level.

Lines 19850 - 20100

Here we read each of the NO(ST) keywords on the leaf page, NR(ST). The data associated with each keyword is found in the storage file by means of the pointer beginning at position T3 within each element. We execute the subroutine of line 21800 to read the storage file record pointed to by the element pointer (represented by the variable TRANSVERSE). When we have read a total of NO(ST) keywords we execute line 20300 to ascend from the leaf page just read (unless this leaf page was also the root page, in which case we are done).

```
20200 ' -------------- ascend from leaf page -------------------
20300 ST = ST - 1
20400 GET BUF2, NR(ST)
20500 IF TV%(ST%) = NO%(ST%) THEN IF ST% <> 0 GOTO 21000 ELSE PRINT
"DONE": GOTO 49600
20600 TRANSVERSE = TV(ST): GOSUB 21800
20700 TV%(ST%) = TV%(ST%) + 1
20800 IF TV%(ST%) = NO%(ST%) THEN ST% = ST% + 1: NR%(ST%) = CVI ( LEFT$
(LE$,2)) : GET BUF2,NR%(ST%): NO%(ST%) = CVI ( MID$ (LE$,3,2)) : GOTO
19850
20900 ST = ST + 1: NR%(ST%) = CVI ( MID$ (REC$,T2 + T*TV%(ST-1),2)): GET
BUF2,NR%(ST%) : NO%(ST%) = CVI ( MID$ (LE$,3,2)) : GOTO 19850
20990 ' -------------- ascend from node page -------------------
21000 ST% = ST% - 1
21100 GET BUF2,NR%(ST%)
21200 IF TV%(ST%) = NO%(ST%) THEN IF ST% <> 0 THEN 21000 ELSE PRINT
"DONE": GOTO 49600
21300 TRANSVERSE = TV(ST): GOSUB 21800
21400 TV%(ST%) = TV%(ST%) + 1
21500 IF TV%(ST%) = NO%(ST%) THEN ST% = ST% + 1: NR%(ST%) = CVI ( LEFT$
(LE$,2)) : GOTO 19400
21600 ST=ST+1: NR(ST) = CVI ( MID$ (REC$, T2 + T*TV%(ST% - 1),2)): GOTO
19400
```

Lines 20300 - 20900

After we have read the leaf page, NR(ST), we ascend to the page NR(ST-1), from which we came down on the way to the leaf page. It may be, however, that we have already read the last keyword on the page (which happens when TV(ST) = NO(ST)). In that case, if page NR(ST) is the root page (i.e. ST is zero), we are finished. If not, we branch to line 21000 to ascend from the current page to the page above it. If we have not already read the last element on the new page, we now read the TV(ST) element. We let TRANSVERSE = TV(ST) and execute the subroutine of line 21800 to retrieve the storage file record. Then we increase TV(ST) by one. If TV(ST)-1 represented the last element on this page (page NR(ST)); that is, if TV(ST) = NO(ST), we will next read the leaf page pointed to by NR(ST)'s page pointer. In doing this, we increase ST by one, set NR(ST) to the page pointer, get the leaf page, page NR(ST), set NO(ST) equal to its element counter, and finally, branch to line 19850 to read the page. If TV(ST)-1 did not represent the last element, we increase ST by one, set NR(ST) to the pointer of the next element, TV(ST-1), get the leaf page NR(ST), set NO(ST) equal to its element counter, and branch to line 19850 to read the page.

Lines 21000 - 21600

After we ascend a level and arrive at a node page, we first look at TV(ST). If TV(ST) = NO(ST), which is the number of elements on the page, we know that the last time we ascended to this page we read out the last element, element NO(ST)-1. Therefore we re-ascend by looping back once more to line 21000, unless this page is the root, in which case we are done.

However, if we have not already read the last element on this page, we read element TV(ST) by means of the subroutine of line 21800. Then we increase TV(ST) by one. If TV(ST)-1 represented the last element on the page, and TV(ST) is now equal to NO(ST), we read down

```
21700 '------------- get pointed record form storage file ------------
-
21800 STORE = CVI( MID$(REC$, T*TRANSVERSE + T3, 2) )
21900 GET BUF1, STORE
21910 E=E+1
22000 PRINT E, WD$; CVI( MID$(MN$,1,2) )
22100 RETURN
```

```
53061 '
59990 '==================================================================
59994 '        reverse transversal of btree (right to left)
59998 '=================================================================
60000 IF count=0 THEN PRINT "No words in file": GOTO 49600
60010 PRINT "Total words in file: "; count
60012 PRINT "order";TAB(14) "storage word and number of times entered"
60090 '
60100 STACK=0: E=0
60140 NR(STACK)=root
60150 '---------- search down to leaf page -----------------------
61000 GET BUF2, NR(STACK)
61005 NO(STACK)=CVI(MID$(LE$,3,2)):NR(STACK+1)=CVI(MID$(LE$,1,2)):
TV(STACK)=NO(STACK)-1
61010 IF NR(STACK+1)<>0 THEN STACK=STACK+1: GOTO 61000
```

to the leaf level, beginning from the page pointer on level ST. In doing this, we increase ST by one, set NR(ST) to the page pointer, and branch to line 19400 to begin reading to the leaf level. If TV(ST)-1 did not represent the last element, we read down to the leaf level beginning from TV(ST), the element pointer on level ST. Next, we increase ST by one, set NR(ST) to the TV(ST-1) element pointer, and branch to line 19400 to begin reading to the leaf level.

Lines 21800 - 22100

Here we show the routine which gets the storage file record pointed to by the TRANSVERSE element of a page (the element you happen to be reading in listing the B-tree). The storage file pointer occupies two bytes, beginning at the T3 position within the element. We set STORE equal to this pointer and get the STORE record from the file. We increase the keyword counter and print it out, along with the current storage file record. This includes the last two bytes of the storage file record, which tell the number of times the current item has been entered.

LISTING THE CONTENTS OF THE B-TREE SYSTEM IN DESCENDING ORDER

Lines 60000 - 60140

If there are keywords on file (COUNT is not zero) we set the level variable, STACK, equal to zero; the keyword counter variable, E, equal to zero; and the record number variable, NR(STACK), equal to ROOT.

Lines 61000 - 61010

Here we read our way down from page NR(STACK) to the page on leaf level containing the largest words. We get there by following the page pointers on the pages we come to. For each page we come to as we drop down, we record the number of elements on that page in the variable NO(STACK). We also initialize to NO(STACK)-1 a

```
61015 '
61017 '----------------- read leaf page ------------------------------
-
61020 FOR I=NO(STACK)-1 TO 0 STEP -1
61030 TRANSVERSE = I: GOSUB 21800
61035 NEXT I
61037 IF NR(STACK)=root THEN PRINT "DONE": GOTO 49600
61038 '
61040 '------------- ascend from leaf page ------------------------
61045 STACK=STACK-1
61055 GET BUF2, NR(STACK)
61065 IF TV(STACK)=-1 THEN IF STACK<>0 GOTO 61200 ELSE PRINT "DONE":
GOTO 49600
61070 TRANSVERSE = TV(STACK): GOSUB 21800
61095 TV(STACK)=TV(STACK)-1
61105 STACK=STACK+1: NR(STACK)=CVI(MID$(REC$, T2 + T*(TV(STACK-1)+1),
2))
61110 GET BUF2, NR(STACK): NO(STACK)=CVI(MID$(LE$,3,2)): GOTO 61020
```

variable, TV(STACK), that tells how far we have to read into the page. Note we are setting TV(STACK) equal to the highest element and are going to read down to the least element, which is TV(STACK)=0. We set NR(STACK+1), the record number of the next page in the search chain, to that page's page pointer. If NR(STACK+1) is zero, then this is the page we have been looking for, which is the leaf page. Therefore, we read that page, using the routine of line 61020. Otherwise, we increase the level counter by one and return to line 61000 to continue the search on the next page.

Lines 61020 - 61037

Here we read, starting with the last element (NO(STACK)-1) and moving toward the first element (element zero), each of the NO(STACK) keywords on the leaf page, NR(STACK). The storage file pointer begins at position T3 within each element. We execute the subroutine of line 21800 (this subroutine serves both the ascending and descending transversal routines) to read the storage file record for the TRANSVERSE element. When we have read all the NO(STACK) keywords we execute line 61045 to ascend from the leaf page (unless this leaf page was also the root page, in which case we are done).

Lines 61045 - 61110

After we have read a leaf page, NR(STACK), we ascend to the page NR(STACK-1), from which we came when we reached the leaf page. It may be, however, that we have already read the first keyword on that page, which is the case if TV(STACK)= -1. If TV(STACK)=-1 then we have passed the first element and are done reading the page. If TV(STACK)=-1, then we check to see if we are on the root page, indicated by STACK=0. If STACK=0 then we are finished. If not, we branch to line 61200 to ascend from this node page to the page above it.

```
61195 '
61197 ' ----------- ascend from node page ---------------------------
61200 STACK=STACK-1
61210 GET BUF2, NR(STACK)
61220 IF TV(STACK)=-1 THEN IF STACK<>0 THEN 61200 ELSE PRINT "DONE":
GOTO 49600
61230 TRANSVERSE = TV(STACK): GOSUB 21800
61240 TV(STACK)=TV(STACK)-1
61250 STACK=STACK+1
61255 NR(STACK)=CVI(MID$(REC$,T2+T*(TV(STACK-1)+1),2)): GOTO 61000
```

If, however, we have not already read the first element on this page as well as the page pointed to by its pointer, we now read the TV(STACK) element. We then let TRANSVERSE = TV(STACK), and execute the subroutine of line 21800 to retrieve the keyword and its data from the storage file. We want to read (in reverse order) the elements on the page pointed to by element TV(STACK) and, after that, test to see if TV(STACK)-1 is -1. If not, we decrease TV(STACK) by one; increase STACK by one; set NR(STACK) to the TV(STACK-1)+1 element pointer; get the leaf page, NR(STACK); set NO(STACK) to its element counter; and finally, branch to line 61020 to read the page.

Lines 61200 - 61255

After we ascend a level (either from a leaf or node page) and arrive at a node page, we first look at TV(STACK). If TV(STACK) is -1, indicating that we have already read the first element on this page as well as all the elements greater than TV(STACK), we know that the last time we ascended to this page we read out the first element, element 0, and then descended to the leaf level from TV(STACK)'s pointer. Therefore (unless this page is the root, in which case we are done), we ascend again by looping back to line 61200.

However, if we have not already read the first element, element 0, we read the TV(STACK) element by means of the subroutine of line 21800. We want to read down from this page to leaf level, starting from the pointer of element TV(STACK), and then read our way back up, so as to read elements less than TV(STACK). Therefore we increase TV(STACK) by one, increase STACK by one, set NR(STACK) to the TV(STACK-1)+1 element pointer, and branch to line 61000 to read down to leaf level.

```
49510 '============================================================
49512 '       search routine
49514 '============================================================
49520 IF count = 0 THEN PRINT "File is empty": GOTO 50000
49525 ST = 0
49530 NR = root
49540 ' -------- search page NR for the word, W$ ----------
49545 GET BUF2, NR
49550 NUMBER = CVI(MID$(LE$,3,2)): NN=CVI(MID$(LE$,1,2))
49555 FOR K=0 TO NUMBER-1
49560 FF$ = MID$(REC$, 1 + T*K, T1)
49565 IF W$ = FF$ THEN 49577
49570 IF W$<FF$ THEN IF NN<>0 THEN NR=CVI(MID$(REC$,T2+T*K,2)): GOTO
49545 ELSE 49575
49572 NEXT
49574 IF NN <> 0 THEN NR = NN: GOTO 49545 ELSE PRINT "Not found": GOTO
50200
49575 PRINT:PRINT "Not found": GOTO 50200
```

SEARCHING THE B-TREE

Lines 49520-49530

If there are keywords on file (COUNT is not zero), we set the level variable, ST, to zero and page number variable, NR, to ROOT. This enables us to enter the page search routine searching the root page.

Lines 49550-49575

Here we get and search page NR for the search word, W$. We are comparing W$ to FF$ which is the keyword (the first T1 bytes off each element). If we find W$, we branch to line 49577 to retrieve it from the storage file. The storage file pointer is located in two bytes, in MKI$ format, starting in position T3 of the B-tree element in which W$ was found. If we don't find W$, then, as we read through the page, we will encounter one of two things:

1) We may come to an FF$ that is greater than W$, in which case, if we are not at leaf level (indicated by the element pointer for this page, NN, being zero), we want to drop to page NW. We set NR equal to the element pointer of FF$ and loop back to line 49545 to continue the search on the new page on the level below. If, however, we are at the leaf level, then we know that W$ is not present on the B-tree. Consequently, we execute line 49575 to print "Not found" and return to the input routine in the search mode.
2) We may come to the end of the page without finding W$. In this case, if we are not at leaf level (as indicated by the page pointer, NN, being zero), we set NR to the page pointer, NN, and loop back to line 49550 to continue the search with a new page on the next level down. If, however, we are at the leaf level, we know that W$ is not present on the B-tree. Consequently, in line 49575, we print "Not found" and return to the input routine in the search mode.

```
49576 '----------- found W$ in tree; retrieve from storage -----------
-
49577 STORE = CVI(MID$(REC$, T3 + T*K, 2))
49579 GET BUF1, STORE
49580 PRINT:PRINT "Storage file contents and number of times
entered:": PRINT WD$, CVI(LEFT$(MN$,2))
49582 GOTO 50200
```

```
23200 '==============================================================
23300 '        allocation & deallocation routines
23400 '==============================================================
23500 ' ---------- allocate new record (NNW) for btree -------------
23600 IF TALLOC = -1 THEN NNW = LOF(BUF2)/RECLN + 1: RETURN
23900 NNW = TALLOC
24000 GET BUF2, TALLOC
24200 TALLOC = CVI(MID$(LE$,1,2))
24400 RETURN
```

Lines 49577-49582

We execute these lines when the searched-for keyword has been found. The found word, along with its data (the number of times this item was input less the number of times it was successfully deleted), is contained in the storage file record. The storage file record has two fields, WD$ and MN$. The word is stored in the storage file in the field variable WD$. The data is stored in the first two bytes of the field variable MN$. We assign the variable STORE the value of the storage file pointer and retrieve the storage file record.

ALLOCATION AND DE-ALLOCATION

Overview of Lines 23600-25540

Here we do the routine that allocates or assigns new records as they are needed for our files (the B-tree file and the storage file). We also de-allocate records which the user wants to delete. For each file we maintain a chain of deleted records. Then, when we need a new record, we get it from the chain, rather than just adding it to the end of the file. Thus, we conserve disk space by recycling records.

Lines 23600-24400

When we delete a record, we put it at the head of our chain of deleted records waiting to be allocated or recycled. The very first record in the chain is called the list head. When the B-tree grows through the addition of a new page, we allocate the list head as our new record, record NNW, to be that page. The variable TALLOC stores the record number of the B-tree allocation list head. Remember, this list head is where the B-tree allocation list starts. When we allocate a record, we use the list head, and the record that was pointed to by the list head is moved up to take its place. The last record in the chain has its list pointer set to -1, so we know that the

```
23200 '================================================================
23300 '        allocation & deallocation routines
23400 '================================================================
23500 ' ---------- allocate new record (NNW) for btree -------------
23600 IF TALLOC = -1 THEN NNW = LOF(BUF2)/RECLN + 1: RETURN
23900 NNW = TALLOC
24000 GET BUF2, TALLOC
24200 TALLOC = CVI(MID$(LE$,1,2))
24400 RETURN
```

allocation list is empty when TALLOC becomes -1. It is also true that in the beginning, before any records are de-allocated and added to the de-allocation list, the value of TALLOC is -1. So a TALLOC of -1 always indicates that the allocation list is empty. Every new (not recycled) record added to the B-tree or storage file, of course, goes on at the end of the file.

Therefore, if TALLOC is -1, and we need a new record, the record number of the new record allocated, NNW, will be one beyond the end of the file. If TALLOC does not have the value of -1, the new record number will be the value of TALLOC, and TALLOC will then be assigned the value of the former TALLOC's allocation chain pointer. We use the first two bytes of the field variable LE$ to store the allocation chain pointer in deallocated records. Remember that our B-tree records are fielded as follows:

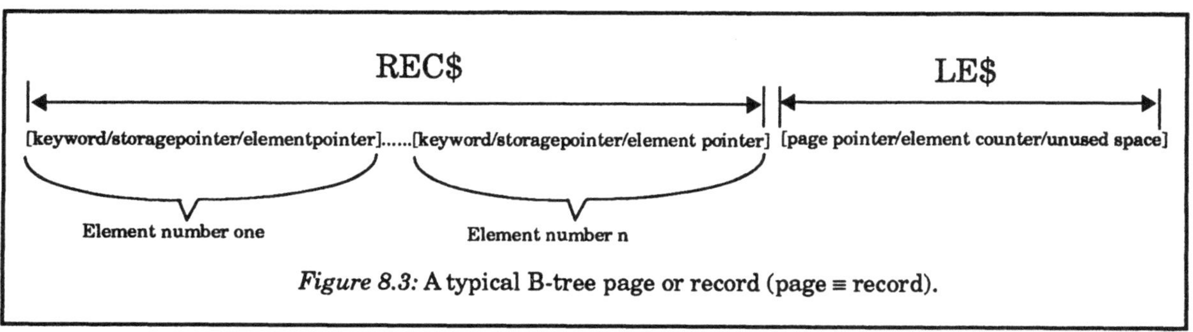

Figure 8.3: A typical B-tree page or record (page ≡ record).

and our storage file records are fielded as follows:

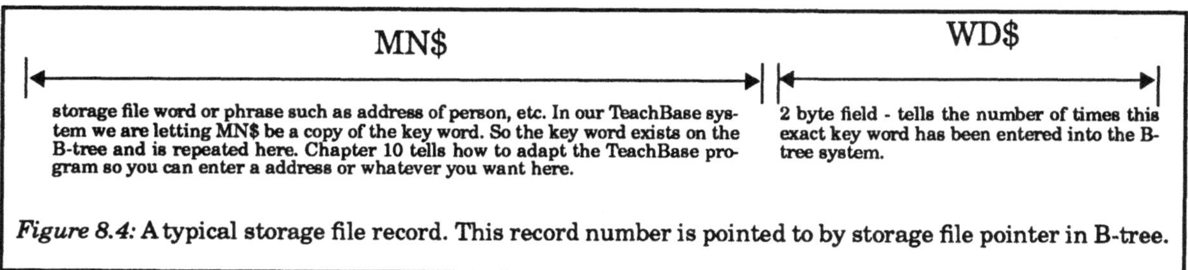

Figure 8.4: A typical storage file record. This record number is pointed to by storage file pointer in B-tree.

```
24405 '--- deallocate a record (OLD) to the btree allocation list -----
24410 LSET LE$ = MKI$(TALLOC) + MKI$(-1)
24420 PUT BUF2, OLD
24430 TALLOC = OLD
24482 RETURN
24500 ' ---------- allocate new record (NNT) for storage file ---------
24600 IF SALLOC = -1 THEN NNT = LOF(BUF1)/LNG + 1: RETURN
24610 NNT = SALLOC
24620 GET BUF1, SALLOC
24630 SALLOC = CVI(MID$(WD$,1,2))
24640 RETURN
25505 '----- deallocate record (OLD) to storage allocation list ------
25510 LSET WD$ = MKI$(SALLOC)
25520 PUT BUF1, OLD
25530 SALLOC = OLD
25540 RETURN
```

Lines 24410-24482

Each time we delete a B-tree page, we perform the de-allocation procedure in these lines to place the deleted page in the allocation chain. A record added to the allocation chain becomes the new allocation list head. This means that the record being de-allocated, the record OLD, gets an allocation chain pointer which points to the previous list head, and TALLOC is set to OLD. Note that, in addition to giving OLD the value of TALLOC, we write a -1, as an allocation list pointer, into the two bytes following the allocation pointer. This acts as a flag in the utility routine, telling us that this record has been deleted from the B-tree.

Lines 24600-24640

Each time we want to add a new keyword to the storage file, we need to allocate a record for it. The record allocated will be NNT. This routine is exactly like the routine explained above for allocating a B-tree record. In this case, however, SALLOC is the variable whose value is the record number of the list head for the storage file allocation list. If SALLOC is -1, the record number of the new record allocated, NNT, will be one beyond the end of the storage file. Otherwise, it will be SALLOC, and the new SALLOC will be the value of the former SALLOC's allocation chain pointer. The storage file allocation list pointers are stored in the first two bytes of the field variable WD$.

Lines 25510-25540

Each time we delete a keyword from the storage file, we place its record in the storage file allocation list so it can be used to store the next keyword added to the storage file. A record added to the storage file allocation chain becomes the new allocation list head. This means that the record being de-allocated, the record OLD, gets an allocation chain pointer which points to the previous list head, and SALLOC is set to OLD.

```
22102 '=============================================================
22104 '       utility routine: record by record list of btree
22108 '============================================================
22250 PRINT STRING$(18,"-"); " Page: 1"; STRING$(30, "-")
22260 PRINT "root", "no words", "tree alloc", "store alloc"
22300 PRINT root, count, TALLOC, SALLOC
22400 FOR IM=2 TO LOF(BUF2)/RECLN
22500 GET BUF2, IM
22550 PRINT STRING$(18,"-"); " Page: "; IM; STRING$(30,"-")
22600 HH = CVI(MID$(LE$,3,2))
22610 IF HH = -1 THEN PRINT "** Deleted ** (in allocation chain)": GOTO
23100
22650 PRINT "word", "Element ptr", "Storage ptr"
22700 FOR IK=0 TO HH-1
22800 PRINT MID$(REC$, IK*T + 1, T1),
22810 PRINT CVI( MID$(REC$, IK*T + T2, 2) ),
22820 PRINT CVI( MID$(REC$, IK*T + T3, 2) )
22900 NEXT
22950 PRINT "Page pointer: "; CVI(MID$(LE$, 1, 2))
23000 PRINT "Words on page: "; CVI(MID$(LE$,3,2))
23100 NEXT
23150 GOTO 49600

2800 '-------------------------------------------------------------
3100 IF count <> 0 THEN 5300 'file is empty
3200 '
3400 GOSUB 23600 'allocate tree record
3500 GOSUB 24600 'allocate storage file record
3600 '---------- increase word counter & set root finder ------------
3700 count = count + 1
3800 root = NNW
4100 '---------- install the root --------------------
4200 LSET REC$ = word$ + MKI$(NNT) + MKI$(0)
4300 LSET LE$ = MKI$(0) + MKI$(1)
4400 PUT BUF2, NNW
4450 GOSUB 17200 'store word in storage file
4455 PRINT "* created a root and installed *": GOTO 50000
4499 '
```

B-TREE EXAMINATION UTILITY

Lines 22250-23150

In this program we first print some headings; then the page number of the root page, the total number; less deletions, of keywords input; the list head for the B-tree allocation list and the list head for the storage file allocation list.

Next, we print the configuration of each page in the B-tree. If the page has been deleted and is in the allocation list, we simply print "** Deleted **" and go on to the next page. Otherwise, we print each keyword on the page, its element pointer, and storage file pointer. Finally, we print the page pointer for the page as well as the number of keywords on the page.

Following the printout of the above information, we branch to the input routine in delete mode.

ADDING TO THE B-TREE

Lines 3100-4450

We arrive here from the input routine with a keyword to install. If there are no elements on the B-tree (COUNT = 0 in line 3100), the keyword we just picked up from the input routine becomes the root. Therefore, we allocate a B-tree record for the root element and a storage file record. We add one to the keyword counter and assign root the record number, NNW, just received from the B-tree page allocation routine. Next, we install the root in the newly allocated B-tree record NNW. Finally, we execute the subroutine of line 17200 to write the keyword to the newly allocated record NNT of the storage file.

Lines 5300 - 6900

If COUNT does not equal zero in line 3100, there are already keywords in the file, and we perform this routine to locate the proper leaf page on which to install a

```
4500 '-----------------------------------------------------------------
4600 ' establishing elements subsequent to the first on the tree
4700 '-----------------------------------------------------------------
4901 '
5000 '-----------------------------------------------------------------
5100 ' searching down the tree for the leaf page on which to put
element
5200 '----------------------------------------------------------------
5300 STACK%=0
5500 NR(STACK) = root
5600 '
5700 GET BUF2, NR(STACK)
5800 NUMBER=CVI(MID$(LE$,3,2))
5900 PAGEPTR = CVI(MID$(LE$,1,2))
5950 LOW=0: HIGH=NUMBER-1
5990 I = (LOW+HIGH)/2
6000 FF$ = MID$(REC$, 1 + T*I, T1)
6300 IF word$ = FF$ THEN 16200 'increase the word counter
6400 IF word$ > FF$ THEN 6800
6500 HIGH=I-1
6600 IF HIGH >= LOW THEN 5990
6650 IF PAGEPTR=0 THEN 8050
6660 LIFT(STACK) = I
6700 STACK=STACK+1: NR(STACK)=CVI(MID$(REC$, T2 + T*I, 2)): GOTO 5700
6800 LOW = I+1
6850 IF LOW <= HIGH THEN 5990
6855 I=I+1
6860 IF I <> NUMBER THEN 6650
6900 IF PAGEPTR = 0 THEN 7050
6910 STACK=STACK+1: NR(STACK)=PAGEPTR: GOTO 5700
7000 '-----------------------------------------------------------------
```

word. Recall that new keywords are added only to leaf pages; the B-tree grows when leaf pages overflow. We start the search at the root page, with STACK set to zero. STACK is the variable that tells us what level of the B-tree we are on. The variable NR(STACK) tells us that at level stack we are at record NR(STACK). We start the search at the root page, so we let NR(0) be root.

Lines 5700 - 6910
Elements are stored, in ascending order on a page, in NUMBER blocks of T bytes per element. The first T1 bytes of each element make up a keyword. After that, two bytes (all our pointers are two-byte integers) make up the storage file pointer and point to the record in the storage file where our information or word is stored. The final two bytes of the element make up the element pointer, which points to the last page on the next lower level, STACK+1, having keywords of lesser value than the keyword to which this pointer belongs. If NR(STACK) is a leaf page, this pointer is zero. Page NR(STACK) contains NUMBER keywords or elements and has a page pointer, PAGEPTR, which points to page PAGEPTR, the first page on level STACK+1 that contains keywords greater than the keywords on NR(STACK). Of course, if NR(STACK) is a leaf page, PAGEPTR is zero.

Starting with the smallest keyword (the first T1 bytes of the leftmost element, the zero element), we search page NR(STACK) to find (1) that the keyword to be installed, WORD$, is already present on the page; or (2) a keyword on page NR(STACK) that is greater than WORD$; or (3) that WORD$ is greater than any keyword on the page. We take action as follows:

1. **A keyword on the page is equal to WORD$:** FF$ represents a keyword stored in one of the elements referenced by I as it runs from 0 to NUMBER-1. If we

```
7300 '
7400 ' 1) adding at the end
7500 '
7600 R$ = MID$(REC$, 1, NUMBER*T) + word$+MKI$(NNT) + MKI$(0)
7700 IF NUMBER = FULLPAGE THEN 9600 ELSE 8800
7800 '
7900 ' 2) adding in the middle
8000 '
8050 GOSUB 24600 'allocate storage file record
8100 IF I=0 THEN 8300 ELSE 8200
8200 R$ = MID$(REC$, 1, T*I) + word$+MKI$(NNT)+MKI$(0) + MID$(REC$, 1 +
T*I, NUMBER*T): GOTO 8400
8300 R$ = word$+MKI$(NNT)+MKI$(0) + MID$(REC$, 1, T*NUMBER)
8400 IF NUMBER = FULLPAGE THEN 9600 ELSE 8800
8500 '------------ adding to leaf, no splitting needed ---------------
-
8700 '
8800 LSET REC$ = R$
8900 LSET LE$ = MKI$(PAGEPTR) + MKI$(NUMBER + 1)
9000 PUT BUF2, NR(STACK)
9200 GOSUB 17200 'write word to new storage file record
9300 count = count + 1 'update word counter
9400 PRINT "* Installed on a leaf with no splitting *": GOTO 50000
```

find WORD$ on this page, that is, if WORD$= FF$ for some element 0 through NUMBER-1, then we execute the routine of line 1620 to increase the keyword counter, stored in the storage file, for WORD$.

2. **A keyword on the page is found that is greater than WORD$:** If, for some I, FF$ is greater than WORD$, we know that WORD$ is not on that page. This means that, if this is a leaf page (PAGEPTR is zero), we execute the routine of line 8100 to insert WORD$ in front of FF$ on page NR(STACK). If, however, page NR(STACK) is not a leaf page, we loop back to line 5700 to continue the search on level STACK+1 using the page pointed to by the element pointer in element I. This pointer consists of the final two bytes of the element I, and begins at byte T2 of the element. For possible use in a later procedure, we save the element number for FF$ in the variable LIFT(STACK).

3. **No keyword on the page is greater than WORD$**: If WORD$ is greater than any of the NUMBER keywords stored on page NR(STACK), then, if the page is a leaf page, we execute the routine of 7600 to add WORD$ onto the end of the page. If, however, page NR(STACK) is not a leaf page, we must continue the search on the next level, STACK+1, on the page pointed to by page NR(STACK)'s page pointer. In this case, we assign I to LIFT(STACK) for possible later use. Note that, in this case, I=NUMBER.

Lines 7600 - 9400

Here we insert WORD$ into the appropriate part of the leaf page NR(STACK). The element WORD$ enters will consist of WORD$, followed by an integer pointing to the record of the storage file, NNT, in which WORD$ is stored, and then the element pointer, which is zero since NR(STACK) is a leaf page.

If WORD$ should be inserted at the end of the page, the

```
9500 ' =============== splitting a leaf ==============================
9600 GOSUB 23600 'allocate new tree page: NNW
9700 A$ = MID$(R$, 1, T*ORDER)
9800 MIDONE$ = MID$(R$, T*ORDER + 1, T0) + MKI$(NR(STACK))
9820 MID$(MIDONE$, T2, 2) = MKI$(NR(STACK))
9900 B$ = MID$( R$, T*(ORDER+1) + 1 )
10000 LSET REC$ = A$
10100 LSET LE$ = MKI$(0) + MKI$(ORDER)
10200 PUT BUF2, NR(STACK)
10300 LSET REC$ = B$
10400 PUT BUF2, NNW
10500 GOSUB 17200 'install new word in storage
10600 count=count+1 'update word counter
10700 IF STACK = 0 THEN GOTO 14950 'form new root on split
10800 '
```

element consisting of WORD$ plus pointers goes into page NR(STACK) as the NUMBER+1 element. Otherwise, it goes in as element I+1 between two elements, unless, of course, I=0 in which case it goes in as the first element.

If NR(STACK) is already full (NUMBER = FULLPAGE), we execute the procedure of line 9600 to split the leaf and raise the middle element to the next level. Otherwise, we write the page, which now contains NUMBER+1 elements or blocks, to the B-tree file as record NR(STACK). Then we execute the routine of line 17200 to install the keyword to the storage file and increase the keyword counter by one. Finally, in line 15000, we enter the input routine to get either another keyword to install or a command to execute a different routine.

Lines 9600 - 10700

This routine is executed when, due to the addition of an element to a leaf page, the page, NR(STACK) overflows because it now contains FULLPAGE+1 or (2)(ORDER)+1 elements. When this occurs, we retain the first ORDER elements on page NR(STACK) and write the last ORDER elements to a newly allocated page, page NNW. The middle element, element ORDER+1, is furnished with an element pointer pointing to page NR(STACK). We do this because, in the routine of line 11100, we must lift the middle element to the next level so that it points to page NR(STACK). After rewriting page NR(STACK) and writing page NNW, we execute the routine of line 17200 to install the new keyword into record NNT. We then increase the keyword counter by one.

If the overflowing page was not the ROOT page, we go on to the lifting procedure of line 11100. Otherwise, we execute the routine of line 14950 to form a new root consisting solely of the middle element.

```
10800 '
10900 ' ---------- Lift middle element to a node page ----------------
11000 '
11100 STACK%=STACK%-1
11200 GET BUF2, NR%(STACK%)
11300 NUMBER = CVI(MID$(LE$,3,2))
11400 IF LIFT(STACK) < NUMBER THEN 11950
11490 '---------------- end pointer ------------------------
11500 R$ = MID$(REC$, 1, T*NUMBER) + MIDONE$
11700 L$ = MKI$(NNW) + MKI$(NUMBER+1) 'page ptr points to newly created
page
11800 GOTO 12600
11900 '---------------- mid pointer ------------------------
11950 IF LIFT(STACK)=0 THEN A$ = "": GOTO 12100 'goes first on page
12000 A$ = MID$(REC$, 1, T*LIFT(STACK))
12100 C$ = MID$(REC$, T*LIFT(STACK) + 1, NUMBER*T)
12200 MID$(C$, T2, 2) = MKI$(NNW) 'elt ptr points to newly created page
12400 L$ = LE$
12500 MID$(L$,3,2) = MKI$(NUMBER + 1)
12550 R$ = A$ + MIDONE$ + C$
12570 '---- if page overflows spits a node; else set the page ---------
12600 IF NUMBER = FULLPAGE THEN 13150
12700 LSET REC$ = R$
12800 LSET LE$ = L$
12900 PUT BUF2,NR(STACK)
12902 IF BRANCHSPLIT$="yes" THEN 12904 ELSE 12990 'what to print
12904 PRINT "* installed; splitting required on branch pages *"
12906 BRANCHSPLIT$="": GOTO 50000
12990 PRINT "* installed on leaf which split with no further splitting
*"
13000 GOTO 50000
```


```
11490 '---------------- end pointer ------------------------
11500 R$ = MID$(REC$, 1, T*NUMBER) + MIDONE$
11700 L$ = MKI$(NNW) + MKI$(NUMBER+1) 'page ptr points to newly created
page
11800 GOTO 12600
11900 '---------------- mid pointer ------------------------
11950 IF LIFT(STACK)=0 THEN A$ = "": GOTO 12100 'goes first on page
12000 A$ = MID$(REC$, 1, T*LIFT(STACK))
12100 C$ = MID$(REC$, T*LIFT(STACK) + 1, NUMBER*T)
12200 MID$(C$, T2, 2) = MKI$(NNW) 'elt ptr points to newly created page
12400 L$ = LE$
12500 MID$(L$,3,2) = MKI$(NUMBER + 1)
12550 R$ = A$ + MIDONE$ + C$
```

Lines 11100 - 13000

These lines constitute the routine by which an overflowing middle element is lifted to the next level, level STACK-1. Therefore, we decrease STACK by one and get page NR(STACK). We get the number of keywords on page NR(STACK) from its position in LE$ and store it in NUMBER. The lifted middle element must be inserted into page NR(STACK), in front of the element whose pointer indicated NR(STACK+1). However, if NR(STACK+1) was pointed to by NR(STACK)'s page pointer, the lifted middle element goes into page NR(STACK) at the end. We determine where to put the lifted element by the value of LIFT(STACK). Remember that LIFT(STACK) stores either the element (0 through NUMBER-1) that pointed to the page that is now NR(STACK+1), or NUMBER, if the page pointer pointed to NR(STACK+1).

Lines 11500 - 11800

We write the lifted middle element onto the end of page NR(STACK). R$ consists of the previous NUMBER elements to which the element MIDONE$, the lifted middle element, has been added. MIDONE$'s element pointer points to NR(STACK+1). The page pointer of page NR(STACK) will now point to page NNW, which was created when NR(STACK) split; formerly, it pointed to NR(STACK+1). Therefore, we assign L$ two bytes, which represent NNW, followed by two bytes to represent the number of elements on the page—now NUMBER+1. Finally, we branch to the routine of line 12570 to set R$ and L$ into page NR(STACK).

Lines 11950 - 12550

We write the lifted middle element, MIDONE$, onto page NR(STACK), somewhere, depending on the value of LIFT(STACK), before the end of the page. MIDONE$ goes into NR(STACK) in front of the LIFT(STACK) element which pointed to NR(STACK+1). MIDONE$ now points to NR(STACK+1), and the LIFT(STACK) element

```
12570 '---- if page overflows spits a node; else set the page ---------
12600 IF NUMBER = FULLPAGE THEN 13150
12700 LSET REC$ = R$
12800 LSET LE$ = L$
12900 PUT BUF2,NR(STACK)
12902 IF BRANCHSPLIT$="yes" THEN 12904 ELSE 12990 'what to print
12904 PRINT "* installed; splitting required on branch pages *"
12906 BRANCHSPLIT$="": GOTO 50000
12990 PRINT "* installed on leaf which split with no further splitting
*"
13000 GOTO 50000
13100 ' ================ splitting a node ===========================
13150 GOSUB 23600 'allocate new record
13200 MIDONE$ = MID$(R$, (T*ORDER)+1, T0) + MKI$(NR(STACK))
13400 OLDPTR$ = MID$(R$, (T*ORDER) + T2, 2 )
13500 A$ = MID$(R$, 1, T*ORDER)
13600 B$ = MID$(R$, T*(ORDER+1) + 1 )
13700 LSET REC$ = B$
13800 MID$(L$,3,2) = MKI$(ORDER)
13900 LSET LE$ = L$
14000 PUT BUF2, NNW
14100 LSET REC$ = A$
14200 LSET LE$ = OLDPTR$ + MKI$(ORDER)
14300 PUT BUF2, NR(STACK)
14400 IF STACK <> 0 THEN BRANCHSPLIT$="yes": GOTO 11100 'lift to next
level
14600 '
```

should now point to NNW, the page created upon the splitting of NR(STACK+1). We then form A$ from the elements before LIFT(STACK) and C$ from the elements after LIFT(STACK). We change the element pointer of the first element in C$ to point to NNW. Note that A$ is null("") if LIFT(STACK) is 0. Finally, using L$, we change the element counter to NUMBER+1, assign R$ the new element configuration, and branch to line 12570 to set the page.

Lines 12570 - 13000
If page NR(STACK) was already full, and the addition of the lifted element to page NR(STACK) results in overflow, we do not execute lines 12700-13000 to set the page. Instead, we branch to the routine of line 13150 to split the over-full page.

Lines 13150 - 14400
Here we split a node page, NR(STACK). This only happens when a node page overflows due to the addition of an element from another overflowing page (leaf or node) on the level below.

The only difference between splitting a node and splitting a leaf is that, since the pointers of a node page are not all zero, like those of leaf pages, we must deal with the pointer left behind when the middle element is lifted. We assign this pointer to OLD$; it becomes the new page pointer of page NR(STACK), which retains the first ORDER elements of the old page NR(STACK). The page pointer of the old NR(STACK) becomes the page pointer of the newly allocated page NNW, which gets the second ORDER elements and, therefore, the page pointer as well.

If the stack is not zero, we loop back to line 11100 to lift the middle element, MIDONE$, to the next level. Otherwise, we continue with the routine of line 14950 and

```
14600 '
14700 '==============================================================
14800 '       create a new root by splitting the old one
14900 '==============================================================
14950 PNNW = NNW 'save old
15000 GOSUB 23600 'allocate new tree record: NNW
15050 LSET REC$ = MIDONE$
15100 LSET LE$ = MKI$(PNNW) + MKI$(1)
15275 PUT BUF2, NNW
15290 '
15300 root = NNW 'update root finder
15800 PRINT "* installed; a new root was formed through splitting *":
GOTO 50000
15900 '--------------------------------------------------------------
16000 '       searched for word is already in file; increase counter
16100 '--------------------------------------------------------------
16200 WHERE = CVI( MID$(REC$, T*I + T3, 2) )
16220 GET BUF1, WHERE
16300 KOUNT = CVI( MID$(MN$, 1, 2) )
16400 KOUNT=KOUNT+1
16500 LSET MN$ = MKI$(KOUNT)
16600 PUT BUF1, WHERE
16750 count=count+1 'increase total word counter
16800 PRINT "* increased the occurrence counter *": GOTO 50000
16900 '--------------------------------------------------------------
17000 '       add new element to the storage storage file
17100 '--------------------------------------------------------------
17200 '
17300 LSET WD$ = word$
17400 LSET MN$ = MKI$(1)
17500 PUT BUF1, NNT
17600 RETURN
```

make the lifted middle element the new root page.

Lines 14950 - 15800
We execute these lines when the lifted middle element comes from the overflowing root page. The lifted element becomes a new, single element root page, page NNW. Its element pointer has already been re-set to point to page NR(STACK). Its page pointer must now be set to point to the number of the new page that was created when the root split. That page is now page PNNW because we saved NNW in PNNW before allocating a new NNW for the new root.

Lines 16200 - 16800
We are sent here from line 6300 to execute these lines, in order to increase the specific keyword counter that is stored in the storage file. This specific keyword counter tells us how many times we have added the identical keyword to the file. It is stored in the first two bytes of the field variable MN$. Since we account for each entering of a word, duplicate or not, we must also increase the total keyword counter, COUNT, by one.

Lines 17300 - 17600
We execute this subroutine whenever we want to actually write a new keyword to the storage file.

DELETING FROM THE B-TREE

Lines 30090-30110
When we get to the deletion routine, the first thing we do is check the keyword counter, COUNT. If COUNT is zero, we have nothing to delete, so we enter the input routine in the installation (add a keyword) mode.

Lines 30120 - 31800
Here we are going to search a chain of records, NR(ST), from the root page, NR(0), to a leaf page, hunting for the

```
30115 '-------- get record number of root ----------------------------
30120 ST=0
30130 NR(ST) = root
30800 '
30900 '------------ search a page for deletion key -------------------
31000 '
31100 GET BUF2,NR(ST)
31200 NUMBER=CVI(MID$(LE$,3,2)): NN=CVI(MID$(LE$,1,2))
31300 FOR K=0 TO NUMBER-1
31310 FF$ = MID$(REC$, 1 + T* K, T1)
31400 IF K$=FF$ THEN 32125
31500 IF K$ < FF$ THEN IF NN<>0 THEN KK(ST)=K%: ST=ST+1:
NR(ST)=CVI(MID$(REC$,T2 + T*K,2)):GOTO 31100 ELSE PRINT "NOT
FOUND":GOTO 49600
31600 NEXT
31700 KK(ST)=-1
31800 IF NN<>0 THEN ST=ST+1: NR(ST)=NN: GOTO 31100 ELSE PRINT "NOT
FOUND":GOTO 49600
31900 '
32000 '==============================================================
32010 'found deletion word: decrease total word counter & specific
counter
32012 '       (also deallocate storage if word occurs only once)
32020 '==============================================================
32100 '
32120 '-------- decrease total word counter ---------------
32125 count = count - 1
32138 --- decrease specific word counter or deallocate completely ----
-
32140 STORAGE$ = MID$(REC$, T3 + T*K, 2)
32145 OLD = CVI(STORAGE$)
32147 GET BUF1, OLD
32150 NZ = CVI(LEFT$(MN$,2))
32154 IF NZ <> 1 THEN LSET MN$ = MKI$(NZ-1): PUT BUF1, OLD: PRINT "**
Reduced count **": GOTO 49600
32156 GOSUB 25505 'deallocate storage record
32157 IF NN=0 THEN 32205 ELSE 48600 'found on leaf else on node
32158 '
```

deletion word, K$. We set ST, the variable which tells us what level we are on, to zero and NR(ST) to root. We then start the repetitive search routine of line 31100, searching the root page. NUMBER is the number of elements on the page being searched, and NN is the page pointer.

We think of a page as consisting of NUMBER elements, numbered 0 through NUMBER-1, which we will search sequentially. If we find the sought-for word, we branch to line 32125 to deal with it. Otherwise, we either come to an element that is greater than K$ or to the end of the page without finding such an element. In either case, if NR(ST) is a leaf page (NN equal to zero), K$ is not in the file. Therefore, we go back to the input routine. However, if NR(ST) is not a leaf page, the search is yet not over. We then go down to the next level, ST+1, and search the page pointed to by either the element pointer of element K or the page pointer, whichever is appropriate. When dropping a level, we save the number of the element doing the pointing in KK(ST). If the page pointer did the pointing, then we save -1. KK(ST) is for possible use in balancing or absorption.

Lines 32125 - 32157

Here we decrease the total keyword counter and go to the storage file to decrease the specific keyword counter stored there along with the word. The storage file pointer consists of two bytes stored in element K and starting in position T3. We get that record and examine the keyword counter stored as the first two bytes of MN$. If it is greater than 1, we simply reduce it by one and go back to the input routine. If it is 1, the keyword must be entirely deleted, so we execute the storage file de-allocation subroutine. We go to line 32205 to delete the element if NR(st) was a leaf page or to line 48700 if it was a node page.

```
32158 '
32178 '=================================================================
32180 'remove element from leaf page: record NR(ST), field block K
32184 '================================================================
32190 '
32205 NUMBER = NUMBER-1
32210 IF K=0 THEN B$ = "" ELSE B$ = MID$(REC$,1,T*K)
32300 C$=MID$(REC$, 1 + T*(K+1))
32500 LSET REC$=B$+C$: LSET LE$ =MKI$(NN)+MKI$(NUMBER): PUT BUF2,
NR(ST)
32550 IF NUMBER >= ORDER THEN PRINT "** DELETED **": GOTO 49600
32555 IF ST <> 0 THEN 33400 'balance or absorption for nonroot leaf
32700 '------- leaf is undersized root ---------
32800 IF NUMBER > 0 THEN PRINT " ** DELETED **": GOTO 49600
32900 PRINT "DELETED & FILE EMPTIED": OLD = NR(ST): GOSUB 24410
32910 root = 0
33000 GOTO 50000
33100 '
33150 '================================================================
33200 ' balance or absorption after leaf deletion
33250 '================================================================
33300 '
33350 ' --- ascend to find the lateral record for balancing or
absorbing ----
33400 L1$=LE$: N1=NR(ST): C1=NUMBER
33450 N1$ = MID$(REC$, 1, C1*T)
33500 ST%=ST%-1
33600 GET BUF2,NR(ST):J$=REC$:L$=LE$: JN = CVI(MID$(LE$,3,2))
33700 IF KK(ST)=-1 THEN N2=CVI(MID$(J$, (JN-1)*T + T2, 2)): GOTO 33900
33800 IF KK(ST) < JN-1 THEN N2=CVI(MID$(J$,T2 + T*(KK(ST)+1),2)) ELSE
N2=CVI(MID$(L$,1,2))
33850 '----- get lateral record for balancing or absorption ----------
33900 GET BUF2, N2
33910 C2 = CVI(MID$(LE$,3,2))
33920 N2$ = MID$(REC$,1,T*C2): L2$ = LE$
34000 IF C2 > ORDER THEN 36300 'do balancing
34100 IF KK(ST)=-1 THEN 35350 ELSE 34550 'do absorption: mid or end
34200 '
```

Lines 32205 - 33000

We delete element K, the T-byte-long element which starts at byte T*K +1, from page NR(ST). We construct R$ from both B$, which comprises the first K-1 elements (B$ is null if K is zero), and from C$ which comprises element K+1 on. (Note that, if K represents the last element, C$ will be null.) We then reform the page with R$, comprising the element section, and with the keyword counter reduced by one. At this point we are finished, unless this deletion causes the page to be undersized. If the page is undersized, and is not the root page (which is permitted to be undersized), we branch to line 33400 to either absorb or balance. If the page is the root, we are finished unless the deletion empties the page. In that case, we de-allocate the page and are finished. When done, we go back to the input routine.

Lines 33400 - 34100

Here we must determine whether to deal with the undersized leaf through absorption or balancing. To make this determination, we must know how many elements are on the appropriate adjacent page. To get to the appropriate adjacent page, we ascend one level to level ST-1. Before we ascend a level, we must save the data pertaining to the page, page NR(ST). This is the function of the variables L1$, N1, C1, and N1$. We then decrease ST by one and get the page, NR(ST), on the previous level which pointed to page NR$(ST+1). In the variables J$, L$, and JN we save the data for this page. It will be convenient to give this page a name, so we will call it the **above page**. From the above page, we can go to the appropriate adjacent page for balancing or absorption. If NR(ST+1) was pointed to by the page pointer of the above page, then the appropriate adjacent page is indicated by the element pointer of the last element on the above page. If this is the case, then, in line 33700, we assign this element pointer to N2 and branch to line 33900. If NR(ST+1) was pointed to by the element pointer of the last element on the above page

definition - above page

```
33850 '----- get lateral record for balancing or absorption ---------
33900 GET BUF2, N2
33910 C2 = CVI(MID$(LE$,3,2))
33920 N2$ = MID$(REC$,1,T*C2): L2$ = LE$
34000 IF C2 > ORDER THEN 36300 'do balancing
34100 IF KK(ST)=-1 THEN 35350 ELSE 34550 'do absorption: mid or end
34200 '
34300 ' ======= absorption =====
34400 '
34500 ' ---------- mid-node pointer: absorb N1 ---------
34550 ABOVE$ = MID$(J$, 1 + T*KK(ST), T0) + MKI$(0)
34600 N2$=MID$(N1$,1,T*C1) + ABOVE$ + MID$(N2$,1,T*C2)
34800 LSET REC$=N2$: LSET LE$=MKI$(0)+MKI$(FULLPAGE): PUT BUF2,N2
34900 OLD = N1: GOSUB 24410 'deallocate absorbed tree page
35000 GOTO 39500 'remove MID(J$,1+T*KK(ST),T) from NR(ST)
35100 '
35200 ' --------- end-node pointer: absorb N2 ----------
35300 '
35350 ABOVE$ = MID$(J$, 1 + T*(JN-1), T0) + MKI$(0)
35400 N1$=MID$(N2$,1,T*C2) + ABOVE$ + MID$(N1$,1,T*C1)
35600 LSET REC$=N1$: LSET LE$=MKI$(0)+MKI$(FULLPAGE): PUT BUF2,N1
35700 OLD=N2: GOSUB 24410 'deallocate absorbed tree page
35800 GOTO 40700 'remove MID$(J$,1+T*JN,T) from NR(ST)
35900 '
```

(meaning that KK(ST) is JN-1), the appropriate adjacent page is pointed to by the above page's page pointer. Otherwise, the appropriate adjacent page is indicated by element KK(ST) + 1 's element pointer.

Lines 33900 - 34100
At this point, we get the appropriate adjacent page, page N2, as determined above, and assign its data to the variables C2, N2$, and L2$. If C2, the number of elements on page N2, is greater than ORDER, we can balance by adding some elements from page N2 to page N1 and still have ORDER or more elements on each page. Therefore, we branch to the balancing routine which starts in line 36300.

However, if C2 contains only ORDER elements, then we must absorb. If page N1 was pointed to by the above page's element pointer, we branch to line 35350 to absorb page N2 into page N1. Otherwise, we execute line 34550 to absorb page N1 into page N2.

Lines 34550 - 35000
Here we absorb page N1 into page N2. This means we reform page N2 so that it contains FULLPAGE elements: the ORDER-1 elements from page N1, followed by the KK(ST) element from the above page (which pointed to page N1 and is now made to point to zero), and the ORDER elements from page N2. This new page becomes page N2 and we de-allocate page N1. Finally, we execute the routine of line 39500 to remove the KK(ST) element from page NR(ST), the above page.

Lines 35350 - 35800
Here we absorb page N2 into page N1. We reform page N1 so that it contains FULLPAGE elements: the ORDER elements from page N2, followed by the last, or JN-1, element on the above page (an element which previously pointed to page N2 and has been changed to

```
36000 '
36100 ' ========== balancing ============
36200 '
36300 O1=INT( (C1+C2)/2 ) 'ORDER-1+C2 is the total on both adjacent
pages
36400 'O1 is no of elements for original page: N1
36500 O2 = C1+C2 - O1 'no of elements for adjacent page: N2
36550 O3 = O1 - C1 'no of elements to add to original page
36700 IF KK(ST)=-1 THEN 38500 'end page pointer
36800 '
36900 ' -------- mid-node pointer --------
37000 '
37100 ABOVE$ = MID$(J$, 1+T*KK(ST), T0) + MKI$(0)
37200 MID$(J$,1+T*KK(ST),T0)=MID$(N2$, 1 + T*(O3-1), T0) 'replace
upper
37250 IF O3 = 1 THEN LAT$ = "" ELSE LAT$ = MID$( N2$, 1, T*(O3-1) )
37300 N1$ = N1$ + ABOVE$ + LAT$
37400 G$ = MID$( N2$, 1 + T*O3 )
37700 LSET REC$=J$: LSET LE$=L$: PUT BUF2,NR(ST)
37800 LSET REC$=N1$: LSET LE$=MKI$(0)+MKI$(O1): PUT BUF2,N1
37900 LSET REC$=G$: LSET LE$=MKI$(0)+MKI$(O2): PUT BUF2,N2
38000 PRINT "** DELETED **"
38100 GOTO 49600
38200 '
```

point to zero) and the ORDER-1 elements from page N1. This new page becomes page N1 and we de-allocate page N2. Finally, we execute the routine of line 40700 to remove the last element from the above page, page NR(ST).

Lines 36300 - 36700

When balancing is called for, we execute these lines to determine how many elements to move from the larger appropriate adjacent page, page N2, to the undersized original page, page N1. We have a total of C1+C2 (C1 is ORDER-1) elements to distribute over both pages. We want to have O1 = INT((C1+C2)/2) elements on page N1, which now contains C1 elements. Therefore, we will have to add O3 = O1-C1 elements to N1, leaving N2 with the rest of the elements, O2 = C1+C2 - O1.

If the above page pointer, formerly pointing to N1, was the page pointer, we execute line 38500. Otherwise we execute line 37100 to begin the balancing process.

Lines 37100 - 38100

We execute these lines if N1 was pointed to by an element pointer. We must remove the first O3 elements from page N2. All but the last of these elements will be added to page N1. The last will take the place of the above page element which pointed to page N1. This above page element will be added to page N1. Thus, we re-form page N1 to N1$+ ABOVE$+ LAT$, where N1$ is the old N1$, ABOVE$ is the element from the above page with its pointer changed from N1 to zero, and LAT$ consists of the first O3-1 element from page N2. If O3 is 1, LAT$ is null. We re-form the above page so that the O3 element from page N2 takes the place of the element which points to page N1. The pointer is not changed; it is the rest of the element that is replaced. Finally, we re-form page N2 so that the first O3 elements have been removed. We then set all of these mod-

```
38200 '
38300 ' ---------- page pointer -------
38400 '
38500 ABOVE$ = MID$(J$, 1 + T*(JN-1), T0) + MKI$(0)
38600 MID$(J$,1+T*(JN-1),T0) = MID$(N2$, 1 + T*(C2 - O3), T0)
38700 N1$ = MID$(N2$, 1+ T*(C2 - (O3-1)) ) + ABOVE$ + N1$
39000 G$=MID$(N2$,1,T*O2)
39100 GOTO 37700
39200 '
39300 ' ========= kill pointer to absorbed branch ========
39400 ' --------- mid-node pointer ---------
39500 IF JN=1 THEN 40300 'N2 --> new root & deallocate old root
39580 IF KK(ST)=0 THEN B$ = "" ELSE B$ = MID$(J$,1,T*KK(ST))
39600 C$=MID$(J$,1+T*(KK(ST)+1),JN*T)
39650 JN = JN - 1
39700 MID$(L$,3,2)=MKI$(JN)
39800 LSET REC$=B$+C$: LSET LE$=L$: PUT BUF2,NR(ST)
39900 IF JN >= ORDER OR (JN<ORDER AND ST=0) THEN PRINT "** DELETED
**":GOTO 49600
40000 GOTO 41900
40290 '--- root consists of a single element: N2 -> new root & dealloc
old ---
40300 OLD = NR(ST): GOSUB 24410 'deallocate old
40310 root = N2
40315 PRINT "** DELETED **"
40400 GOTO 49600
40500 '
```

ified pages where they belong, with the element counters for pages N1 and N2 suitably changed.

Lines 38500 - 39100

We execute these lines if N1 was pointed to by a page pointer. We restructure the elements of page N1 so that it contains the last O3-1 elements of page N2 (the O3th element from the last replaces, except for element pointer, the last element in the above page), followed by the last element on the above page, with its pointer changed to zero, and finally, the elements of page N1 as they originally were. We restructure page N2 so that it now contains only the first O2 elements. We then go to line 37700 to set these modified pages and change the element counter on pages N1 and N2.

Lines 39500 - 41200

In these lines we eliminate from page NR(ST) the element which pointed to the page eliminated during the absorption process. This element was incorporated into the page that absorbed the eliminated page.

Lines 39500 - 40400

We use these lines when the pointer that pointed to the absorbed page was not the last element pointer. In that case, we simply form a new page from which the pointing element is excluded and with the element counter, JN, reduced by one. Then, if JN is not less than ORDER, we are done and go back to the input routine. Even if JN is less than ORDER, we are done if the above page, NR(ST), is the root and JN was not equal to one at the start of the routine. If, at the start of the routine, JN was one, we immediately branch to line 40300 to delete the old root and make the surviving page the new root.

However, if JN is less than ORDER, and NR(ST) is not the root page, we must branch to the routine of line 41900 to carry out either the absorption or the balancing

```
40500 '
40600 ' -------- end-page pointer --------
40700 IF JN=1 THEN N2=N1: GOTO 40300 'N2 --> new root & deallocate old
root
40710 JN=JN-1
40800 MID$(L$,3,2)=MKI$(JN)
40900 LSET REC$=MID$(J$,1,T*JN): LSET LE$=L$: PUT BUF2, NR(ST)
41000 IF JN >= ORDER OR (JN<ORDER AND ST=0) THEN PRINT "** DELETED
**":GOTO 49600
41600 '
41700 ' ========= option for either balancing or absorbing =====
41710 '       after deletion of an element form a node page
41800 '
41900 N1=NR(ST): N1$=REC$: L1$=LE$: C1= JN
42000 ST%=ST%-1
42100 GET BUF2,NR(ST):J$=REC$: L$=LE$: JN = CVI(MID$(LE$,3,2))
42110 IF KK(ST)=-1 THEN N2 = CVI( MID$(J$, T*(JN-1) + T2, 2) ): GOTO
42300
42200 IF KK(ST) < JN-1 THEN N2=CVI(MID$(J$,T2+T*(KK(ST)+1),2)) ELSE
N2=CVI(MID$(L$,1,2))
42300 GET BUF2,N2: C2=CVI(MID$(LE$,3,2)): N2$=REC$: L2$=LE$
42400 IF C2 > ORDER THEN 44700 'do balancing
42500 IF KK%(ST%)=-1 THEN 43850 ELSE 42950 'absorb end else mid
42600 '
```

process. For, when an element is eliminated from this page, NR(ST), we have created an undersized node page.

Line 40700 - 41000

We use these lines when the above page pointer that pointed to the absorbed page is the last element pointer on the page. This can happen if N1 was pointed to by the page pointer (meaning the page to be eliminated through absorption is N2) or if N1 was pointed to by the last element pointer (meaning the page to be eliminated through absorption is N1). Thus, we simply form a new page, excluding this element and reducing the element counter by one. Then, if JN is not less the ORDER, we are done and go back to the input routine. If JN is less than ORDER, we are done if the above page, NR(ST), is the root page and JN was not one at the start of the routine. If JN was one, we immediately branch to line 40300 to delete the old root and make the surviving page the new root.

However, if JN is less than ORDER, and NR(ST) is not the root page, we must branch to the routine of line 41900 to carry out either the absorption or the balancing process. This is because, due to the elimination of an element from this page, NR(ST), we have created an undersized node page.

Line 41900 - 42500

After the elimination of an element from a node page causes the page to become undersized, we use these lines to determine whether balancing or absorption is required. We make this determination by finding out how many elements, C2, are on the appropriate adjacent page. If C2 contains only ORDER elements, absorption is required; otherwise, balancing is called for.

The appropriate adjacent page is located by going up one level (letting ST = ST-1) and getting page NR(ST). The

```
42600 '
42700 ' ======= absorbing ========
42800 ' --------- mid-node pointer: absorb N1 ----------
42900 '
42950 ABOVE$ = MID$(J$, 1 + T*KK(ST), T0) + MID$(L1$,1,2)
43000 N2$=MID$(N1$,1,T*C1) + ABOVE$ + MID$(N2$,1,C2*T)
43200 LSET REC$=N2$: LSET LE$=MID$(L2$,1,2) + MKI$(FULLPAGE): PUT
BUF2,N2
43300 OLD = N1: GOSUB 24410 'deallocate N1
43400 GOTO 39500
43500 '
43700 ' ------ end-node pointer: absorb N2 ------
43800 '
43850 ABOVE$=MID$(J$, 1 + T*(JN-1), T0) + MID$(L2$,1,2)
43900 N1$ = MID$(N2$,1,T*C2) + ABOVE$ + MID$(N1$,1,T*C1)
44100 LSET REC$=N1$: LSET LE$=MID$(L1$,1,2)+MKI$(FULLPAGE): PUT
BUF2,N1
44200 OLD = N2: GOSUB 24410
44300 GOTO 40700
44400 '
```

value of KK(ST) tells us where on page NR(ST) we can find the pointer to the appropriate adjacent page. This page is back on level ST+1, from which we have just ascended. Page N1 is the undersized page; page N2, the appropriate adjacent page; and NR(ST), the above page, which points to both N1 and N2. If KK(ST) is -1, the appropriate adjacent page is pointed to by the last element on the page; thus in line 42110, we set N2 accordingly. Otherwise, we set N2 in line 42200, depending on whether or not N2 is pointed to by the page pointer (in other words, depending on whether or not KK(ST) represents the last element).

Once we have N2, we get page N2 and look at C2. If C2 is greater than ORDER, we branch to line 44700 to balance. Otherwise, we absorb. If KK(ST) represents the page pointer, we will absorb page N2 into page N1; therefore, we branch to line 43850. Otherwise, we execute line 42950 to absorb page N1 into page N2.

Lines 42950 - 43400

Here we absorb page N1 into page N2. This involves forming a new page N2, made from the C1 elements of page N1, followed by the above page element that points to page N1 (with its pointer replaced by page N1's page pointer), and finally, by the C2 elements of page N2. This configuration becomes the next page N2 with its element counter changed to FULLPAGE. Page N1 is deallocated. Finally, we branch to line 39500 to eliminate the element that pointed to page N1 and was absorbed into page N2.

Lines 43850 - 44300

Here we absorb page N2 into page N1. This entails forming a new page. This new page consists of the C2 elements of N2, followed by the last element on the above page, with its pointer replaced by N2's page pointer, and by the C1 elements of page N1. This configuration

```
44500 '
44600 ' ====== balancing ==========
44700 O1 = INT((C1+C2)/2) 'for N1
44900 O2 = C1 + C2 - O1 'for N2
44950 O3 = O1 - C1 'to be added to N1
44980 I=0 'snake around counter
45000 N1$=MID$(N1$,1,T*C1)
45100 IF KK%(ST%)=-1 THEN 47200 ELSE 45500
45200 '
45300 ' ----------- mid-node pointer --------
45400 '
45500 P1$ = MID$(L1$,1,2) 'N1 page pointer
45600 P2$ = MID$(N2$,T2 + T*I,2) 'N2 Ith element pointer
45700 MID$(L1$,1,2) = P2$
45800 F1$ = MID$(J$, 1 + T*KK(ST), T0) + P1$
45900 MID$(J$,1+T*KK(ST),T0)=MID$(N2$,1+T*I,T0)
46000 N1$=N1$+F1$
46100 I=I+1
46200 IF I < O3 THEN 45500 'O3 to be add to N1
46300 MID$(L1$,3,2)=MKI$(O1): MID$(L2$,3,2)=MKI$(O2)
46400 N2$=MID$(N2$,1+T*I,C2*T)
46500 LSET REC$=J$: LSET LE$=L$: PUT BUF2,NR(ST)
46600 LSET REC$=N1$: LSET LE$=L1$: PUT BUF2,N1
46700 LSET REC$=N2$: LSET LE$=L2$: PUT BUF2,N2
46800 PRINT "*** DELETED ***": GOTO 49600
46900 '
```

becomes the next page N1 with its element counter changed to FULLPAGE. Page N2 is de-allocated. Finally, we branch to line 40700 to eliminate the element on the above page, page NR(ST), that pointed to page N2 and was absorbed into N1.

Lines 44700 - 45100

We are sent to these lines from line 42400, when we know that we can balance because C2 is greater than ORDER. The total number of elements on both pages is C1+C2. We want page N1 to contain about half, O1 = INT((C1+C2)/2), of these. This means that we have to add O3 = O1-C1 elements to page N1, and consequently, take O3 elements from page N2, leaving page N2 with O2 = C1+C2-O1 elements.

We are going to be following an iterating element-adding process in which we add elements before the first element or following the last element of page N1. Therefore, we initialize N1$ to consist of the C1 elements originally on page N1. The variable I will count the times we perform the process. If page N1 was pointed to by page NR$(ST)'s page pointer, we branch to line 47200 to begin this process; otherwise, we begin it at line 45500.

Lines 45500 - 46800

Here we repeat this process O3 times—while I is less than O3. We take the element on the above page that points to page N1, replace its pointer with page N1's page pointer, and add it to the end of N1$. We replace page N1's page pointer with the pointer on element I on page N2. The rest of element I goes to the above page to replace the element that came down to page N1.

When this process is over, we change the element counter for pages N1 and N2, respectively, to O1 and O2. We then change N2$ so that it consists of the C2 ele-

```
46900 '
47000 ' -------------- end-page pointer --------------
47100 '
47200 P1$ = MID$(L2$,1,2) 'N2 page pointer
47300 P2$ = MID$(N2$,T2 + T*(C2-1-I),2)
47400 MID$(L2$,1,2) = P2$
47500 F1$ = MID$(J$, 1 + T*(JN-1), T0) + P1$
47600 MID$(J$,1+T*(JN-1),T0)=MID$(N2$,1+T*(C2-1-I),T0)
47700 N1$=F1$+N1$: I%=I%+1
47800 IF I < O3 THEN 47200
47900 MID$(L2$,3,2)=MKI$(O2%)
48000 MID$(L1$,3,2)=MKI$(O1%)
48100 N2$=MID$(N2$,1,T*O2)
48200 GOTO 46500
48300 '
48390 '================================================================
48400 '        replace a branch element with the highest lower element
48410 '================================================================
48500 '
48570 '
48600 RR$=REC$: LR$=LE$: RR=NR(ST) 'save the node page
48650 '------ move down to the "greatest lower" leaf page ------
48700 KK(ST) = K
48710 ST=ST+1
48800 NR(ST)=CVI(MID$(RR$,T2 + T*K,2))
48850 GET BUF2,NR(ST)
48875 NN = CVI(MID$(LE$,1,2))
48880 IF NN <> 0 THEN KK(ST)=-1: ST=ST+1: NR(ST) = NN: GOTO 48850
48940 '
48950 '------- found "greatest lower" leaf page -----
48960 '
49000 NUMBER=CVI(MID$(LE$,3,2)): N1$=REC$
49010 NUMBER=NUMBER-1
49090 '------- change node ------------
49100 MID$(RR$,1+T*K,T0)=MID$(REC$,1+T*NUMBER, T0)
49200 LSET REC$=RR$: LSET LE$=LR$: PUT BUF2, RR
49290 '------- change leaf --------------
49300 B$=MID$( N1$,1,T*NUMBER )
49350 LSET REC$ = B$
49375 LSET LE$ = MKI$(0) + MKI$(NUMBER)
49400 PUT BUF2,NR(ST)
49500 IF NUMBER > = ORDER THEN PRINT "** DELETED **":GOTO 49600 ELSE
33400
```

ments following element I. We then set the modified pages NR(ST), N1, and N2 and go back to the input routine.

Lines 47200 - 48200

In this case, page N1 was pointed to by NR(ST)'s page pointer. We repeat the following process O3 times - while I is less than O3. We replace the pointer of the last element on page NR(ST), the above page, with page N2's page pointer and place the modified element at the beginning of page N1$. We replace page N2's page pointer with the pointer on element C2-I-1 of page N2 and use the rest of element C2-I-1 to replace the above page pointer element that was brought down to page N1.

When we have completed this process, we change the element counters for page N1 and N2, respectively, to O1 and O2. We change N2$ so that it consists of only the first C2 elements. We then branch to line 46500 to set the modified pages NR(ST), N1, and N2 and return to the input routine.

Lines 48600 - 49500

We are sent here from line 32157 to delete an element found on a node page - element K on page NR(ST). To do this, we replace the node element to be deleted with the greatest element on the B-tree that is less than the node element. This element is the last element on the leaf page that can be reached by going to the page pointed to by the element to be deleted, and then following page pointers down to leaf level. Then, in the standard way described above, we delete this leaf element.

First, in the variables RR$ and LR$, we save the configuration of the page containing the keyword to be deleted. We save its record number in the variable RR. Then, following page pointers from the page pointed to

```
48600 RR$=REC$: LR$=LE$: RR=NR(ST) 'save the node page
48650 '------ move down to the "greatest lower" leaf page ------
48700 KK(ST) = K
48710 ST=ST+1
48800 NR(ST)=CVI(MID$(RR$,T2 + T*K,2))
48850 GET BUF2,NR(ST)
48875 NN = CVI(MID$(LE$,1,2))
48880 IF NN <> 0 THEN KK(ST)=-1: ST=ST+1: NR(ST) = NN: GOTO 48850
48940 '
48950 '------- found "greatest lower" leaf page -----
48960 '
49000 NUMBER=CVI(MID$(LE$,3,2)): N1$=REC$
49010 NUMBER=NUMBER-1
49090 '------- change node -------------
49100 MID$(RR$,1+T*K,T0)=MID$(REC$,1+T*NUMBER, T0)
49200 LSET REC$=RR$: LSET LE$=LR$: PUT BUF2, RR
49290 '------- change leaf --------------
49300 B$=MID$( N1$,1,T*NUMBER )
49350 LSET REC$ = B$
49375 LSET LE$ = MKI$(0) + MKI$(NUMBER)
49400 PUT BUF2,NR(ST)
49500 IF NUMBER > = ORDER THEN PRINT "** DELETED **":GOTO 49600 ELSE
33400
```

by the element to be deleted, we descend until we come to leaf level. Note that we set up the KK(st) chain as we descend. This enables us carry out balancing or absorption later on, in the event that deletion of this highest numbered lower element results in an undersized leaf.

We let NUMBER be the number of elements on the leaf page we find. We save the elements of this page in N1$. We decrease NUMBER by one since we are going to remove the last element from this page.

Next, we replace keyword K on the node page with the last keyword, keyword NUMBER, from the leaf page. Then, we eliminate element NUMBER from the leaf page, NR(st). If this results in an undersized leaf page, we branch to line 33400 for either balancing or deletion; otherwise, we go back to the input routine.

SECTION IV

Changing the B-tree System

9

Optimizing the B-tree Performance

CHAPTER SUMMARY

This chapter is dedicated to optimizing the performance of your B-tree. Since we will be going through a lot of analysis, it is probably best if we summarize the chapter's conclusions, so those readers that do not want to wade through the analysis can go on with their work. Here are the highlights of Chapter 9:

Items to consider:

There are only three things that need to be addressed: the speed of our B-tree, the size of the B-tree file and future enhancements that can be made to the Teach-Base system. We assume you are using the average hard disk one would find in an office (standard 512-byte sectors, no special formatting, etc.).

Speed:

1) **The seek:** It turns out that the slowest step by far in the performance of a B-tree is the mechanical act of the hard disk seeking (i.e. locating and moving to) data that is stored on the disk.

2) **Sector reading:** It turns out that almost all hard disks are divided into 512-byte sectors, and every time the computer goes to read a sector it has to read the entire sector (whether or not it is full of information).

3) **512 byte page:** Therefore, as far as speed is concerned, the ideal page size is 512 bytes or the smallest multiple of 512 bytes that our keyword will fit into.

4) **Keyword only needed:** Notice that the user always supplies the keyword. The keyword is all our program needs to create an optimal B-tree, because as soon as the user types in the keyword we know the length of the keyword and length of the B-tree page. All other variables are simply calculations that use these two items.

equation for fitting elements into 512-byte page

5) **Example:** This means, as a programmer, that you should take the keyword size selected by the user, create your element, and fit as many elements as you can into a 512-byte page. A few simple lines of code can perform this operation. The equation is simple: given a keyword of length X, we create an element Y so that Y=X+4 (element = key + 2 bytes for element pointer + 2 bytes for storage pointer). Y fits into 508 bytes (512 bytes - 2 byte page pointer - 2-byte element counter) Z times. Thus our order is Z/2, rounded down to the nearest integer. **Note:** A problem can occur if there is too much waste. For example, a 212-byte key, if forced into a 512-byte B-tree page, would produce a waste of 76 bytes. So for a 100,000 keyword B-tree we would have a waste of (100,000/2)(76) = 3.8 megabytes! This seems like a lot of waste but the elements alone in a 100,000 element B-tree take up 21.6 megabytes. The

programmer has to decide if 3.8 megs, or about 15% of the file, is too much waste.

Size of B-tree file:

1) **Waste:** What we are talking about here is waste, or how much waste should be tolerated in a B-tree page.

2) **BASIC-base addresses waste:** The TeachBase system, being limited to 32,000 entries, does not concern itself with this problem but the BASIC-base program (the more professional version of the TeachBase program) does. This is available from the publisher.

3) **Waste solution:** The solution is fairly simple. As soon as the user gives us the keyword size we compute the smallest B-tree page (this would be 512 bytes or the lowest multiple of 512 bytes possible). We then see what percentage of the page will be waste when the page is full. If this percentage waste is greater than what we want to allow, then we go to the next multiple of 512 bytes and see what the waste is there. We can do this for several multiples of 512 bytes and then pick the page size that has the smallest amount of waste .

4) **Trade- off:** Be aware that there is a trade- off here. As your page size gets bigger and bigger you are sacrificing speed to save space because your hard disk will have to read a bigger and bigger record. Unless you have a really enormous database and very restrictive storage, the speed problem is generally more important than the waste problem.

Enhancements:

There are enhancements that we can make to the classic B-tree presented in this book. Some of these will be incorporated in upgrades, but even with these enhancements you will not get a much faster B-tree than what is presented in this book. Most of the enhancements will save space. Here they are:

1) **Optimize B-tree waste:** This is already discussed above and addressed in the BASIC-base program.

increased space utilization

2) **Redistribution upon addition:** This is a routine that can be added to the B-tree to inspect and balance the pages as a keyword is entered. This keeps the amount of wasted space to a minimum. Tests conducted show average space utilization going from 67% to 85%. A more balanced and full B-tree, as we will see in this chapter, means not only saved space but fewer levels being created. The end result is fewer seeks, hence a faster B-tree. The downside is that you have to add another routine to your B-tree, and what you gain might not be significant, except in very large cases.

3) **B* trees:** This is a variation on B-trees put forth by Knuth [1973]. The idea is that if you are doing redistribution upon addition, then your pages are pretty full most of the time. Therefore, when it comes time to split a page, instead of splitting one record to get two records, each of which are about half-full, why not take the adjacent page to the page you are about to split, which should also be fairly full, and use it in the splitting process, causing a 2 to 3 split instead of a 1 to 2 split? The result will be pages that are 2/3 full instead of only half-full. This, of course, will require a rewrite of the procedures for addition and redistribution.

holding pages in memory

4) **Buffering of pages:** We mention in this chapter that it is a good idea to hold the root page in memory, because you will always be asking for it and it saves making a lot of disk accesses. It is possible, of course, to hold other pages in memory as well. The most called-for pages are usually the pages close to the root, and you can select the first few levels to put in memory.

5) **LRU replacement:** Carrying Step 3 a little further, you could have some kind of arrangement where the pages held in memory are the pages that are called for the most frequently. For example, we could hold in memory the pages visited during insertion, so we

don't have to get them if splitting is required. The pages visited during descent to a leaf during transversal should also be kept, because we will use them again.

6) **B-tree in memory:** Ideally, of course, if memory permits we should keep the entire B-tree in memory or as much of it as we can. This will affect speed dramatically because there are no hard disk seeks.

7) **Rapid importing:** This is covered in the BASIC-base version. In general, rather than read in a foreign file one record at a time, you can simply view the entire foreign file as one giant string and read it all into memory with one read (actually you are limited to 32,000 bytes of reading at a time). Once in memory, you can tree the foreign elements. If your B-tree is in memory too, then the entire process of absorbing a foreign file will occur in memory.

This concludes our summary. Now for the analysis.

ANALYSIS

The sector

When a hard disk is first manufactured it has no data on it. The operating system you are working with needs to "map" where the data is going to be located on the disk. To do this, the operating system employs a grid by creating concentric electronic bands, called tracks, that start from the center and emanate out (much like the rings in a tree). Each of these tracks are then segmented into 512-byte sections, called **sectors**.

definition: sector

This configuration is true for all major operating systems. It is possible to override the standard, or default, formatting scheme and create an unusually formatted hard disk with larger sectors. We will not concern ourselves with these unusual cases. Thus under normal conditions a hard disk is formatted into sectors, each containing 512 bytes. The data you are reading or writ-

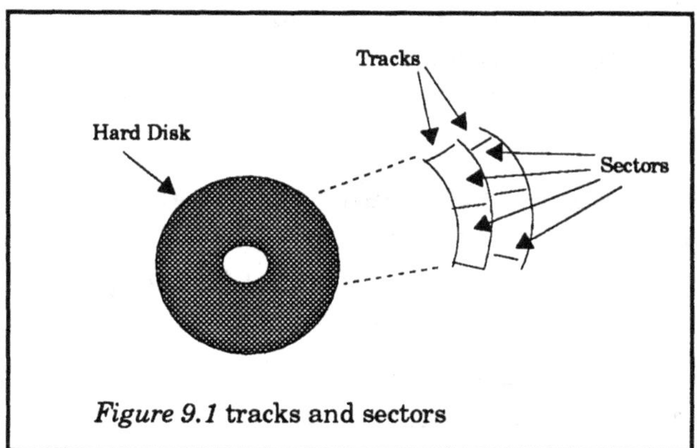

Figure 9.1 tracks and sectors

division of information between sectors

ing goes into one of these sectors. If the data you are reading or writing in a sector exceeds 512 bytes, there is a pointer at the end of the sector. This pointer tells the operating system where the next sector is located, so it can go there and continue reading or writing data. When reading more than 512 bytes of data from the disk, the sectors you are looking for are not necessarily contiguous. In other words, part of your data could be in a sector on one track and the next part in a sector on another track. This is necessary because in the normal course of usage the user is deleting data randomly and the operating system must reuse these sectors.

wasted space: what is acceptable?

definitions: seek time & transfer time

When you look at the advertising literature put out by popular hard disk manufacturers, you see the "speed" of the hard disk described with terminology like "....has an average seek time of 12 ms (milli-seconds)". The **seek time** is the average amount of time (actually, statistical mean time) that it takes a hard disk to find a random sector. It should also be stated that once a sector has been located and the read head mechanically positioned at the start of a sector of data, there is some time needed to transfer the data to memory. The time required to transfer one sector of data to memory we define as **transfer time** and it is much faster than the seek time.

When you look at the literature describing the speed of

popular computer memory, you'll find that the rate at which the computer finds data that is already loaded in the computer's memory is many times faster than either the seek time or the transfer time. This means that seek time is clearly going to be the slowest part of our B-tree performance.

From the literature we can then observe the following:

1) 512-byte sectors are generally used by operating systems as the default formatting procedure.
2) The seek time is clearly what determines how fast our B-tree is. The fewer seeks you encounter in reading your B-tree, the faster it is.
3) Each time a hard disk sector is read, the entire 512-byte sector is read regardless of how much data you have stored in the sector.
4) Therefore, any B-tree page that is not an even multiple of 512 bytes is not going to be efficient. This is because once the page exceeds 512 bytes in length, or any multiple of 512 bytes, you have to read all of the next 512-byte sector whether you like it or not.

512 bytes vs. multiple of 512: which is better?

Our investigation has now come down to a simple question: Since the basic unit of disk access is 512 bytes, is it better to have your page 512 bytes long, or some multiple of 512 bytes? There are arguments for either position.

In favor of multiple sectors per page

The argument in favor of having pages whose length is some multiple of 512 bytes is that you can reduce the number of seeks needed to get the page containing the searched-for key. This is because you have a higher probability of reading sectors that are contiguous, since when you created the page you requested disk space that was several sectors long. Contiguous sectors would require no extra seek time. Once the starting sector is

probability of reading contiguous sectors

found the time required to transfer data contained in contiguous sectors is small compared to the time required to find the starting sector. With long pages (consisting of say, k sectors) we could do one seek and then very quickly read in k sectors of data. With pages one sector in length we would have to do k seeks to read in k sectors of data.

Against having multiple sectors per page

The argument against long pages is that you have to read the entire page into memory, which will require several seeks, if the sectors are not contiguous, and, even if the sectors are contiguous, you will be reading in many elements that you have no need for. Even if you have fewer seeks and read in fewer pages, since those you read in will be longer, more data transfer time will be needed. Also, it takes longer to search long pages for your element.

Calculations and performance results

We will now proceed with some mathematical calculations and performance tables, in the following manner:

1) **Maximum & Minimum B-tree:** Assume we have a B-tree page that is exactly one sector (512 bytes) long. We will determine formulas that relate the height, or level, of the B-tree to the number of elements on the B-tree. For a given number of elements we will determine this for the worst-case B-tree (tallest B-tree that can be grown), and then the best-case B-tree (smallest B-tree that can be grown) that will have to be performed.

2) **Oversized pages:** We will use the formulas we develop to investigate whether B-trees having pages of lengths greater than 512 bytes are actually faster than pages of only 512 bytes.

3) **Performance charts:** We present results of tests

demonstrating the effect on B-tree performance due to having page sizes that are various multiples of 512 bytes.

Maximum and minimum B-trees

How quickly a B-tree locates a given keyword depends on how many keys are stored on a page and on how many pages have to be searched. If the B-tree has 10 levels and the keyword we are searching for is on leaf level, we must search on 10 levels. We will always have to search all the way to leaf level to determine whether or not a given keyword is absent from the tree, or to determine where to place a keyword that is to be added to the tree, since new keywords go on leaf level.

This means that if we increase the height of the B-tree by making pages longer we will be searching fewer pages, but those we search will be longer. For a B-tree containing a given number of elements, let's examine how the number of elements per page affects the tree height.

minimally loaded tree

Minimum tree: A B-tree, whose pages all contain order number of elements, with the root page containing a single element, will grow to the greatest height and give the worst-case performance. We will call such a tree **minimally loaded**.

maximally loaded trees

Maximum tree: Conversely, a B-tree whose pages all contain twice the order will grow to the least height and give the best performance. We will call this tree **maximally loaded**.

Note that if we delete one element from a minimally loaded tree, its height will decrease one level, and if we add one element to a maximally loaded tree, its height will increase one level.

We will now develop formulas relating tree height (measured by the number of levels), the B-tree order, and the total number of elements on the B-tree for both minimally- and maximally-loaded trees. We will then use these formulas to arrive at a conclusion as to what the optimum page length should be.

Formula for a minimally loaded tree of order n:

Problem: Find, for a minimally-loaded B-tree of order n, a mathematical expression that relates the B-tree level, L, to the number of elements N_{min}.

Given: We are given that each page contains the minimum number of elements, which is the order n.

Solution:

(1) We say the root is on level 1.

(2) The number of pages and elements per level is as follows: the root has one element, and points to two pages; other pages contain order, n, elements and point to n+1 pages.

(3) Table 9.1 is a chart that shows the growth of a B-tree of order n to level L.

Table 9.1: Minimally-loaded B-tree of order n

Level	Pages	Elements on Level
1	1	1
2	2	2n
3	2(n+1)	2n(n+1)
4	$2\,(n+1)^2$	$2n\,(n+1)^2$
.....	......	......
L	$2(n+1)^{L-2}$	$2n\,(n+1)^{L-2}$

We find the total number of elements N_{min} on the tree by summing the elements on each level. This produces:

$$N_{min} = \sum 1 + 2n + 2n(n+1) + 2n(n+1)^2 + \ldots\ldots\ldots + 2n(n+1)^{L-2}$$

We also know that the sum of the geometric series is:

$$\sum a + ar + ar^2 + \ldots\ldots\ldots + ar^{n-1} = \frac{a(1-r^n)}{1-r}$$

So, with n=L-1, a=2n, r=n+1, and an extra 1, we have:

$$N_{min} = 2(n+1)^{L-1} - 1$$

or solving for L we have: $L = Log_{n+1}(\frac{N_{min}+1}{2}) + 1$

We learn from Table 9.1 (above) that the number of pages on the leaf level of a minimally-loaded B-tree of L levels is one more than the total number of elements on a minimally-loaded B-tree of L-1 levels! The same is true for a maximally -loaded B-tree, as we will see.

We can also say that for any B-tree, since the number of pages on any level is equal to the number of elements plus the number of pages on the previous level, the number of pages on the leaf level is greater by one than the total number of elements on all the levels above.

This means most of the elements on a B-tree are on the leaf level.

Formula for a maximally -loaded tree of order n:
Problem: Find, for a maximally -loaded B-tree of order n, a mathematical expression that relates the B-tree level, L, to the number of elements N_{max}.

Given: All pages contain 2n elements.

Solution:

(1) We say the root is on level 1.

(2) All pages including the root contain 2n elements and point to 2n+1 pages on the next level.

(3) Table 9.2 is a chart that shows the growth of a maximally -loaded B-tree of order n:

Table 9.2: maximally loaded B-tree of order n

Level	Pages	Elements on Level
1	1	2n
2	2n+1	2n (2n+1)
3	$(2n+1)^2$	$2n\ (2n+1)^2$
4	$(2n+1)^3$	$2n\ (2n+1)^3$
....	....	....
L	$(2n+1)^{L-1}$	$2n\ (2n+1)^{L-1}$

Again, we find the total number, N_{max}, by summing the elements on each level and noting the occurrence of the geometric series. We have:

$$N_{max} = \sum 1 + 2n + 2n(2n+1) + 2n(2n+1)^2 + \dots\dots\dots + 2n(2n+1)^{L-1} = (2n+1)^L - 1$$

and

$$L = Log_{2n+1}(N_{max} + 1) + 1$$

Order 9 example

To understand what these formulas tell us, we have created Table 9.3, which shows how many elements per level there are in minimally-loaded and maximally-loaded B-trees of Order 9 at various levels.

This means that even if this tree grows so that it is always minimally loaded (impossible if the keywords are

Table 9.3: Order 9 B-tree

Level	Elements on maximally loaded B-tree	Elements on minimally loaded B-tree
1	18	1
2	366	19
3	6858	199
4	130,320	1999
5	2,476,098	19,999
6	47,045,880	199,999
7	893,871,739	1,999,999
8		19, 999,999
9		199,999,999
10		1,999,999,999

installed on the tree in random order) a tree of only six levels can hold up to 1,999,998 keywords and a tree of eight levels can hold up to 199,999,998 keywords. Even a billion keywords require a minimally-loaded tree of only nine levels! To have a billion keywords on a maximally-loaded tree you need seven levels, so with even a billion keywords, to search all the way to the bottom of the tree you can expect to have to search between only seven and nine pages, and never more than nine.

What, in practical terms, is a B-tree of Order 9? Suppose we require a keyword of 24 bytes. A page element would then be 28 bytes, because we need 2 bytes for an element pointer and 2 bytes to point to a storage file record number. For each page we also need 2 bytes for the element counter and another two bytes for the page pointer.

retrieving all the data in one seek

We will pick the B-tree page length to be one sector; in other words, the number of bytes the hard disk reads in one disk access. This way we can retrieve all the data in one page of our B-tree with one seek. For our hard disk let's say this number is 512 bytes. This means with 28-byte elements and 4 bytes of pointers and counters, one of our B-tree pages, in order to be a sector, will hold 18 elements. There will be 4 bytes of unused space at the end of the record. This is our B-tree of Order 9.

Suppose our keywords are just 14 bytes long. Then, with a 512-byte page, we would have a B-tree of Order 14 and would have 8 bytes of unused space per record. Such a B-tree could, minimally loaded, contain up to 1,518,748 keywords in just five levels or 22,781,248 keywords in six levels.

Worst-case growth

Let's consider how a B-tree could grow so that it was minimally loaded. If a key to be added to the tree could go onto any leaf with equal likelihood, the resulting B-tree would be somewhere between minimally and maximally loaded. For a B-tree to grow so as to be minimally loaded, keywords have to be added to a page until that page splits, then added again to just one page until it splits. One way to ensure this worst-case growth would be to grow a B-tree by adding keys that are in sorted order. This is something to be aware of when growing a tree from an existing file. It is best if the file is in random order with respect to keywords. If it is not, consider using a shuffling routine to break up the order when installing the keys to the B-tree.

PAGE LENGTHS GREATER THAN ONE SECTOR

In the B-tree examples we have just considered, a B-tree page was picked to be exactly one sector in length, since a sector is the physical unit of disk access.

most economical method of searching

One may wonder whether it might be more economical, in terms of number of sectors read in search of a key, if we were to let a tree page be very large and require several sectors to be retrieved. This would increase the order of the B-tree and give fewer levels as well as fewer pages. The hoped-for economy would be gotten by having to search a tree of fewer levels, and therefore not having to read as many pages.

It turns out, as we will show using the equations developed earlier in this chapter relating levels and number of elements on a tree, that although fewer pages would be read using this strategy, there would be an increase in the number of sectors read in searching for a keyword! We will then calculate a specific example and follow it with actual performance results.

Calculating the seeks

For a B-tree of order n containing a certain number, N, of elements we will calculate the number of levels l. Then, for the same number of elements we will increase the number of sectors in a B-tree page by a factor of k and recalculate the number of levels, L.

1 sector = 1 seek

Since the order of the new B-tree is greater than the previous order, L will be smaller than l. The question is, which will be greater, kL, or l? In other words, since a search of a new B-tree page now requires reading into memory k times as many sectors, if there is to be saving in number of sectors read, k times L must be less than l.

On a B-tree of order n, when we increase the number of seeks in a page by a factor of k, the new order will be, at most, kn+k-1. It will always be kn, but because of unused space that could be almost 2 page elements in length, we could have an order as great as kn+k-1. Since we already know, from earlier in the chapter, that

$$L - 1 = Log_{kn+k}(\frac{N+1}{2})$$

and

$$(\frac{N+1}{2}) = (n+1)^{l-1}$$

we have a relation between L and l, namely:

$$L - 1 = (l-1) \log_{kn+k}(n+1)$$

so...

$$\frac{k(L-1)}{l-1} = \log_{kn+k}(n+1)^k$$

formula for calculating the B-tree page size

and this must be less than one for k(L-1) to be less than l-1. But $(n+1)^k \geq kn+k$ for all k and n, with equality holding only for k=2 and n=1 (we are not interested in k=1). So if $(kn+k)^x = (n+1)^k$, x must be greater than or equal to 1.

Thus k (L-1) is always greater than (l-1) except for n=1, k=2, when k(L-1) = l-1. But this means kL is always greater than l, indeed, $kL \geq l+k-1$.

Example

Let's look at a concrete case. Suppose we have a tree of order 7 containing 524,286 elements and the length of each page is one sector. The height of this tree, minimally loaded, is six levels. Therefore, it would require reading six sectors to search to leaf level.

If we double the page size and suppose the order is now 15, this new tree, minimally loaded, has four levels. But this means that to search to leaf level we would have to read eight sectors instead of the original six. Tripling the record size means the tree would be three levels, but that would mean reading nine sectors. And what about our previous tree of Order 9 containing a billion elements on nine levels? If we increase the order to 19, only six levels are required, but this means reading twelve sectors instead of nine.

Note that our argument shows that if we have a B-tree whose page length corresponds to the quantity of data the computer actually reads in a disk access (one sector), we do not achieve saving in actual sectors read during a B-tree search through the strategy of increasing the number of sectors per page by a factor of k, where k is an integer.

We have shown that in the usual case when a B-tree page consists of one sector the above strategy fails and it also fails in the unusual case in which keywords are so long that it takes more than one sector to comprise a B-tree page consisting of just 2 elements. That is, if B-tree pages were first made up of m sectors, where m is one or more, if we now let the B-tree pages be made up of k times m sectors, in searching to leaf level we will have to read into memory more sectors than we did with just m sectors.

Calculating the B-tree page size

What we have concluded is that increasing the page size of a B-tree by a factor of k results in having to read more sectors and therefore there is no advantage to larger page sizes. This, however, assumes that the time required to read each sector is the same. This would be the case if a separate seek were needed to get each sector as when pages are made up of non-contiguous sectors. However, to the degree that pages consist of contiguous disk sectors, the time required to read in a page of k sectors would be less than the time required to read in k completely non-contiguous sectors. This is because k seeks would be required to read in k completely non-contiguous sectors, but only one seek is required to locate the start of k contiguous sectors of data. Although the transfer time involved with longer pages is greater since more sectors of data have to be transferred to memory, if the pages consist of contiguous sectors the total seek time could be less since each page could be gotten in just one seek. This could represent a total saving in time since seek time is far greater than transfer time.

We will deal with the case of contiguous sectors in the next section. For now let's assume there is no advantage to having pages that are longer than the minimum number of sectors needed to form a B-tree page (which will be one sector in the usual case).

This means that picking the page size for a B-tree of a given sized key is simple. In the usual case in which a sector-sized B-tree page of length x can hold at least two elements of length y, we calculate the order by simply dividing the page length x minus 4 bytes for the two pointers at the end of each record by 2y. This division may not come out evenly, and the remainder is unused or wasted space.

In doing your calculations remember that a page element consists of a keyword plus an element pointer and a storage file pointer. For example, consider the B-tree of Order 9 discussed previously. The keywords are 24 bytes long, so each element is 28 bytes long. The sector length is 512 bytes, and subtracting 4 bytes from that gives us

508 bytes. Fifty-six divides 508 nine times, with a remainder of 4, so we have a tree of Order 9 with 4 bytes of unused space.

In the unusual case in which the B-tree page is longer than one sector-sized record, just set up a B-tree of Order 1.

CONTINUOUS RECORDS ON THE HARD DISK

We now consider B-tree pages that span several sectors, with the sectors being contiguous on the hard disk.

From a practical point of view this is something that seldom, if ever, happens. The average hard disk that you will find in the work place is formatted for in 512-byte sectors. In the normal operating environment the location of the sectors on the disk will be fairly random, since the operating system will be constantly reassigning deleted sectors to new incoming information. It is still very worthwhile, however, to investigate further what happens in an environment where sectors are contiguous, which we will do now.

increasing page size: faster or slower searching?

Once again our problem is whether increasing the page size means faster searching because we look at fewer pages, or slower searching, because of having to handle more sectors per page. There are two consideration here. (1) Time retrieving a page from hard disk and (2) Time processing or searching through a page for our element once it is in memory.

Most hard disks have "seek time" and "transfer time": seek time is the time required to physically locate a sector, and transfer time is the time required to get the sector into memory. Typically seek time is far greater than the time required to transfer in a sector. This means that it is more economical to do one seek and read in many sector-sized, contiguously-located, records than to do a separate seek for each record. This is why we consider letting a B-tree page consist of several sector-sized records.

Let's look at both the time to retrieve a page from hard disk and the time to process the page once in memory.

Retrieving time:
Let us say that l is the number of levels when a page consists of a record that is one sector in length, L is the number of levels when a page consists of k sectors, S_t is the seek time (the average time required to come to the start of a sector), and T_t is the transfer time (the time required to read into memory one sector of data). Lastly, let's define d = l-L.

The time required to access a leaf originally (before increasing page size) is:

$$T_0 = lS_t + lT_t$$

and the time T_1, needed to access a leaf after making pages greater by a factor of k is:

$$T_1 = LS_t + LK\ T_t = (l\text{-}d)\ S_t + (l\text{-}d)k\ T_t$$

Thus if by increasing k, d is greater, then we can get a savings, but if by increasing k, d is not greater than zero, T_1 will actually increase.

This will eventually happen (that is, that increasing k does not result in non-zero d) since the number of levels is related to $\log_{(order)}$(number of tree elements).

For instance, 4 million keys can be accommodated on a

minimally-loaded B-tree of Order 19 in five levels. Increasing the order to 38 uses four levels. Increasing the order to 76 still requires four levels. The order would have to be increased to 125 to accommodate 4 million keys in three levels!

Also note that if T_t is, say, $\frac{1}{75}$ of S_t, then if d is just 1 and k is 25 and there are 3 levels now, there is almost no time saving. But if k is 2 to 4, there is substantial savings. If T_t is about $\frac{1}{10}$ of S_t, as appears to be the case in the following time trials, even getting to Level 2 from Level 3 with k=5 does not achieve a savings.

Processing time:

processing time: multiple sectors vs. single sector

Now let us consider the time involved in processing pages consisting of a multiple of sectors, as opposed to pages consisting of a single sector. Here it is clear that we lose time per page because our pages are larger, but again we have less pages. If we use a sequential search in locating an element on a page and increase the size of the page by a factor of k, then the search time will also increase by a factor of k. But our formula giving the number of physical records accessed, Lk> l, applies in this case, showing that we will in fact have a greater search time, although few levels are searched.

This clearly means we have to use a binary search to locate elements in a B-tree page if we intend to multiply the page size. Actually, since a binary search of n elements requires the comparison of only $\log_2 n + 1$ elements as opposed to about $\frac{n}{2}$ comparisons using sequential searching, if we intend to have pages of approximately order 8 or more we should use binary search anyway. Using binary search, if we increase the page size by a factor of k we will introduce a $\log_2 k$ term into the expression for the page searching time. If the original order is n and the time to make a comparison is C, then the searching time on l levels would be $lC\text{int}((\log_2 n) + 1)$. If we increase the order to kn and have to search L levels we have a searching time of:

$$LC\text{int}(\log_2(kn)+1) = LCint(\log_2 k + \log_2 n + 1)$$

We want to know which searching time is shorter, so let's divide the new time by the original time:

$$\frac{L\text{int}(\log_2 k + \log_2 n + 1)}{l\text{int}(\log_2 n + 1)}$$

This formula indicates a saving if its value is less than 1. This means that L must be less than l, and even if L is less than l, k must not be too large. For example, if l is 5 and L is 4 and n is 16, there is no saving for any k beyond 3.

The problem is that a decrease in height of a tree of a larger order is unlikely, and even with small-order trees k must not be large. For example, for $\frac{L}{l}$ to be $\frac{1}{2}$ when the order of the tree is 4, k must be less than 8.

Thus, even with a binary search for your element, increasing the page size will likely increase the processing time, unless the order is quite small.

Table 9.4 number of comparisons in a binary search of a page of various orders

sequential vs. binary searching

While it is clear from Table 9.5 (giving the times to grow a B-tree of 10,000 elements using both sequential and binary searching) that the reduction of comparisons afforded by replacing sequential searching with binary searching is significant, it turns out that when binary searching is used and the question is just whether increasing a page's size is advantageous in reducing comparisons, the answer is perhaps surprising. This can be seen by looking at Table 9.4, the table depicting the number of elements on minimally-loaded B-trees of dif-

Level	**Order Class:** 4 **Orders:** 4 through 7 **Greatest order:** 7 **Comparisons per page:** 3	Comparisons	**Order Class:** 8 **Orders:** 8 through 15 **Greatest order:** 15 **Comparisons per page:** 4	Comparisons	**Order Class:** 16 **Orders:** 16 through 31 **Greatest order:** 31 **Comparisons per page:** 5	Comparisons	**Order Class:** 32 **Orders:** 32 through 63 **Greatest order:** 63 **Comparisons per page:** 6	Comparisons	**Order Class:** 64 **Order:** 64 through 127 **Greatest order:** 127 **Comparisons per page:** 7	Comparisons	
1	1		1		1		1		1		
2	15	4	31	5	63	6	127	7	255	8	$2^1=2$
3	127	7	511	9	2,047	11	8,191	13	32,767	15	$2^2=4$
4	1,023	10	8,191	17	65,535	16	524,287	19	4,194,303	22	$2^3=8$
5	8,191	13	131,071	21	2,097,151	21	33,554,431	25	536,870,911	29	$2^4=16$
6	65,535	16	2,097,151	25	67,108,863	26					$2^5=32$
7	524,287	19	33,554,431	31							$2^6=64$
8	4,194,303	22									$2^7=128$
9	33,554,431	23									$2^8=256$

Level	**Order Class:** 128 **Orders:** 128 through 255 **Greatest order:** 255 **Comparisons per page:** 8	Comparisons	**Order Class:** 256 **Orders:** 256 through 511 **Greatest order:** 511 **Comparisons per page:** 9	Comparisons	**Order Class:** 512 **Orders:** 512 through 1,023 **Greatest order:** 1,023 **Comparisons per page:** 10	Comparisons	**Order Class:** 1024 **Orders:** 1,024 thru 2,047 **Greatest order:** 2,047 **Comparisons per page:** 11	Comparisons			
1	1		1		1		1				
2	511	9	1,023	10	2,047	11	4,095	12			$2^1=2$
3	131,071	17	524,287	19	2,097,151	21	8,388,607	23			$2^2=4$
4	33,554,431	25	268,434,943	28							$2^3=8$

Table 9.4: Number of comparisons in a binary search of a page of various orders.

For minimally-loaded B-trees of orders of the form $2^{n+1}-1$, where n is an integer with values 2,3,.....14. This table gives for various levels the number of elements on t tree when the height of the tree reaches the given level and also the number of comparisons needed to search down to and including the given level. These trees are s to be in order class 2^n. The pages of these trees of orders 2^n to $2^{n+1}-1$ can be searched using binary search in n+1 comparisons. Notice that the number of elements o tree of k levels, of order $2^{n+1}-1$, in order class 2^n, is $2^{(n+1)(k-1)+1}-1$. This means that having obtained the left-most columns, we can obtain all the other columns by m tiplying by 2 to the appropriate power, depending on the level. That is, if we know, N, the number of elements on a tree of a certain order of k levels, the number of e ments on the same level in the tree of the next order class is $2^{k-1}(N+1)-1$. This multiplier for each level is given in the last column.

ferent orders and of various levels, and showing the number of comparisons that would have to be made in searching to a particular level.

In Table 9.4 we have shown the number of elements on various levels for nine minimally-loaded B-trees of particular order (orders of the form 2^k-1). The reason for picking trees of these orders is that a binary search of a page of 2^k-1 elements requires k comparisons. Since k comparisons are also needed for any pages which contain between 2^{k-1} and 2^k-1 elements, with trees of such order we have a tree of the greatest order that requires k comparisons for a binary search of its pages.

For example, a tree of Order 31 requires four comparisons per page search, as do all trees of orders between 16 and 31. If we pick the tree that has the greatest possible order for any given number of comparisons, we will be able to minimize comparisons while having as short a tree as possible.

order class-definition

In this table the number to the right of the number of elements on a tree of a given level and order is the number of comparisons needed to search a tree of that level and order. These numbers were obtained from the formula: $(L-1)(\log_2 n + 1) + 1$, where L is the number of levels and n is the "**order class**" of the tree. The order class refers to the whole range of orders searchable with a particular number of comparisons. For example, pages of orders 16 through 31 which can be searched in five comparisons, $\log_2 16 + 1$, are in Order Class 16; similarly Order Class 32 comprises pages of orders 32 through 63 that can be searched in six comparisons $\log_2 32 + 1$, and so forth.

This table tells us that in terms of comparisons needed for binary searching, in one sense, one order class is just about as good as another. For example, in Order Class 4,

16 comparisons are needed to search to Level 6, which can hold up to 524,286 elements while the same number of elements can be searched using 13 comparisons in Order Class 32. If you want 65,534 elements, however, you would need 11 comparisons in Order Class 16, and 13 in Order Class 32. In general, though, it is better to increase the page size so that the number of intended elements can be held in two levels. This can be done for 2,097,150 elements in order class 512 using 11 comparisons to do the search. 8,388,606 elements require Order Class 1024 and 12 comparisons, etc.

What is the significance of all this? If you are growing a B-tree in memory, where there is neither seek time nor transfer time, then you might as well pick your page sizes to be Order Class 512 or greater, and make them the highest order in the class. But if your tree is grown in a storage medium where seek time is a factor, then the relative comparisons involved in binary searching are a minor consideration. The two important considerations are:

1) The order of a B-tree whose page length is that of a sector.
2) The number of times the size of this sector-sized page may be multiplied and still be efficient. This depends on the seek time and the transfer time.

We have shown, then, that the strategy of increasing page size beyond the sector size is not likely to yield faster searching unless the height of the tree falls dramatically (in only an increase of a few-fold), as can happen if the order of the tree is small.

The following tables illustrate in actual B-trees the dynamics we have been discussing. Wee used a standard Macintosh SE computer with no hardware enhancements, and ran the TeachBase program in the interpreted mode.

Table 9.5: B-tree Performance for Building Tree of 10,000 Elements (in sec)

Table 9.5 Creating a B-tree of 10,000 keywords.

Page length / Order	level/number of elements on B-tree when it reaches that level	B-tree creation time using binary Search (time in seconds)	B-tree creation time using sequential search (time in seconds)	B-tree creation tim e using elements that are already in order (time in seconds)	multiple of physical unit of disk access	B-tree size
128/3	1/1 2/7 3/38 4-/86 5/816	5051	4951	1411	1/4	307K
256/7	1/1 2/15 3/164 4/1618	4505	4562	1340	1/2	261K
512/14	1/1 2/57 3/561	4245	4796	1316	1	264K
1024/28	1/1 2/57 3/2158	4486	5845	1313	2	260K
2560/71	1/1 2/143	4613	7986	1302	5	283K
5120/ 142	1/1 2/285	5127	10706	1285	10	295K
10240/ 284	1/1 2/569	6085	17264	1301	20	310K
30720/ 853	1/1 2/1707	10091	------	1281	60	300K

Here we have installed 10,000 records using the Teach-Base B-tree system and then read them from the B-tree.

From an import file, we imported 10,000 different keys, each of which is a random number composed of 14 characters. As we input each key, we also saved the key in a storage file whose records consisted of the key plus a 2-byte field representing the number of times the word occurred (there were, however, no duplicates). Each record in the storage file is pointed to, or indexed, by a pointer that comes right after the key on the B-tree. Also, each time a key is installed on the B-tree we print a message on the screen telling us if it was simple leaf addition, whether splitting occurred or not, and if so, whether it was limited to leaf level.

We do this twice, once using sequential searching to search a page and once using binary search to search a page. Of course, binary searching is superior except with Order 3.

It takes the same time to read a page of 128 bytes, 256 bytes or 512 bytes (since the computer reads in 512 byte sectors) but the orders change from 3 to 7 to 14, causing the height of the trees to drop from 6 to 4 to 3 levels. Thus the saving, especially in the binary case, is expected.

Although pages of multiple sectors were of no help in improving installation performance, the larger page size was a distinct advantage in reading back the tree. This would be even more dramatic if we stored records we visited, in reading to leaf level in memory, since after reading a leaf we have to do a seek just to read one element.

Table 9.6

In Table 9.6 we do exactly the same thing we did for Table 9.5, except we eliminate the on-screen messages each time a key is installed. We also do not use sequential searching, drop the last two large page sizes, and added some intermediate page sizes. Note that with order 56 most keys are going in on Level 2, and we have a saving over Order 28, where most keys are going in on level 3. But order 14, representing pages one sector long, is the fastest, although most keys go into Level 3.

Table 9.6 10,000 keys with sequential search

Page size / order	Level / number of elements on the B-tree when it formed a new root to reach this level	Multiple of physical unit of disk access	Time (sec) to install 10,000 random 14-digit character keys
128/3	1/1	1/4	3521
	2/7		
	3/38		
	4/186		
	5/816		
	6/4212		
256/7	1/1	1/2	2995
	2/15		
	3/164		
	4/1618		
512/14	1/1	1	2776
	2/29		
	3/561		
1024/28	1/1	2	3038
	2/57		
	3/2158		
2048/56	1/1	4	3030
	2/113		
	3/8515		
2560/71	1/1	5	3162
	2/143		
4096/113	1/1	8	3411

Page size / order	Level / number of elements on the B-tree when it formed a new root to reach this level	Multiple of physical unit of disk access	Time (sec) to install 10,000 random 14-digit character keys
	2/227		
4680/127	1/1 2/255	9	3557
5120/142	1/1 2/285	10	3668
8192/227	1/1 2/455	16	4193

In other words, increasing the page size by a factor of just 5, from 512 to 2560, resulted in the order increasing from 14 to 71. However, this did not improve the insertion time, even though the tree height decreased from three to two levels.

If we disregard savings due to less frequent page splitting with larger pages, this indicates that the transfer time involved in reading a physical unit of disk access was greater than 1/5 of the seek time to locate the start of a page. The number of binary search comparisons as a factor can be ruled out, since a look at the order classes shows that the number of comparisons actually drops. The 512-page size is in order class 8, so it takes around 80,000 comparisons to insert 10,000 elements. The page size of 2560 bytes is in Order Class 64, so it takes more like 70,000 comparisons.

limit of multiplying physical records to form pages

This means that in our computer system the limit of multiplying physical records to form pages is four-fold, but even that achieves no savings.

If we assume a seek time of five times the transfer time, we can predict or explain the times of 3,038, 3,030, and 3,162 obtained respectively for page sizes of 1,024,

converting seek time to transfer time

2,048,and 2,560 by expressing the time needed to locate and read in a key in transfers, where a transfer is the time required to read in one sector of data. We convert seek time to transfers at the rate of one seek = five transfers.

In the case of a page of 1024 bytes, the number of transfers per page is two, and so the total time to access a page is seven transfers (one seek + two transfers). Thus, since there are about 7,850 keys to be inserted on Level 3, and about 2,150 on Level 2, we may calculate the total transfers to insert 10,000 as (7,850) (3) (7) + 2,150 (2) (7) = 194,950. Similarly, for a page of 2,048 bytes, with nine transfers per page, we have 193,500 transfers involved, since we have about 1,500 keys for Level 3 and 8,500 for Level 2. This is just slightly less than 194,950, as 3,030 is slightly less than 3,038. Finally, with a page of 2,560 bytes we have no keys that require three levels. We have about 10,000 keys for Level 2, and each page requires five transfers plus seek time equivalent to five transfers, so we have (10,000) (2) (10) = 200,000 transfer equivalents.

Table 9.7: Large Keys

Here we have installed on B-trees the same file of 10,000 keys that we used to generate Table 9.5. We have done nothing differently except that the 18-character key element was left-set into fields of 250 and 500. So in this table we present the results of using large keys of 250 and 500 bytes, so that it takes file records greater than one physical unit of disk access (512 bytes) to form a B-tree page. Here, the dynamics discussed above can also be seen working. If we form a page of Order 1 or 2, then the tree will be quite high, thus making it possible to have dramatic reduction in height by forming larger pages. Thus, even with pages as large as 8, 16, and 20 physical units of disk access we have substantial savings. This is expected because we expect in going from Order 1 or 2 to Order 8 or more, to have the tree height

Key element size: 500

page size	order	install time	read time	multiple of physical records
2048	2	7381	1627	4
8192	8	6772	1413	16
16384	16	7746	1375	32

Key element size: 250

page size	order	install time	read time	multiples of physical records
512	1	7994	1782	1
4096	8	5846	1398	8
10,240	20	6531	1344	20
21,504	43	8503	1330	42

Table 9.7 Large keys

fall six or seven levels from 10 to 3. Calculating that a 5-fold multiple achieves a level drop but makes up for it in added transfer time, we could expect to have to multiply by about 30 before losing our savings. This is exactly what we observe in Table 9.7.

Table 9.8 Installing 100,000 elements

generating keys one at a time vs. generating from an input file

The last table of results we present is the result of installing 100,000 10-digit keys on B-trees. We proceed differently than we did previously, in that we do not get our keys from an input file; instead, we have the program generate them one at a time. Also, we do not form a storage file of keys and index by the B-tree, instead we just install the key on the B-tree. The keys are ten-digit random integers which we store on the B-tree as an eight-byte double precision number in the MKS format.

Table 9.8 Installing 100,000 elements

Page size / order	Level / number of keys added when new root formed	Multiple of Physical units of disk access	Time (sec) to generate & install 100,000 10-digit keys at random
512/25	1-1 2-51 3-1700 4-59124	1	45003
1024	1-1 2-103 3-6861	2	47,556
2048/102	1-1 2-205 3-27743	4	47,064
4096/204	1-1 2-409	8	48,857

Here, note the saving in going from Order 51 to Order 102; but in increasing the page size from 512 bytes to 1,024 we expect a small savings. This seems evident from the fact that with a small increase in page size, the height of the tree is reduced. That there was no savings is perhaps due to the fact that we started with order 25, which is already fair-sized compared with 1, 2, 3, or 4.

contiguous sectors

We have been assuming that when we create pages consisting of several sectors of data, these sectors are contiguously located on the disk. This may not be true depending on how free space is allocated in the disk. To the degree that page sectors are not contiguous on the disk we find that no time saving is achieved in making page size greater than one sector. Previously we observed that because of less saving than we had expected the transfer time might be as large as 1/5 of seek time. It is likely that non-contiguous page sectors are to some degree involved.

Summary of Results

picking proper page size

In summary, we can say that if a B-tree is being grown in the computer's main memory, (and we can begin a binary search of a page from its beginning in only the time it takes to access its storage location), then page size should be picked according to Table 9.4: Order 127 if it is to contain up 32,766 elements, Order 255 if it is to contain up to 131,070 bytes, Order 256 if it is to contain up to 524,286 elements, Order 1,023 if it is to contain up to 2,097,150 bytes, and so forth.This is because processing time depends on the time required to search a page and the number of pages. The dynamics of the relation of number of pages to page size has been discussed above.

If a B-tree is being grown in on disk where there is significant seek time involved in locating the start of a page and after that transfer time, then it may be advantageous to make the page consist of several units of disk access if they are contiguously located on the disk so that many sectors of data can be transferred to memory with only one seek.

There is trade-off, however, since the number of units of disk access that have to be transferred to main memory is increased. If the seek time is very large compared to transfer time, it may be possible to allow a page to consist of enough units of disk access so that the order of the page is large enough to allow the tree to grow to two, or at most three levels. This, of course, improves performance. Also, with larger orders, the number of comparisons needed to do binary searching to locate an element on leaf can fall by a factor of two. However, if the seek time is only 10 or 12 times the transfer time, improvement in tree performance through letting pages consist of multiple physical units of disk access is limited to a multiple, maybe 4 or 5. Finally, when the seek time is zero, or very small compared to transfer time, if we let a page consist of several physical records we will have more transfer time. This is because we have to read more physical records into memory. Whether there is any advantage in performance to be gained by increasing page size depends on whether a reduction in binary search comparison can be made which will offset the increased transfer time.

Algorithm for finding Optimal Page Size with Contiguous Sections

We take the above considerations into account, but also assume the B-tree is being grown on a disk with non-zero seek time and with key size such that one physical record can be a B-tree page. We can then give the following algorithm to find optimal order and page size. The basis of this algorithm is that the page size can be increased to only a certain multiple, say 4, of physical records. If the height of the tree falls within that limit, saving occurs. Beyond that limit, even if the tree height falls, no saving results.

If the key size is such that it will take more than one physical record to make up a page, this algorithm still works, the only change being that instead of initializing the variable *pagesize1* to *recsize* (the size of a sector), *pagesize1* is initialized to the minimum number of sectors needed to make up a B-tree page.

Constants that must be assigned by the user:

eleptr: Size of element pointer

fileptr: record number for key in storage file

electr: size of the element counter

pageptr: size of page pointer

recsize: size of a unit of file access;physical record; one disk sector.

keysize: size of indexing key

N: number of elements the tree is expected to hold

kmax: maximum multiple of sectors comprising a page

Initializing variables:

page size1=recsize

k=0

Calculate original order and height of minimally-loaded B-tree

order1=int

int[(pagesize1-(pageptr+eleptr)2*(keysize +fileptr+eleptr)]

level 1 = int [$\log_{order\ 1+1}$ ((N+1)/2)] +1

loop to see if increasing the order until k reaches kmax lowers tree height

loop: k=k+1

if k>kmax Done (use the values of pagesize1 & order 1)

pagesize=pagesize*k

order = int[pagesize-(pageptr+electr)/2*(keysize +filptr+eleptr)]

level = int [$\log_{order\ +1}$ {(N+1)(2)}+1

if level<level1 then pagesize1=pagesize, order 1=order

10

Changing the TeachBase B-tree System

Changing the TeachBase system so that it will use your own custom keywords, and store in the storage file whatever information you desire, is not as hard as you might think. In fact, the program is designed with this in mind, and you will see how easy it is in this chapter.

We will look at making the following changes:

1) **Change storage file use:** You want to add something to the storage file such as people's addresses, etc.

2) **Change keyword use:** You want to use a keyword length other than the one that comes set up in the program.

3) **Change output:** You want to interrupt the listings and send it to a printer or some other file.

4) **Change inputting procedure:** You want to add a lot of names from another file.

5) **Refuse duplicate entries:** Adjust program so there will be no duplicate keywords allowed into the system.

Now let's do the above items:

1) Change Storage File Use:

Line 400 - In line 400 you are asked for the length of your record in the storage file:

```
400 LNG =16 'record length for storage file
```

Simply change the length to whatever record length you desire and include two bytes to go at the end of the record for keeping track of how many entries have been made. Most users want the records in their files to be "32-bit friendly" or a record length that is evenly divisible by 32.

Line 1300 - This is the fielding of your storage file record. Change it to read:

```
1300 Field BUF1, LNG AS WD$, 2 AS MN$
```

Line 50020-50100- Use the space between these two lines to ask what the user wants to send to storage. Set the entire expression equal to sword$. For example:

```
50030 PRINT:PRINT "What is the item you want to store in the storage file? ";

50032 LINE INPUT sword$
```

Of course, you can doctor up the input query. For example, you could ask for each line of addresses, and then add them all together with a semicolon or some marker between the lines of the address. Then set sword$ equal to that expression.

Line 17300 - This is where your storage word is buffered before sending to storage file. Change this line from its current status:

```
17300 LSET WD$ = word$
```

To be equal to your sword$. So it will read:

```
17300 LSET WD$ = sword$
```

That's all that is necessary!

Note that you will now be asked for both a keyword and for your storage file information. This means you will make up some kind of ID for the information you will be storing in the storage file and that ID is what will be stored on the b-tree.

2) Change keyword use:

This is fairly simple because we designed the program so that all the variables are defined at the start of the program and they are in the lines 300 to 1500, as follows:

```
300 RECLN =128 'length of page on btree

400 LNG =16 'record length for storage file

500 T = 18 'length of a page element

600 T1 = 14 'length of key word

610 T0 = 16 'length of key-word plus store pointer

700 T2 = 17 'start of element pointer

710 T3 = 15 'start of storage pointer

800 ORDER = 2 'order of btree: half of no of ele-
ments on a full page

900 FULLPAGE = 2*ORDER

1000 BUF1 = 1 'file number for storage file

1100 BUF2 = 2 'file number for btree index

1200 OPEN "R", BUF1, "storage.fil", LNG

1300 FIELD BUF1, T1 AS WD$, LNG - T1 AS MN$

1400 OPEN "R", BUF2, "btree.fil", RECLN
```

```
1500 FIELD BUF2, T*FULLPAGE AS REC$, RECLN -
T*FULLPAGE AS LE$
```

As we have stated previously, in order to change the TeachBase B-tree system, all you really have to know is what you want your new keyword length to be - the rest can be calculated very easily.

Let's assume you want a new keyword of 24 characters.

We will now go through lines 300 to 1500 and show you how easy it is to change the values. We will give you the original line and then show you what the change should be.

We know from Chapter 9 that we want our page length to always be a multiple of 512 bytes and we want the shortest page length possible.

```
300 RECLN =128  'length of page on b-tree
```

Change line 300 so RECLN = 512

```
400 LNG =16  'record length for storage file
```

You would simply change this to whatever length you want your storage file record to be.

```
500 T = 18   'length of a page element
```

The new value would be T=24+2+2 = 28 characters (24 bytes is our keyword length plus two bytes for the storage file pointer plus two bytes for the element pointer).

```
600 T1 = 14 'length of keyword
```

The new value would be T1=24

```
610 TO = 16 'Length of keyword plus store pointer
```

The new value would be TO=24+2 = 26

```
700 T2 = 17 'start of element pointer
```

The new value would be T2=24+2+1= 27

```
710 T3 = 15 'start of storage pointer
```

The new value would be T3=24+1=25

```
800 ORDER = 2 'order of b-tree: half of no of ele-
ments on a full page
```

The new value would be ORDER=9

lines 900 to 1500:

Nothing needs to be done to lines 900 to 1500 unless you want to change the name of the B-tree file or the name of the storage file. If you want to change the name of the B-tree file, it is in line 1400, and the current name is "btree.fil". Simply change that name. If you want to change the name of the storage file, it is in line 1200 and the current name is "storage.fil". Simply change that name. Nothing else need be changed.

3) Change Output:

What you want to do here is simply have the ability to interrupt the listing of storage file words which is currently going to screen. The listing of the storage file words to screen is done in lines 21800 to 22100. The actual print statement is line 22000. Your keyword is the first T1 bytes of REC$. The variable WD$ is the description you sent to the storage file, and the 2-byte field called MN$ tells how many times a keyword identical to the one being looked at has been entered on the B-tree. Change these lines to do whatever you want.

4) Change Inputting Procedure:

The actual input of a new item occurs in lines 50000 - 50100. If you are inputting data from another file these lines would be modified so that they work in a loop to read in the foreign file.

5) Refuse Duplicate Entries:

There are two places you would want to affect the program. First of all is line 1300:

```
1300 FIELD BUF1, T1 AS WD$, LNG - T1 AS MN$
```

If you are to going to have duplicates in the database, then you do not need MN$. Simply change the fielding to:

```
1300 FIELD BUF1, LNG AS WD$
```

You now need to interrupt the program where a duplicate entry is discovered. This occurs in the lines 15900 to 16800:

```
15900 '----------------------------------------
16000 'searched for word is already in file;
increase counter
16100 '----------------------------------------
16200 WHERE = CVI(MID$(REC$, T*I + T3, 2))
16220 GET BUF1, WHERE
16300 KOUNT = CVI(MID$(MN$, 1, 2))
16400 KOUNT=KOUNT+1
16500 LSET MN$ = MKI$(KOUNT)
16600 PUT BUF1, WHERE
16750 count=count+1 'increase total word counter
16800 PRINT "* increased the occurrence counter *":
GOTO 50000
16900 '----------------------------------------
```

What you want to do is get rid of or deactivate lines 16200 to 16800 and simply replace them with a notice to the user that this keyword is already taken. So a solution would be to replace lines 16200 to 16800 with the line:

```
16200 PRINT:PRINT "I'm sorry but your keyword
";WWW$;" is taken.":print "Please try again.":goto
50000
```

The other thing you have to fix is all the places that the counter MN$ is mentioned. Those lines are as follows:

```
17400 LSET MN$ = MKI$(1)
```

Delete line 17400.

```
22000 PRINT E, WD$; CVI(MID$(MN$,1,2))
```

You will not be displaying MN$ so change line 22000 to:

```
22000 PRINT E, WD$
```

The next occurrence of MN$ is when a deletion is made and we need to decrease the counter in MN$ by one. This occurs in lines 32150 to 32154:

```
32150 NZ = CVI(LEFT$(MN$,2))
32154 IF NZ <> 1 THEN LSET MN$ = MKI$(NZ-1): PUT
BUF1, OLD: PRINT "** Reduced count **": GOTO 49600
```

Since we have no word counter to decrease, lines 32150 and 32154 should be deleted.

In line 49580 we are displaying contents of storage file:

```
49580 PRINT:PRINT "Storage file contents and number
of times entered:": PRINT WD$, CVI(LEFT$(MN$,2))
```

Since WD$ does not exist, we delete that part of the statement. It will now read:

```
49580 PRINT:PRINT"Storage file contents:":PRINT WD$
```

CODE AVAILABLE FROM PUBLISHER:

There are two items available from the publisher that will be of interest to the reader:

TeachBase code
If you want the TeachBase code, we will send you the following items:

1) The TeachBase program itself - this saves you typing errors.

2) File generator - This program will generate a file with as many records of random numbers as you like.

3) Editor for file made by the file generator. This allows you to go into the file created above and change any record or read what has been input.

4) Input B-tree - This program is the same as the TeachBase program except it has been modified to automatically read in all the contents of a foreign file (such as the one created with your file generator).

All of the above programs are in interpreted BASIC and easy to edit if you wish. With them you can create a file of whatever size records and whatever file length you want, edit the file, and then have it automatically read into your TeachBase B-tree system. The TeachBase program can then be called to work with the newly created database.

Cost: $45.00 (major credit cards accepted)

Contact:
BALDAR
P.O. Box 4340
Berkeley, CA 94704 USA
Tel. (800) 367-0930
or (510) 841-2474
FAX (510) 841-2695

BASIC-base

The advanced TeachBase program:

There are a few items that we did not have time to go into in this book. They are covered in a advanced version of the TeachBase program called BASIC-base. Available from the publisher shortly, this program will have the following, more-advanced items:

1) Extended size of B-tree: The TeachBase B-tree system in this book is limited in size by the highest value of the pointers. We use the short integer MKI$ format, so the limit with the TeachBase system is 32,000 keywords. In BASIC-base we use long integers which allow the database to accept over 2 billion entries.

2) Routines listed separately: The routines for deleting, listing, searching, and adding keywords are listed separately so you can incorporate them into your other programs as needed.

3) Search with hints: In Teachbase you either knew all of the keyword you were searching for or you did not find your item. In BASIC-base you need only give a hint of what is in your keyword (maybe the first letter or two) and the program will find it.

4) Listing with hints: In TeachBase you listed everything in your B-tree when you asked for a listing. In BASIC-base, you can give a hint of the keyword you want to start with and a hint of the keyword you want the listing to end with.

5) Controlling wasted space: As you can imagine, for a given keyword and a page length of 512 bytes you probably have some wasted space at the end of your page. In TeachBase we did not concern ourselves with the amount of space that might be wasted. In BASIC-base this problem is addressed.

6) Object-oriented interface: There is an object-oriented interface being done for BASIC-base as well as a system-independent, character-based version. Obviously, the MAC, WINDOWS, etc. versions will require different code.

Contact:
BALDAR
P.O. Box 4340
Berkeley, CA 94704 USA
Tel. (800) 367-0930 or (510) 841-2474
FAX (510) 841-2695

SECTION V

Appendices

APPENDIX A

Review of Standard File Procedures

OVERVIEW

In this chapter we review the fundamentals of how to open files, send data to files, get data from files and close files. This will familiarize you with all the fundamental information about files that you need in order to study this book.

The first order of business is to cover some very simple definitions.

Data

Data is simply any information that you can input to your computer (usually by striking keys on your keyboard). What the data consists of in the way of letters, numbers and other characters is obviously up to the person operating the computer.

File

When you go to store data on a disk, you are required to give a name to the location where you are storing the data on disk so you can find it later. This location is referred to as a **file**. So, a **file** is simply the data that you stored on a disk and the name you give to the file is called the **file name**. You can, of course, have many different files. One other concept we should mention now is that of **records**. When you send data to your file you usually want to have some kind of "dividers" in the data you are sending out to disk. For example, you would want to have a marker that tells you where the end of the first line of a person's address is and the start of the second line of the address. These "groups" of data, which the user defines, are called **records**.

Sequential and Random Access files

In the BASIC language there are two types of files available, and you must tell the computer which type you want your file to be when you first create it. You have the option of storing your data as a **sequential file** or as a **random access file** (sometimes also called a **direct file**).

What is the difference between a sequential file and a random access file? In the beginning of computer history there existed only the sequential file. When you went to store data to your file, you simply sent each character of your data, one after another (including your record markers), to disk, and every character of data you sent to your file was added to the end of the file. When you wanted to find a piece of data, you would read through your sequential file, from the front to the back, one character after another, until you found the data you were looking for.

As time went on, people noticed that in many of the programs they wrote, the records were always exactly the same length throughout the entire file. An example would be a program that always stored exactly one five-character name in a sequential file every time the program was run.

Programmers decided that in this unique situation, they could expedite the reading and writing of data to the sequential file if they declare, when the file is created, that it is a sequential file in which every record will be the same length. Having done that, you can start reading or writing to almost any location in the file. For example, if you say that your records are all five characters long and you want the 154th record, the computer knows instantly that you want to start reading with character 766, and stop reading after reading character 770. As you can imagine, this makes reading and writing of data to files much faster, and since you can randomly access data anywhere in the file without having to read all the way through the file to your data, this type of special file has become known as the **random access** file. The name **direct file** is also sometimes used since you can directly access any data in the file. Random access, however, has become the most favored industry name.

In summary, we now have two types of files: the sequential file and a variation of it called the random access file. What are the advantages and disadvantages of the two files? The advantage of a random access file is speed. It can be many orders of magnitude faster then the sequential file and absolutely must be used under certain circumstances. The beauty of the sequential file is that there is no waste. You are not forced to fit your data into any pre-specified record size and consequently there is no wasted space in any of your records. We will discuss, with examples, how you send data to and get data from both the sequential and random access files.

Sequential Files

How to open, write to, and read from a sequential file.

Opening a new file is also called creating a file. We call the process of inserting information into a file **writing to a file**. We can open a previously existing sequential file in order to read its data. This is called **reading a file**. We can open an already existing sequential file to add data onto the end of that file. This is called **appending data to a file**. Another set of terms we should define at this point is the **end of file** marker (**EOF** marker) and the **file pointer**. The EOF marker is a physical character written at the very end of your file. It is automatically put there by the computer at the file's creation, and, when read, it means you are at the end of your file. The file pointer, on the other hand, is a variable held in cpu memory and is controlled by the user. It simply points to the last character that you read in the file.

Whenever we open a sequential file we must provide the computer with three things.

(1) **The access code:** This tells the computer the mode of access for this opening of the file. You have a choice of three possible access codes for a sequential file: O, I, and A. We will give examples of these shortly.

(2) **A buffer number:** This is a dedicated space in cpu memory, which the programmer requests when opening a file and uses temporarily (while the file remains open) to shuttle data between the cpu memory and the disk (hence the name buffer).

(3) **The file name:** If the file was created earlier, this is the name given the file when it was created. If the file is being created by this opening, this is the name by which this file will always be known.

The access codes

Here is what the three codes O, A and I are used for:

O opens the sequential file so it will receive output from the computer (hence the letter O). When you open a sequential file using the "O" command, the computer puts the EOF marker and the file pointer at the very first character of the file (indicating that file is empty). As you send data to file, the computer adds your data to the end of the file. This continues until you close the file.

A opens a sequential file for output, with the file pointer positioned at the end of the file. This mode is called "open for appending." Suppose you open a file using the "O" command, put data in the file, and then close it. Later you want to add data to the file. You can't use the "O" mode because you will start writing at the front of the file, typing over what exists. The "A" mode allows you to start writing to the file where you left off--at the end of the file.

I opens a sequential file for input to the computer. The file is open for input. This means that you can read the file but not write to it. The file pointer will be positioned at the first character of the file when it opens.

The Open Statement for Sequential Files.

```
10 OPEN "O", 2, "FILE1"
```

As an example, the above statement at line 10 of a program creates a new file, "FILE1", which is open and ready to receive data. This file is being opened to memory buffer number 2. Remember that if a file called "FILE1" already exists this statement kills the existing "FILE1".

```
10 OPEN "A", 4, "FILE4"
```

The above statement opens for appending the already existent file, "FILE4", using memory buffer 4. If file "FILE4" does not already exist this statement achieves the same result as the "O" mode achieves. It opens the file and starts writing at the end which, of course, is the beginning since the file has never been opened.

```
10 OPEN "I", 6, "FILE1"
```

Finally, the statement above opens for reading a file that already exists, "FILE1". The "I" means the CPU is open for input from the file. Memory buffer 6 is used.

Program A.1: Using a Sequential File

Let us now open a sequential file for output, write data to it, close it, reopen it for input, and read back the just written data. Program A.1 writes five records to a newly-created file. When you use the Print # statement to write data to your file, the computer will send a carriage return+line feed to file at the end of your print statement unless you put a semicolon at the end of the command. We will designate carriage return + line feed from now on as (CR+LF). Our records, in the short program below, are delineated by commas and by (CR+LF).

Program A.1: monkey.bas

```
2 'monkey.bas   **writes to a sequential file
10 OPEN "O", 1, "FILE"
15 A$ = "I"
```

```
16 PRINT#1, A$;",";
21 A$ = "AM"
22 PRINT#1, A$;",";
25 A$ = "A"
26 PRINT#1, A$;",";
30 A$ = "MONKEY"
31 PRINT#1, A$
35 A$ = "I am a monkey"
36 PRINT#1, A$
38 CLOSE 1
40 '-------- read back these five records ---------
50 OPEN "I", 1, "FILE"
52 IF EOF(1) THEN PRINT "DONE": CLOSE 1: END
54 INPUT#1, A$
58 PRINT A$
59 GOTO 52
```

Analysis of Program A.1

Your output from running the program will be the following:

```
I
AM
A
MONKEY
I AM A MONKEY
DONE
```

Let's inspect the main features of the input part of the program (lines 10 through 38). Note that we use the PRINT#1 command to write to the file. It looks like this:

```
PRINT#1, A$; ",";
```

What does the statement do? Let's inspect it item by item:

Print #1, Says print to the sequential file that is using buffer number 1. The comma tells the computer that what comes next will be what we want written to buffer number 1.

**A$;** The string A$ is going to be written to the file. The semicolon tells the computer: "do not write a (CR+LF) to file after you have written A$ to file."

","; This command says write what is between the quotation marks, namely one comma, to file using buffer number one. Again, the semicolon tells the computer: "do not write a (CR+LF) to file."

In summary, the above commands first write the string A$ to the file. This string is immediately followed by a comma. If the computer does not see a semicolon after you write a statement to file, it will write a line feed - carriage return to file. So semicolons hold the file pointer at the position immediately following the last printing; hence, in line 16, 22 and 26, the final semicolon serves only to hold the file pointer at the position immediately following the comma. The absence of any punctuation in line 31 and 36 after the A$ means that a line feed - carriage return is written. Thus the file written to the disk looks like this:

```
I,AM,A,MONKEY(CR+LF)I AM A MONKEY(EOF)
```

Now let's look at the output of the program (lines 40 to 59). In line 54 we ask the computer to input, or read from, buffer number one. How does the computer know when to stop reading? The input statement is designed to read until it hits a comma, a (LF+CR) or an EOF mark. The loop of line 52 to line 59 checks, after reading and printing each record, to see if we have come to the EOF mark. Note that if "FILE" had been empty, that is, previously opened but never written to, the first encounter of line 52 would have detected the EOF mark.

Program A.2: Storing Data in a Sequential File

Numbers can also be stored in sequential files. Program A.2 generates, stores, and then reads back a list of ten random integers between 1 and 100.

Program A.2: numbers.bas

```
5 ' numbers.bas **writes and reads ten random numbers ranging
1 - 100
10 OPEN "O", 1, "NUMBERS"
15 FOR J = 1 TO 10
16 RANDOMIZE TIMER
17 PRINT#1, INT(RND*100);
20 NEXT J
23 CLOSE 1
24 ' -------- read back the numbers ---------
25 OPEN "I", 1, "NUMBERS"
26 WHILE NOT EOF(1)
27 INPUT#1, I
28 PRINT I;
29 WEND
30 PRINT "DONE": CLOSE 1
```

Analysis of Program A.2

The output looks something like this (of course your numbers will vary):

```
12 36 82 17 96 44 78 53 27 81 DONE
```

In the above program, positive numbers are printed to the file preceded and followed by a blank. We will not analyze the above program because it is so similar to program A.1.

Program A.3: Storing fixed length records consisting of numbers and strings in a sequential file.

In order to randomly access data in a file you have to declare it a random access file at creation. You can, however, create a sequential file that has fixed-length records. As an academic exercise, program A.3 generates a sequential file of fixed-length records.

In this file a record is made up of twenty characters. The twenty characters are broken down as follows:

1 blank
12 digits
1 blank
1 comma
4 digits
1 line feed + carriage return
----
20 characters

The twelve digits are random positive integers. The first four digits of the twelve random positive digits are repeated in the second four-digit spot. We can define a record to be delineated by whatever item we want. In this case, our records will be delineated by (CR+LF). In a random access file the record is defined at the creation of the file. Note that if we want to we can, at any time, stop writing records that are twenty characters long and write any length records we wish. In the program below we will store five of the above records and then read them back from file, printing on screen the record, the twelve-character number and the five-character number from the file.

Program A.3: seqrnd.gen

```
1 'seqrnd.gen   **generates sequential files
2 'Generates sequential files; each record is 20 bytes long:
3 'blank, 12 digits, blank, comma, 4 characters, line feed -
carriage return.
4 'Each record consists of random 12 digit integers and 4
characters of data.
5 '==================================================
6 '--- set number of records and open the file -----
```

```
7 LNGTH% = 5: 'The number of records to create.
10 OPEN "O", 1, "origin.fil"
22 '---- do for each of the LNGTH% records --------
25 FOR J% = 1 TO LNGTH%
30 B% = RND*10: B$ = STR$ (B%): B$ = MID$ (B$,2,1) '1st digit
of string is blank.
31 if B%=0 then 30:' Let's make the first digit non-zero.
33 '------- do to get next 11 random digits for record key --
------
40 FOR I% = 1 TO 11
45 RANDOMIZE TIMER
50   D% = RND*10: IF D% = 10 THEN D% = 0
55   D$ = STR$ (D%): D$ = MID$ (D$,2,1)
60   B$ = B$ + D$
70 NEXT I%
80 B# = VAL (B$) 'convert string to number
100 DTA$ = LEFT$(B$,4) 'data is first 4 bytes of string
110 PRINT #1, B#;",";DTA$ 'write record to file
120 NEXT J%
122 CLOSE
128 '------- open file and read it ---------------
130 OPEN "I", 1, "origin.fil"
131 IF EOF(1) THEN CLOSE: END
132 I=I+1
133 INPUT #1, A#, A$
134 PRINT I; A#, A$
135 GOTO 131
```

Analysis of Program A.3

Line 7
Here we assign LNGTH%, the number of records we want in our file.

Line 10
Here we open for output from the computer to the disk using memory buffer 1 the file "origin.fil".

Lines 25 - 122
These lines generate and write each of the LNGTH% records to the file. The outer loop in J% simply runs LNGTH% times so that LNGTH% records are written. In line 30 we get the first random digit between 1 and 9. Then in the loop in I% we get the next 11 digits. These run between 0 and 9. Note that we first get a number. Then we convert this number to a single character that is added onto the string B$ started in line 30. When this string consists of twelve

digits it is converted to a number in line 80. The first four characters of this string are used to create the data portion, DTA$, of a record. In line 110, delineated by a comma and followed by a line feed - carriage return, we print the numeric key and the data to the file. In line 122, after writing the last record to the file, we close the file.

Lines 130 - 135
Here we re-open "origin.fil" for input to the computer. In line 133 we input a record. The twelve-digit number goes into A#. The four-digit number goes into A$.

Program A.4: Removing records from the sequential file generated by program A.3
The final sequential program we provide searches the sequential file "origin.fil", generated by program A.3, for a record with a key beginning with the digit specified in the program. We want to remove any such records from the file and write them to a file called "special.fil".

Program A.4: pick.bas
```
5 ' pick.bas ** picks out all records from origin.fil starting
with the number in line 20
10 '----------- digit to search for to determine a special
record ---------
20 cls:print “Give me the first digit of a record I can find
and delete”;:input N%
30 '-------- open file that will be the modified file -------
--
40 OPEN "O", 1, "changeme"
50 '--------- open the original file --------------
60 OPEN "I", 2, "origin.fil"
70 '--------- open the special file to hold wanted records --
---------
80 OPEN "O", 3, "special.fil"
90 '------ scan and print# to files ---------------
100 WHILE NOT EOF(2)
110 INPUT#2, I#, D$
120 TEST% = INT(I#/10^11)
130 IF TEST%=N% THEN PRINT#3, I#;",";D$ ELSE PRINT#1, I#;",";
D$
140 WEND
150 CLOSE
155 '------ test to see if any special records were found ---
--
160 OPEN "I", 1, "special.fil"
```

```
170 IF EOF(1) THEN 300: 'Special file empty. No items found.
180 KILL "origin.fil"
190 NAME "changeme" AS "origin.fil"
200 '------- read special file --------------
210 WHILE NOT EOF(1)
220 INPUT#1, I#, D$
230 PRINT I#, D$
240 WEND
250 CLOSE 1: END
299 '------- no special file was formed -----------300 CLOSE 1
303 PRINT "No items found so no special file was formed"
305 KILL "changeme": KILL "special.fil"
```

Analysis of Program A.4

Lines 20-80

These lines open for input the file to be searched, "origin.fil"; and two files for output, "changeme" which will become the new "origin.fil" less those records whose key begins with the digit, N%, specified in line 20, and "special.fil", which will contain all the records whose key begins with N%.

Lines 100-140

Here we read each record in "origin.fil" into memory, the key into I#, and the data into D$. In line 120 we put the first digit of the key into TEST%. If TEST% is equal to N% we must write this record into "special.fil", otherwise we write it into "changeme".

Line 150

We are done with the all the files, so then we close. Note that with a sequential file data is not actually written to the disk until the buffer is full, or until the file is closed; therefore, closing is essential to avoid losing data. (With random access files data is immediately written with each PUT statement.)

Lines 160 - 190

Here we open "special.fil" for input. If no records were printed to "special.fil", the file pointer will be at the end of file marker. If it is, we branch to line 300 to close "special.fil" and also kill "special.fil" and "changme" because they are both empty. Otherwise, the special file was written to. In that case we want to keep "changeme" as the modified original file, and kill the old original file. This we do in line 180 and line 190.

Lines 210-250
Here we get a reading of the special file which now contains all the records whose key has N% as the first digit.

RANDOM ACCESS FILES

Creating and using a Random Access file

Sequential access files are more primitive than random access files. Sequential files only allow sequential access when reading or writing data. Random access files, on the other hand, allow records to be accessed in any order. Thus we can open a random access file and read from or write to a record in the middle of the file if we wish. The drawback, of course, is that all records must be exactly the same length (which you declare on opening the file).

There are benefits beyond just the speed of input and output that come with declaring all records to be the same length. This restriction allows us to think of random access files mathematically, as one-dimensional arrays. That means all the mathematical laws for manipulating arrays can apply to random access files. Random access files can be seen as one-dimensional arrays because each record number in a random access file can be thought of as a array address. Just as an array element can be accessed directly though its array address, a record in a random access file can be accessed directly through its record number.

To open a random access file, you have to execute both an open statement and a field statement. Let's look at how this is done.

The OPEN statement

The main parts of an open statement are

1) The word "OPEN"

2) The code "R" to specify that this file is a random access file.

3) The buffer number.

4) The length you want each record to be in this file.

For example, the statement below is line 10 in a program and it opens a file named "monkey". Each record is sixteen bytes long and the program uses memory buffer number 1 for shuttling data to and from the file.

```
10 OPEN "R", 1, "MONKEY", 16
```

The FIELD statement

Somewhere in the program, after the OPEN statement and before accessing the file, you must make a FIELD statement. In the FIELD statement, you tell the computer how much memory you want to set aside (it must be equal to the amount declared in the OPEN statement) and you assign one or more buffer variables to represent this amount of memory.

Thus we can have one field for buffer number 1, or, as shown below, we can have several fields and provide each with its own name. The only rule is that the total memory used by all the variables must add up to the amount of memory you are fielding.

The following statement divides the buffer into four fields, starting at the left of the buffer. The first, A$, is six bytes long; the second, A1$, is two bytes long; the third, B$, is six bytes long; and the fourth, B1$, is two bytes long.

```
10 OPEN "R", 1, "MONKEY", 16
20 FIELD 1, 6 AS A$, 2 AS A1$, 6 AS B$, 2 AS B1$
```

The FIELD statement of line 20 is associated with the file of line 10 because it references the same buffer number, 1. Note that the sum of the lengths of the field variables in the FIELD statement must, and do, equal the record length listed in the OPEN statement (6+2+6+2=16).

Variables, such as A$, A1$, B$, and B1$, that occur in a FIELD statement are known as **field variables**. Field variables are very important to random access files. It is by means of field variables that we have quick access to every character in the record of a random access file.

WRITING TO AND READING FROM RANDOM ACCESS FILES

LSET and RSET

PUT and GET

Random access files require that every time you write data to file you have to write an entire record. Because of this we need to make sure our data, before it is sent to the file, has the right number of characters (the amount we fielded for file for) and if we are short of characters the computer needs to know whether to add blanks to the right or left side (before or after) our data. To accomplish this, we assign data to our field variables using one of the two commands: LSET or RSET. **LSET** left-justifies a string of characters in a field variable, and fills any unused space to the right with blanks. Likewise, **RSET** righ- justifies a string of characters in a field variable and fills any unused space to the left with blanks.

The **PUT** and **GET** statement, respectively, put the contents of your field variables into a record of the file, and, when you want to read a record in a file, GET retrieves the contents of the file record and assigns it to our field variables so we can access the data.

If we want to write the phrase, "You of a burnt b" to record 5 of the file opened above in line 10 and fielded in line 20, we use this program segment:

```
10 OPEN "R", 1, "MONKEY", 16
20 FIELD 1, 6 AS A$, 2 AS A1$, 6 AS B$, 2 AS B1$
30 LSET A$ = "You of"
32 RSET A1$ = "a"
34 RSET B$ = "burnt"
36 RSET B1$ = "b"
38 PUT 1,5
```

After executing line 36 the field variables are as follows (note that we use "_" to represent a leading blank):

```
A$=You of
A1$=_a
B$=_burnt
B1$=_b
```

Note how LSET left-justifies the string of characters in the field variable, and fills any unused space to the right with blanks. Likewise RSET right-justifies the string of characters in the field variable and fills any unused space to the left with blanks.

In general, PUT x,y writes the contents of buffer x to record number y of the random access file open to buffer x. Thus, PUT 1,5 writes the contents of buffer 1, "You of a burnt b", to record 5 in file "monkey".

A major point to be noted is that if this is the first time we have written to the file "monkey", "monkey" will now have five records of sixteen bytes each, since the number of records in a random access file is determined by the highest record number written to the file. We just requested our record be written to record number 5. What about the contents of records 1-4? These records contain garbage from whatever was previously on the disk in their locations. If nothing was previously on the disk these records contain the null character, "".

Over-fielding

Another fielding option, which we have not yet discussed, is that of over-fielding. The concept is very simple. Once you have fielded a buffer, you can field it again using different variables. The only requirement is that the lengths of the second set of buffers add up to the amount of memory declared in the open statement. Program A.5 exemplifies this:

Program A.5:demo1.bas

```
5 ' demo1.bas **creates and writes to the fifth record of "monkey"
10 OPEN "R", 1, "monkey", 16
20 FIELD 1, 6 AS A$, 2 AS A1$, 6 AS B$, 2 AS B1$
30 FIELD 1, 16 AS R$
32 LSET R$ = "You of a burnt b"
35 PUT 1,5
37 CLOSE
```

Note that line 20 is superfluous; we included it to emphasize the point that we can field a buffer simultaneously in several ways.

Reading with the GET statement

In general, GET x,y transfers the data in record y of a random access file open to buffer x into memory in buffer x. Once this data is in the buffer it may be accessed by means of the field variables for that buffer. For example, we use Program A.6 to read the five records of the file "monkey" set up previously.

Program A.6:demo2.bas

```
5 'demo2.bas   **reads the five records of "monkey"
10 OPEN "R", 1, "monkey", 16
20 FIELD 1, 16 AS REC$
30 FOR I% = 1 TO 5
32 GET 1, I%
33 PRINT I%, REC$
35 NEXT I%
37 CLOSE I%
```

This program prints whatever garbage was in the records 1 - 4, as well as the familiar "You of a burnt b" of record 5.

Program A.7: Changing Records in a Random Access file

Suppose we want to keep all the data in the five records of "monkey", but that we wish to write the character "*" into the seventh byte of each record. We can do it this way:

Program A.7:demo3.bas

```
5 'demo3.bas   **modifies the five records of "monkey"
10 OPEN "R", 1, "monkey", 16
20 FIELD 1, 6 AS ONE$, 1 AS IT$, 9 AS TWO$
30 FOR I% = 1 TO 5
32 GET 1, I%
33 LSET IT$ = "*"
35 PUT 1, I%
37 NEXT I%
39 CLOSE 1
```

Here we get the data for each record into the buffer. Then we write "*" into the seventh byte by setting only the field variable IT$. The PUT 1,I% then puts the modified buffer back into the record from which it came.

We could achieve this same result using program A.8.

The LOF function

Program A.8: The LOF function and MID$ function

Program A.8 illustrates an important use of the LOF function. LOF (x) yields the total number of bytes in the file open to buffer x. Here the file open to buffer 2 is "monkey" which contains five sixteen-byte records for a total of 80 bytes. Thus, LOF(2)/16 gives the number of records, five, in the file. The number of records in a random access file open to buffer x is always found by dividing LOF (x) by the length of a record.

Program A.8: demo4.bas

```
5 'demo4.bas**modifies the five records of "monkey"
10 OPEN "R", 2, "monkey", 16
12 FIELD 2, 16 AS REC$
14 FOR I% = 1 TO LOF(2)/16
16 GET 2, I%
18 HOLD$ = REC$
20 MID$(HOLD$, 7, 1) = "*"
22 LSET REC$ = HOLD$
35 PUT 2, I%
37 NEXT I%
39 CLOSE 2
```

Analysis of Program A.8

This program also illustrates the method of inserting something into a record using a field variable covering the entire record. In line 18 we assign the value of the record, REC$, to a temporary variable, HOLD$. In line 20 we use the MID$ function to remove the seventh character in HOLD$ and replace it with "*". In line 22 we set the modified HOLD$ into the buffer. We put the buffer into the desired record. NOTE: The only correct way to assign a value to a field variable is to use LSET or RSET. Field variables differ from other variables in this way.

SAVING NUMBERS AS FIXED LENGTH STRINGS

The MKI$, MKL$, MKS$, MKD$ functions

Numbers written to random access files have to be converted to strings before they are stored. The above three functions convert numbers to storable strings of a specific length. Table 1 shows that we have precise control over the number

Table 1: Variable limits

Variable	Maximum	Minimum	Space Occupied
MKI$	32,767	-32,768	2 bytes
MKL$	2,147,483,647	-2,147,483,647	4 bytes
(positive) MKS$	3.402823 E38	1.401298 E-45	4 bytes
(negative) MKS$	-1.401298 E-45	-3.402823 E38	4 bytes
(positive) MKD$	1.797693134862315 D308	4.940656458412465 D-324	8 bytes
(negative) MKD$	-4.940656458412465 D-324	-1.797693134862315 D308	8 bytes
variable names	40 characters	1 character	
string length	32,767 characters	0 characters	
static array size	65,535 bytes	1 byte	
dynamic array size	Available memory	1 byte	
Array dimensions	8	1	
Array subscripts	32,767	32,768	

of bytes used in storing numbers with random access files since only two, four or eight bytes are used.

Large numbers

Let's say you are someone who really does use huge numbers. You are probably wondering what the "E" in MKS$ and the "D" in MKD$ represent. They both mean an exponent to the power of 10, but MKS$ format is called a single precision number (meaning you can have up to seven significant digits including the period) and MKD$ is a double precision number (meaning you can have up to fifteen significant digits including the period). The power of 10 exponent, however, is good up to 38 in the case of single precision, etc. Thus if you multiply two single precision numbers together the resulting answer will have seven significant digits and a power of 10 exponent good up to the power of 38. With large numbers, the computer needs to know if your answer is suppose to be good for single precision or double precision. You use the "E" or the "D" to let it know if you want a single or double precision answer. In normal calculations, with no indicators, the computer calculates things in single precision mode.

The CVI, CVL, CVS, and CVD functions

The CVI, CVL, CVS and CVD functions convert, respectively, the MKI$, MKL$, MKS$, AND MKD$ strings back to their original numbers.

Using the above functions, program A.9 stores ten random, single-digit integers in a random access file in the first ten records, then reads them back again.

Program A.9:demo5.bas

```
5 'demo5.bas   **writes integers to a random access file
10 OPEN "R", 2, "number", 2
20 FIELD 2, 2 AS REC$
30 FOR I% = 1 TO 10
35 LSET REC$ = MKI$(RND*10)
37 PUT 2, I%
39 NEXT I%
40 '-------- read them back ---------
45 FOR I% = 1 TO 10
46 GET 2, I%
47 N% = CVI(REC$)
48 PRINT N%
49 NEXT I%
50 CLOSE 2
```

Storing many numbers in one record

Instead of storing these ten numbers in ten records we can store them in, and then get them from, one record of twenty bytes. We need 20 bytes because each MKI$ uses 2 bytes. We do this as follows:

Program A.10:demo6.bas

```
5 'demo6.bas   **writes ten integers to one random access file
record
10 OPEN "R", 2, "number", 20
```

```
20 FIELD 2, 20 AS REC$
25 BLANK$ = STRING$(20, "*")
30 FOR I% = 0 TO 9
32 MID$(BLANK$, 1 + I% * 2, 2) = MKI$(RND*10)
34 NEXT I%
36 LSET REC$ = BLANK$
38 PUT 2,1
40 '-------- read them back -------------
45 GET 2,1 'not needed; done for emphasis
46 FOR I% = 0 TO 9
47 N% = CVI(MID$(REC$, 1 + I% * 2, 2))
48 PRINT N%
49 NEXT I%
50 CLOSE 2
```

Generating a file of random numbers & strings.

Program A.11 generates a random access file of 32-byte records, where the first eight bytes of each record represents a double precision number stored in MKD$ format. This double precision number is a 12-digit integer generated from twelve random digits, zero through nine. The first digit cannot be zero. LNGTH%, set to 10, tells us how many records will be generated.

Program A.11: dirrnd.gen

```
0 'dirrnd.gen **generates random access files of LNGTH%
records
4 '====================================
5 '----- set record length, number of records, open file, and
field buffer ----
8 LNGTH% = 10   'number of records in file
9 RECLEN% = 32   'record length
10 OPEN "R",1, "origin.fil", RECLEN%
20 FIELD 1, 8 AS KEY$, RECLEN%-8 AS DTA$
23 '---- do for each of LNGHT% records -----------
25 FOR J% = 1 TO LNGTH%
30 B% = RND *10: B$ = STR$ (B%): B$ = MID$ (B$,2,1) '1st digit
is non-zero
31 if B%=0 then 30
33 '--------- do to get last 11 random digits for the record
key ----------
40 FOR I% = 1 TO 11
50   D% = RND *10: IF D% = 10 THEN D% = 0
55   D$ = STR$ (D%): D$ = MID$ (D$,2,1)
60   B$ = B$ + D$
70 NEXT I%
80 B# = VAL (B$)     'convert string to number
90 LSET KEY$ = MKD$ (B#) 'set in key field of 8 bytes
```

```
100 LSET DTA$ = B$+STRING$(RECLEN%-20,"*") 'set in data field
of 24 bytes
110 PUT 1,J%      'write record to file
120 NEXT J%
122 '---------- read file -----------------
125 FOR I%=1 TO LOF(1)/RECLEN%
127 GET 1, I%
129 PRINT CVD(KEY$), DTA$
132 NEXT
135 CLOSE
```

Analysis of Program A.11

Lines 8 and 9
Here we set LNGTH%, the number of records we wish to write to the file. LNGTH% can be anything up to the two-billion-record limit set by BASIC. We assign a value to RECLEN%, the record length for the file; it could be anything up to 32,767 bytes, but we have designed this program so that it is expected to be at least twenty bytes long.

Lines 10 and 12
Here we open "origin.fil" with a record length of RECLEN%, field it with two field variables, KEY$ of length 8 to hold a double precision number stored using MKD$, and DTA$ of length RECLEN%-8 to hold everything except the key.

Lines 25 - 120
These lines form LNGTH% records and write them to the file. These lines consist of two loops. The outer loop counts from one to LNGTH% so that we form LNGTH% records. To form the key for a record we get a twelve-digit character string, B$, of random digits which we then convert to a double precision number and store in the key field using MKD$. For consistency, each number contains exactly twelve digits. For this reason we use line 30 to ensure that the first character in B$ is not zero. The purpose of the inner loop of lines 40 through 70 is to add the next eleven digits to the string B$. Then in line 80 we use the VAL function to get a double precision number, B#, from B$. Finally in line 90 we convert B# to a MKD$ string and left-set it in the buffer field. In line 100 we form a data string consisting of B$, the character string of twelve random digits, plus enough "*"s to fill up the record. We then left-set this string into the buffer field.

Lines 125 - 135
Finally, we read the LOF(1)/RECLEN% records we have just written.

Summary

In this appendix we have reviewed the fundamental concepts of opening a file and getting data out to disk and back. The next step is to be able access and manipulate the data you have on disk. That is what the B-tree system will do for you.

Some people argue that learning a B-tree system is unnecessary because "You don't need an atomic weapon to kill an ant", but more often than not,the data you begin to store on disk, especially if it is valuable, grows to the point that you later wish you had started with the B-tree. At that point it takes too much time and energy to learn the B-tree system, so you eventually transfer your data into somebody else's B-tree and live your life at their mercy.

It is better to take the time and do it right the first time. This book provides you with all the fundamental tools you need to do the job. Good luck, and don't give up!

APPENDIX B

Other Methods that Compete with a B-tree

As we mentioned in the main text of this book, there are several methods one may think of to try and do the same job a B-tree does. Let's look at some of those methods and examine the good and bad points they have to offer. I assume you are familiar with other methods, such as prime division hashing, and we will not take time to explain the theory behind these methods because it would take far too much time. In order to discuss the value of other approaches, let us again pretend we have the problem of making a mailing list.

The Mailing List Problem

Suppose we have a mailing list file, which we will call the main file, in which each record consists of the following fields: a numeric identification key, a name, an address, and a zip code. This list must be updated constantly so that, at any time, we can search the list by name, key, or zip code, and retrieve the most current information from a given record. We must also be able to print portions of the entire list, ordered according to name, key, or zip code. How can we best implement these functions? You guessed it: with B-trees.

It is certainly possible to implement these functions by keeping the mailing list file sorted, and doing a binary search whenever we wanted to find a record. We could also obtain a sorted printout easily using this strategy. But then how would we get a printout ordered by some other field? That task would necessitate a re-sorting of the whole file. Moreover, we would have to re-sort the file after every addition or deletion. The time required for all these manipulations--made longer if the file is large--may make constant updating impractical.

Another possible solution is to leave the main file static by constructing a sorted index file for it. In our example we would actually need three sorted index files, one for each searchable field. Although it is easier to sort three index files rather than three copies of the main file, sorting index files between main file updates may be too time-consuming. Once again, our solution is impractical, especially in the case of large files.

Another possibility is to avoid sorting by maintaining a three-fold system of pointer chains for our three search fields: key, name, and zip code. This allows us to carry out additions and deletions without extensive file manipulation. For deletions, we simply close up the lists, and for additions, we break the list and insert. And producing printouts with various ordering becomes easy because we can now read the file in sequential order by following a pointer chain for a given field. But even this solution is not perfect; the problem of efficient searching remains unsolved. To locate a given record by key, for instance, we would have to use our key list pointer chains to search sequentially, following the chain until we came to the record having the sought-for key. This means that we would be forced, on average, to search half the file to find a record. This problem could be overcome to a large extent by maintaining an index for the main file. This index could tell us the record of the first key starting with A, B, C, and so on.

We might turn to prime division hashing. We could then add records to the main file by prime division hashing (hashing by key, perhaps), rather than by simply adding them to the end of the file. This would solve the problem of finding a record by key, but not by name or zip code. If we decide that sequential searching is unacceptable for these fields, we could then hash names and zip codes into hash-coded index files in which each record would be composed of a name or zip code, and the main file record number would contain the rest of the data.

Since this would not allow us an ordered read-out, one final option for the solution of our mailing list problem is a variation on the last. It involves a totally static main file with pointers implementing a three-fold list structure, and three hash-coded index files indexing the main file by key, name, and zip code. This combination of linked lists and hashing allows for easy deletions and additions and for searching that is, on average, very fast. Moreover, the file may be read in order by means of any one of its pointer chains. This combination of hashing and linked lists presents an excellent solution to the mailing list problem. Hashing, in fact, usually allows faster look-up than is possible with B-trees. So, after all of our deliberation, you might again ask: why should I learn about B-trees? The following discussion explains why.

The Performance of B-trees vs. hashing

Although it is sometimes slower than hashing, a B-tree mailing system with a static main file indexed by three B-trees has some distinct advantages over our hashing solution. For one thing, the B-tree look-up, though not the fastest in all cases, is still very fast. If there are a lot of elements on a B-tree page, the worst case B-tree look-up could even be faster than the average prime division hashing look-up, depending on the loading factor of the hash-coded file. Moreover, the worst-case performance for B-tree look-ups is very close to the average hashing performance. The worst-case hashing performance, although extremely unlikely, is unthinkably bad. With hashing we may encounter elements which require more disk accesses than the worst-case number using B-trees. This is particularly true for an unsuccessful search of a hash-coded file.

B-trees, then, offer no surprises: there is a limit to bad performance and, happily, this limit keeps the number of disk accesses low. Consider, for example, a B-tree which contains 1,999,999 elements, and which is capable of holding 18 elements per page. This B-tree is minimally loaded (a situation that is impossible with random data) so that the root contains only one element and all the rest of the pages contain nine elements. We choose a minimally loaded B-tree because, given a limited number of elements, it will be the highest tree possible. The higher the tree, the slower the worst-case look-up will be because we must search the tree from top to bottom. A worst-case look-up in this tree never requires more than six disk accesses to find a given element or to determine it is absent. A tree capable of holding 38 elements per page and containing 6,399,998 elements requires only five disk accesses for a worst case look-up when minimally loaded with 19 elements per non-root page. If we were to increase the number of elements on such a tree to 127,999,998 elements, a worst-case look-up would require only six disk accesses. With a tree capable of holding only four elements per page and containing 39,365 elements, the worst-case look-up in a minimally-loaded tree with two elements per non-root page requires nine disk accesses.

These disk access figures are low enough to be considered fast and are relative to logarithms of the number of elements to the bases 10, 20, and 3, respectively. B-tree look-up is much faster than binary searching, which is related to the logarithm to the base 2 of the number of elements being searched.

Thus, while B-trees are not always faster on look-up than hashing, they are still very fast and have the advantage of avoiding hashing's worst case disaster. With B-trees there is also no need to link the main file with pointers in order to read it in order. A B-tree functions automatically as an ordered index. As it turns out, we need only three B-tree indexing files in addition to the main file to solve our mailing list problem.

The main strength of B-trees is that they create an ordered index that enables us to search a file quickly and read it in order. B-trees also avoid the tendency of binary trees to grow in an unbalanced manner. As a binary tree become more unbalanced, it behaves less like a tree and more like a linear list. The growth of B-trees is always perfectly balanced, and so we maintain the primary advantage of using a tree structure.

In summary, not only does the B-tree indexing method solve the problems caused by frequent main file modifications, but in terms of retrieval speed, its performance is actually superior to that of a binary search on an ordered index file. In fact, retrieval speed for a B-tree is usually only slightly slower than the average retrieval speed for prime division hashing. And unless you have only a handful of records in the hash-coded file, the worst-case B-tree retrieval speed is never as bad as the worst-case retrieval of prime division hashing. Please note that the B-trees' streamlined structure makes possible its remarkable performance. And this performance is achieved at the cost of disk space. However, the B-tree's high performance is usually worth the price--especially as the price of disk space drops! In addition, B-trees generally waste less space than hashing since B-trees use at least 50 percent of the disk space needed to implement the B-tree structure for actual storage of data. In hashing terms, the loading factor for a B-tree must be at least .50.

Clearly, for a unsorted file of any length the B-tree is the best possible way to keep your data in order and defeats its competitors by quite some margin.

APPENDIX C

The TeachBase B-tree System

```
95 'Copyright © 1992 BALDAR
98 'this is TeachBase - version 1.0
100 ' This code runs without any changes under Mcrosoft's QBASIC
102 ' on MAC, MSDOS and UNIX (SCO Xenix) operating systems.

110 ' ********* PROGRAMMERS NOTE **********
112 ' In some versions of QBASIC the very first time you open a
114 ' random access file you must first open the file as a sequential
116 ' file in the output format, then close the file,then reopen it as a
118 ' random access file.
120 ' Once a file has been created as a random access file, you do not
122 ' want to open it again as a sequential file in the output format
124 ' because that will destroy all the information in the file.
132 '
134 ' This program comes to you with the storage file and btree file
136 ' having already been created (opened sequentially) but empty.
138 ' If you want to erase the files and start over, simply activate lines
140 ' 150, 152 and 155 by removing the comment markers for the
142 ' first time and FIRST TIME ONLY that you use the database.
144 ' In a professional program, of course, you would have menus that query the
146 ' user as to whether or not they wanted to create a new database, kill old databases,
etc.
150 ' OPEN "O",1,"storage.fil"
152 ' OPEN "O",2,"btree.fil"
155 ' CLOSE
160 '***************************************

200 DEFINT A-Z:CLS
```

```
300 RECLN =128 'length of page on btree
400 LNG =16 'record length for storage file
500 T = 18 'length of a page element
600 T1 = 14 'length of of key word
610 T0 = 16 'leng of key-word plus store ptr
700 T2 = 17 'start of element ptr
710 T3 = 15 'start of storage ptr
800 ORDER = 2 'order of btree: half of no of elements on a full page
900 FULLPAGE = 2*ORDER
1000 BUF1 = 1 'file number for storage file
1100 BUF2 = 2 'file number for btree index
1200 OPEN "R", BUF1, "storage.fil", LNG
1300 FIELD BUF1, T1 AS WD$, LNG - T1 AS MN$
1400 OPEN "R", BUF2, "btree.fil", RECLN
1500 FIELD BUF2, T*FULLPAGE AS REC$, RECLN - T*FULLPAGE AS LE$
1590 '----------- need to initialize control record ? ----------------
1600 IF LOF(BUF2) <> 0 THEN 1955
1690 '----------- initialize control record ------------------------
1700 LSET REC$ = MKI$(0) + MKI$(0) 'set root finder and ele counter to 0
1800 LSET LE$ = MKI$(-1)+MKI$(-1) 'set allocation ptrs to ground
1900 PUT BUF2, 1
1950 '----------- read control record ----------------------------
1955 GET BUF2, 1
1959 root = CVI( MID$(REC$,1,2) )
1962 count = CVI( MID$(REC$,3,2) )
1965 TALLOC = CVI( MID$(LE$,1,2) )
1970 SALLOC = CVI( MID$(LE$,3,2) )
1975 '------- input routine: install or give command -----------------
1980 GOTO 50000
2100 '==========================================================
2200 'generation of a B-tree: the installation routine
2300 '==========================================================
2500 '
2600 ' -------------------------------------------------------
2700 ' establishing the first element on the tree
2800 '---------------------------------------------------------
3100 IF count <> 0 THEN 5300 'file is empty
3200 '
3400 GOSUB 23600 'allocate tree record
3500 GOSUB 24600 'allocate storage file record
3600 '---------- increase word counter & set root finder -------------
3700 count = count + 1
3800 root = NNW
4100 '---------- install the root --------------------
4200 LSET REC$ = word$ + MKI$(NNT) + MKI$(0)
4300 LSET LE$ = MKI$(0) + MKI$(1)
4400 PUT BUF2, NNW
4450 GOSUB 17200 'store word in storage file
4455 PRINT "* created a root and installed *": GOTO 50000
4499 '
4500 '---------------------------------------------------------
4600 ' establishing elements subsequent to the first on the tree
4700 '---------------------------------------------------------
4901 '
5000 '---------------------------------------------------------
```

```
5100 ' searching down the tree for the leaf page on which to put element
5200 '-----------------------------------------------------------------
5300 STACK%=0
5500 NR(STACK) = root
5600 '
5700 GET BUF2, NR(STACK)
5800 NUMBER=CVI(MID$(LE$,3,2))
5900 PAGEPTR = CVI(MID$(LE$,1,2))
5950 LOW=0: HIGH=NUMBER-1
5990 I = (LOW+HIGH)/2
6000 FF$ = MID$(REC$, 1 + T*I, T1)
6300 IF word$ = FF$ THEN 16200 'increase the word counter
6400 IF word$ > FF$ THEN 6800
6500 HIGH=I-1
6600 IF HIGH >= LOW THEN 5990
6650 IF PAGEPTR=0 THEN 8050
6660 LIFT(STACK) = I
6700 STACK=STACK+1: NR(STACK)=CVI(MID$(REC$, T2 + T*I, 2)): GOTO 5700
6800 LOW = I+1
6850 IF LOW <= HIGH THEN 5990
6855 I=I+1
6860 IF I <> NUMBER THEN 6650
6900 IF PAGEPTR = 0 THEN 7050
6905 LIFT(STACK)=I
6910 STACK=STACK+1: NR(STACK)=PAGEPTR: GOTO 5700
7000 '-----------------------------------------------------------------
7050 GOSUB 24600 'allocate storage file record
7100 ' adding on a leaf page at either 1) the end or 2) the middle
7200 '-----------------------------------------------------------------
7300 '
7400 ' 1) adding at the end
7500 '
7600 R$ = MID$(REC$, 1, NUMBER*T) + word$+MKI$(NNT) + MKI$(0)
7700 IF NUMBER = FULLPAGE THEN 9600 ELSE 8800
7800 '
7900 ' 2) adding in the middle
8000 '
8050 GOSUB 24600 'allocate storage file record
8100 IF I=0 THEN 8300 ELSE 8200
8200 R$ = MID$(REC$, 1, T*I) + word$+MKI$(NNT)+MKI$(0) + MID$(REC$, 1 + T*I, NUMBER*T):
GOTO 8400
8300 R$ = word$+MKI$(NNT)+MKI$(0) + MID$(REC$, 1, T*NUMBER)
8400 IF NUMBER = FULLPAGE THEN 9600 ELSE 8800
8500 '------------ adding to leaf, no splitting needed ----------------
8700 '
8800 LSET REC$ = R$
8900 LSET LE$ = MKI$(PAGEPTR) + MKI$(NUMBER + 1)
9000 PUT BUF2, NR(STACK)
9200 GOSUB 17200 'write word to new storage file record
9300 count = count + 1 'update word counter
9400 PRINT "* Installed on a leaf with no splitting *": GOTO 50000
9500 ' =============== splitting a leaf =============================
9600 GOSUB 23600 'allocate new tree page: NNW
9700 A$ = MID$(R$, 1, T*ORDER)
9800 MIDONE$ = MID$(R$, T*ORDER + 1, T0) + MKI$(NR(STACK))
```

```
9820 MID$(MIDONE$, T2, 2) = MKI$(NR(STACK))
9900 B$ = MID$( R$, T*(ORDER+1) + 1 )
10000 LSET REC$ = A$
10100 LSET LE$ = MKI$(0) + MKI$(ORDER)
10200 PUT BUF2, NR(STACK)
10300 LSET REC$ = B$
10400 PUT BUF2, NNW
10500 GOSUB 17200 'install new word in storage
10600 count=count+1 'update word counter
10700 IF STACK = 0 THEN GOTO 14950 'form new root on split
10800 '
10900 ' ---------- Lift middle element to a node page ----------------
11000 '
11100 STACK%=STACK%-1
11200 GET BUF2, NR%(STACK%)
11300 NUMBER = CVI(MID$(LE$,3,2))
11400 IF LIFT(STACK) < NUMBER THEN 11950
11490 '--------------- end pointer -----------------------
11500 R$ = MID$(REC$, 1, T*NUMBER) + MIDONE$
11700 L$ = MKI$(NNW) + MKI$(NUMBER+1) 'page ptr points to newly created page
11800 GOTO 12600
11900 '--------------- mid pointer -----------------------
11950 IF LIFT(STACK)=0 THEN A$ = "": GOTO 12100 'goes first on page
12000 A$ = MID$(REC$, 1, T*LIFT(STACK))
12100 C$ = MID$(REC$, T*LIFT(STACK) + 1, NUMBER*T)
12200 MID$(C$, T2, 2) = MKI$(NNW) 'elt ptr points to newly created page
12400 L$ = LE$
12500 MID$(L$,3,2) = MKI$(NUMBER + 1)
12550 R$ = A$ + MIDONE$ + C$
12570 '----- if page overflows spits a node; else set the page ---------
12600 IF NUMBER = FULLPAGE THEN 13150
12700 LSET REC$ = R$
12800 LSET LE$ = L$
12900 PUT BUF2,NR(STACK)
12902 IF BRANCHSPLIT$="yes" THEN 12904 ELSE 12990 'what to print
12904 PRINT "* installed; splitting required on branch pages *"
12906 BRANCHSPLIT$="": GOTO 50000
12990 PRINT "* installed on leaf which split with no further splitting *"
13000 GOTO 50000
13100 ' =============== splitting a node ==========================
13150 GOSUB 23600 'allocate new record
13200 MIDONE$ = MID$(R$, (T*ORDER)+1, T0) + MKI$(NR(STACK))
13400 OLDPTR$ = MID$(R$, (T*ORDER) + T2, 2 )
13500 A$ = MID$(R$, 1, T*ORDER)
13600 B$ = MID$(R$, T*(ORDER+1) + 1 )
13700 LSET REC$ = B$
13800 MID$(L$,3,2) = MKI$(ORDER)
13900 LSET LE$ = L$
14000 PUT BUF2, NNW
14100 LSET REC$ = A$
14200 LSET LE$ = OLDPTR$ + MKI$(ORDER)
14300 PUT BUF2, NR(STACK)
14400 IF STACK <> 0 THEN BRANCHSPLIT$="yes": GOTO 11100 'lift to next level
14600 '
14700 '=======================================================
```

```
14800 '          create a new root by splitting the old one
14900 '==========================================================
14950 PNNW = NNW 'save old
15000 GOSUB 23600 'allocate new tree record: NNW
15050 LSET REC$ = MIDONE$
15100 LSET LE$ = MKI$(PNNW) + MKI$(1)
15275 PUT BUF2, NNW
15290 '
15300 root = NNW 'update root finder
15800 PRINT "* installed; a new root was formed through splitting *": GOTO 50000
15900 '-----------------------------------------------------------
16000 '          searched for word is already in file; increase counter
16100 '-----------------------------------------------------------
16200 WHERE = CVI( MID$(REC$, T*I + T3, 2) )
16220 GET BUF1, WHERE
16300 KOUNT = CVI( MID$(MN$, 1, 2) )
16400 KOUNT=KOUNT+1
16500 LSET MN$ = MKI$(KOUNT)
16600 PUT BUF1, WHERE
16750 count=count+1 'increase total word counter
16800 PRINT "* increased the occurrence counter *": GOTO 50000
16900 '----------------------------------------------------------
17000 '          add new element to the storage storage file
17100 '----------------------------------------------------------
17200 '
17300 LSET WD$ = word$
17400 LSET MN$ = MKI$(1)
17500 PUT BUF1, NNT
17600 RETURN
18600 '===========================================================
18650 '          btree transversal - normal (left to right) order
18700 '===========================================================
18800 IF count = 0 THEN PRINT "No words in file": GOTO 49600
18850 PRINT "Total words in file: "; count
18860 PRINT "order";TAB(14) "storage word and number of times entered"
18900 ST = 0: E = 0
19100 NR(ST) = root
19300 '-------------- drop to bottom ---------------------------
19400 GET BUF2, NR%(ST%)
19500 NO%(ST%) = CVI ( MID$ (LE$,3,2)) : TV%(ST%) = 0: NR%(ST% + 1) = CVI ( MID$ (REC$,T2
+ T*TV(ST),2))
19600 IF NR%(ST% + 1) <> 0 THEN ST% = ST% + 1 : GOTO 19400
19700 ' ============= READ LEAF PAGE ===========================
19850 FOR I=0 TO NO(ST) - 1
19900 TRANSVERSE = I: GOSUB 21800
20000 NEXT I%
20100 IF NR(ST)=root THEN PRINT "DONE": GOTO 49600
20200 ' -------------- ascend from leaf page -------------------
20300 ST = ST - 1
20400 GET BUF2, NR(ST)
20500 IF TV%(ST%) = NO%(ST%) THEN IF ST% <> 0 GOTO 21000 ELSE PRINT "DONE": GOTO 49600
20600 TRANSVERSE = TV(ST): GOSUB 21800
20700 TV%(ST%) = TV%(ST%) + 1
20800 IF TV%(ST%) = NO%(ST%) THEN ST% = ST% + 1: NR%(ST%) = CVI ( LEFT$ (LE$,2)) : GET
BUF2,NR%(ST%): NO%(ST%) = CVI ( MID$ (LE$,3,2)) : GOTO 19850
```

```
20900 ST = ST + 1: NR%(ST%) = CVI ( MID$ (REC$,T2 + T*TV%(ST-1),2)): GET BUF2,NR%(ST%) :
NO%(ST%) = CVI ( MID$ (LE$,3,2)) : GOTO 19850
20990 ' -------------- ascend from node page ------------------
21000 ST% = ST% - 1
21100 GET BUF2,NR%(ST%)
21200 IF TV%(ST%) = NO%(ST%) THEN IF ST% <> 0 THEN 21000 ELSE PRINT "DONE": GOTO 49600
21300 TRANSVERSE = TV(ST): GOSUB 21800
21400 TV%(ST%) = TV%(ST%) + 1
21500 IF TV%(ST%) = NO%(ST%) THEN ST% = ST% + 1: NR%(ST%) = CVI ( LEFT$ (LE$,2)) : GOTO
19400
21600 ST=ST+1: NR(ST) = CVI ( MID$ (REC$, T2 + T*TV%(ST% - 1),2)): GOTO 19400
21700 '------------- get pointed record form storage file -------------
21800 STORE = CVI( MID$(REC$, T*TRANSVERSE + T3, 2) )
21900 GET BUF1, STORE
21910 E=E+1
22000 PRINT E, WD$; CVI( MID$(MN$,1,2) )
22100 RETURN
22102 '============================================================
22104 '           utility routine: record by record list of btree
22108 '============================================================
22250 PRINT STRING$(18,"-"); " Page: 1"; STRING$(30, "-")
22260 PRINT "root", "no words", "tree alloc", "store alloc"
22300 PRINT root, count, TALLOC, SALLOC
22400 FOR IM=2 TO LOF(BUF2)/RECLN
22500 GET BUF2, IM
22550 PRINT STRING$(18,"-"); " Page: "; IM; STRING$(30,"-")
22600 HH = CVI(MID$(LE$,3,2))
22610 IF HH = -1 THEN PRINT "** Deleted ** (in allocation chain)": GOTO 23100
22650 PRINT "word", "Element ptr", "Storage ptr"
22700 FOR IK=0 TO HH-1
22800 PRINT MID$(REC$, IK*T + 1, T1),
22810 PRINT CVI( MID$(REC$, IK*T + T2, 2) ),
22820 PRINT CVI( MID$(REC$, IK*T + T3, 2) )
22900 NEXT
22950 PRINT "Page pointer: "; CVI(MID$(LE$, 1, 2))
23000 PRINT "Words on page: "; CVI(MID$(LE$,3,2))
23100 NEXT
23150 GOTO 49600
23200 '============================================================
23300 '           allocation & deallocation routines
23400 '============================================================
23500 ' ---------- allocate new record (NNW) for btree -------------
23600 IF TALLOC = -1 THEN NNW = LOF(BUF2)/RECLN + 1: RETURN
23900 NNW = TALLOC
24000 GET BUF2, TALLOC
24200 TALLOC = CVI(MID$(LE$,1,2))
24400 RETURN
24405 ' --- deallocate a record (OLD) to the btree allocation list -----
24410 LSET LE$ = MKI$(TALLOC) + MKI$(-1)
24420 PUT BUF2, OLD
24430 TALLOC = OLD
24482 RETURN
24500 ' ---------- allocate new record (NNT) for storage file ---------
24600 IF SALLOC = -1 THEN NNT = LOF(BUF1)/LNG + 1: RETURN
24610 NNT = SALLOC
```

```
24620 GET BUF1, SALLOC
24630 SALLOC = CVI(MID$(WD$,1,2))
24640 RETURN
25505 '------ deallocate record (OLD) to storage allocation list ------
25510 LSET WD$ = MKI$(SALLOC)
25520 PUT BUF1, OLD
25530 SALLOC = OLD
25540 RETURN
30090 '===========================================================
30094 '            Deletion routine
30098 '===========================================================
30110 IF count = 0 THEN PRINT "File is empty": GOTO 50000
30115 '-------- get record number of root --------------------------
30120 ST=0
30130 NR(ST) = root
30800 '
30900 '------------ search a page for deletion key ------------------
31000 '
31100 GET BUF2,NR(ST)
31200 NUMBER=CVI(MID$(LE$,3,2)): NN=CVI(MID$(LE$,1,2))
31300 FOR K=0 TO NUMBER-1
31310 FF$ = MID$(REC$, 1 + T* K, T1)
31400 IF K$=FF$ THEN 32125
31500 IF K$ < FF$ THEN IF NN<>0 THEN KK(ST)=K%: ST=ST+1: NR(ST)=CVI(MID$(REC$,T2 +
T*K,2)):GOTO 31100 ELSE PRINT "NOT FOUND":GOTO 49600
31600 NEXT
31700 KK(ST)=-1
31800 IF NN<>0 THEN ST=ST+1: NR(ST)=NN: GOTO 31100 ELSE PRINT "NOT FOUND":GOTO 49600
31900 '
32000 '===========================================================
32010 'found deletion word: decrease total word counter & specific counter
32012 '           (also deallocate storage if word occurs only once)
32020 '===========================================================
32100 '
32120 '-------- decrease total word counter --------------
32125 count = count - 1
32138 --- decrease specific word counter or deallocate completely -----
32140 STORAGE$ = MID$(REC$, T3 + T*K, 2)
32145 OLD = CVI(STORAGE$)
32147 GET BUF1, OLD
32150 NZ = CVI(LEFT$(MN$,2))
32154 IF NZ <> 1 THEN LSET MN$ = MKI$(NZ-1): PUT BUF1, OLD: PRINT "** Reduced count **":
GOTO 49600
32156 GOSUB 25505 'deallocate storage record
32157 IF NN=0 THEN 32205 ELSE 48600 'found on leaf else on node
32158 '
32178 '===========================================================
32180 '           remove element from leaf page: record NR(ST), field block K
32184 '===========================================================
32190 '
32205 NUMBER = NUMBER-1
32210 IF K=0 THEN B$ = "" ELSE B$ = MID$(REC$,1,T*K)
32300 C$=MID$(REC$, 1 + T*(K+1))
32500 LSET REC$=B$+C$: LSET LE$ =MKI$(NN)+MKI$(NUMBER): PUT BUF2, NR(ST)
32550 IF NUMBER >= ORDER THEN PRINT "** DELETED **": GOTO 49600
```

```
32555 IF ST <> 0 THEN 33400 'balance or absorption for nonroot leaf
32700 '------- leaf is undersized root ---------
32800 IF NUMBER > 0 THEN PRINT " ** DELETED **": GOTO 49600
32900 PRINT "DELETED & FILE EMPTIED": OLD = NR(ST): GOSUB 24410
32910 root = 0
33000 GOTO 50000
33100 '
33150 '===============================================================
33200 ' balance or absorption after leaf deletion
33250 '===============================================================
33300 '
33350 ' --- ascend to find the lateral record for balancing or absorbing ----
33400 L1$=LE$: N1=NR(ST): C1=NUMBER
33450 N1$ = MID$(REC$, 1, C1*T)
33500 ST%=ST%-1
33600 GET BUF2,NR(ST):J$=REC$:L$=LE$: JN = CVI(MID$(LE$,3,2))
33700 IF KK(ST)=-1 THEN N2=CVI(MID$(J$, (JN-1)*T + T2, 2)): GOTO 33900
33800 IF KK(ST) < JN-1 THEN N2=CVI(MID$(J$,T2 + T*(KK(ST)+1),2)) ELSE
N2=CVI(MID$(L$,1,2))
33850 '----- get lateral record for balancing or absorption -----------
33900 GET BUF2, N2
33910 C2 = CVI(MID$(LE$,3,2))
33920 N2$ = MID$(REC$,1,T*C2): L2$ = LE$
34000 IF C2 > ORDER THEN 36300 'do balancing
34100 IF KK(ST)=-1 THEN 35350 ELSE 34550 'do absorption: mid or end
34200 '
34300 ' ======= absorption =====
34400 '
34500 ' ---------- mid-node pointer: absorb N1 ---------
34550 ABOVE$ = MID$(J$, 1 + T*KK(ST), T0) + MKI$(0)
34600 N2$=MID$(N1$,1,T*C1) + ABOVE$ + MID$(N2$,1,T*C2)
34800 LSET REC$=N2$: LSET LE$=MKI$(0)+MKI$(FULLPAGE): PUT BUF2,N2
34900 OLD = N1: GOSUB 24410 'deallocate absorbed tree page
35000 GOTO 39500 'remove MID(J$,1+T*KK(ST),T) from NR(ST)
35100 '
35200 ' --------- end-node pointer: absorb N2 ----------
35300 '
35350 ABOVE$ = MID$(J$, 1 + T*(JN-1), T0) + MKI$(0)
35400 N1$=MID$(N2$,1,T*C2) + ABOVE$ + MID$(N1$,1,T*C1)
35600 LSET REC$=N1$: LSET LE$=MKI$(0)+MKI$(FULLPAGE): PUT BUF2,N1
35700 OLD=N2: GOSUB 24410 'deallocate absorbed tree page
35800 GOTO 40700 'remove MID$(J$,1+T*JN,T) from NR(ST)
35900 '
36000 '
36100 ' ========== balancing ============
36200 '
36300 O1=INT( (C1+C2)/2 ) 'ORDER-1+C2 is the total on both adjacent pages
36400 'O1 is no of elements for original page: N1
36500 O2 = C1+C2 - O1 'no of elements for adjacent page: N2
36550 O3 = O1 - C1 'no of elements to add to original page
36700 IF KK(ST)=-1 THEN 38500 'end page pointer
36800 '
36900 ' -------- mid-node pointer --------
37000 '
37100 ABOVE$ = MID$(J$, 1+T*KK(ST), T0) + MKI$(0)
```

```
37200 MID$(J$,1+T*KK(ST),T0)=MID$(N2$, 1 + T*(O3-1), T0) 'replace upper
37250 IF O3 = 1 THEN LAT$ = "" ELSE LAT$ = MID$( N2$, 1, T*(O3-1) )
37300 N1$ = N1$ + ABOVE$ + LAT$
37400 G$ = MID$( N2$, 1 + T*O3 )
37700 LSET REC$=J$: LSET LE$=L$: PUT BUF2,NR(ST)
37800 LSET REC$=N1$: LSET LE$=MKI$(0)+MKI$(O1): PUT BUF2,N1
37900 LSET REC$=G$: LSET LE$=MKI$(0)+MKI$(O2): PUT BUF2,N2
38000 PRINT "** DELETED **"
38100 GOTO 49600
38200 '
38300 ' ---------- page pointer -------
38400 '
38500 ABOVE$ = MID$(J$, 1 + T*(JN-1), T0) + MKI$(0)
38600 MID$(J$,1+T*(JN-1),T0) = MID$(N2$, 1 + T*(C2 - O3), T0)
38700 N1$ = MID$(N2$, 1+ T*(C2 - (O3-1)) ) + ABOVE$ + N1$
39000 G$=MID$(N2$,1,T*O2)
39100 GOTO 37700
39200 '
39300 ' ========= kill pointer to absorbed branch ========
39400 ' --------- mid-node pointer ---------
39500 IF JN=1 THEN 40300 'N2 --> new root & deallocate old root
39580 IF KK(ST)=0 THEN B$ = "" ELSE B$ = MID$(J$,1,T*KK(ST))
39600 C$=MID$(J$,1+T*(KK(ST)+1),JN*T)
39650 JN = JN - 1
39700 MID$(L$,3,2)=MKI$(JN)
39800 LSET REC$=B$+C$: LSET LE$=L$: PUT BUF2,NR(ST)
39900 IF JN >= ORDER OR (JN<ORDER AND ST=0) THEN PRINT "** DELETED **":GOTO 49600
40000 GOTO 41900
40290 '--- root consists of a single element: N2 -> new root & dealloc old ---
40300 OLD = NR(ST): GOSUB 24410 'deallocate old
40310 root = N2
40315 PRINT "** DELETED **"
40400 GOTO 49600
40500 '
40600 ' -------- end-page pointer --------
40700 IF JN=1 THEN N2=N1: GOTO 40300 'N2 --> new root & deallocate old root
40710 JN=JN-1
40800 MID$(L$,3,2)=MKI$(JN)
40900 LSET REC$=MID$(J$,1,T*JN): LSET LE$=L$: PUT BUF2, NR(ST)
41000 IF JN >= ORDER OR (JN<ORDER AND ST=0) THEN PRINT "** DELETED **":GOTO 49600
41600 '
41700 ' ========= option for either balancing or absorbing =====
41710 '                             after deletion of an element form a node page
41800 '
41900 N1=NR(ST): N1$=REC$: L1$=LE$: C1= JN
42000 ST%=ST%-1
42100 GET BUF2,NR(ST):J$=REC$: L$=LE$: JN = CVI(MID$(LE$,3,2))
42110 IF KK(ST)=-1 THEN N2 = CVI( MID$(J$, T*(JN-1) + T2, 2) ): GOTO 42300
42200 IF KK(ST) < JN-1 THEN N2=CVI(MID$(J$,T2+T*(KK(ST)+1),2)) ELSE N2=CVI(MID$(L$,1,2))
42300 GET BUF2,N2: C2=CVI(MID$(LE$,3,2)): N2$=REC$: L2$=LE$
42400 IF C2 > ORDER THEN 44700 'do balancing
42500 IF KK%(ST%)=-1 THEN 43850 ELSE 42950 'absorb end else mid
42600 '
42700 ' ======= absorbing ========
42800 ' --------- mid-node pointer: absorb N1 ----------
```

```
42900 '
42950 ABOVE$ = MID$(J$, 1 + T*KK(ST), T0) + MID$(L1$,1,2)
43000 N2$=MID$(N1$,1,T*C1) + ABOVE$ + MID$(N2$,1,C2*T)
43200 LSET REC$=N2$: LSET LE$=MID$(L2$,1,2) + MKI$(FULLPAGE): PUT BUF2,N2
43300 OLD = N1: GOSUB 24410 'deallocate N1
43400 GOTO 39500
43500 '
43700 ' ------ end-node pointer: absorb N2 ------
43800 '
43850 ABOVE$=MID$(J$, 1 + T*(JN-1), T0) + MID$(L2$,1,2)
43900 N1$ = MID$(N2$,1,T*C2) + ABOVE$ + MID$(N1$,1,T*C1)
44100 LSET REC$=N1$: LSET LE$=MID$(L1$,1,2)+MKI$(FULLPAGE): PUT BUF2,N1
44200 OLD = N2: GOSUB 24410
44300 GOTO 40700
44400 '
44500 '
44600 ' ====== balancing ==========
44700 O1 = INT((C1+C2)/2) 'for N1
44900 O2 = C1 + C2 - O1 'for N2
44950 O3 = O1 - C1 'to be added to N1
44980 I=0 'snake around counter
45000 N1$=MID$(N1$,1,T*C1)
45100 IF KK%(ST%)=-1 THEN 47200 ELSE 45500
45200 '
45300 ' ----------- mid-node pointer --------
45400 '
45500 P1$ = MID$(L1$,1,2) 'N1 page pointer
45600 P2$ = MID$(N2$,T2 + T*I,2) 'N2 Ith element pointer
45700 MID$(L1$,1,2) = P2$
45800 F1$ = MID$(J$, 1 + T*KK(ST), T0) + P1$
45900 MID$(J$,1+T*KK(ST),T0)=MID$(N2$,1+T*I,T0)
46000 N1$=N1$+F1$
46100 I=I+1
46200 IF I < O3 THEN 45500 'O3 to be add to N1
46300 MID$(L1$,3,2)=MKI$(O1): MID$(L2$,3,2)=MKI$(O2)
46400 N2$=MID$(N2$,1+T*I,C2*T)
46500 LSET REC$=J$: LSET LE$=L$: PUT BUF2,NR(ST)
46600 LSET REC$=N1$: LSET LE$=L1$: PUT BUF2,N1
46700 LSET REC$=N2$: LSET LE$=L2$: PUT BUF2,N2
46800 PRINT "*** DELETED ***": GOTO 49600
46900 '
47000 ' -------------- end-page pointer --------------
47100 '
47200 P1$ = MID$(L2$,1,2) 'N2 page pointer
47300 P2$ = MID$(N2$,T2 + T*(C2-1-I),2)
47400 MID$(L2$,1,2) = P2$
47500 F1$ = MID$(J$, 1 + T*(JN-1), T0) + P1$
47600 MID$(J$,1+T*(JN-1),T0)=MID$(N2$,1+T*(C2-1-I),T0)
47700 N1$=F1$+N1$: I%=I%+1
47800 IF I < O3 THEN 47200
47900 MID$(L2$,3,2)=MKI$(O2%)
48000 MID$(L1$,3,2)=MKI$(O1%)
48100 N2$=MID$(N2$,1,T*O2)
48200 GOTO 46500
48300 '
```

```
48390 '===========================================================
48400 '          replace a branch element with the highest lower element
48410 '===========================================================
48500 '
48570 '
48600 RR$=REC$: LR$=LE$: RR=NR(ST) 'save the node page
48650 '------ move down to the "greatest lower" leaf page ------
48700 KK(ST) = K
48710 ST=ST+1
48800 NR(ST)=CVI(MID$(RR$,T2 + T*K,2))
48850 GET BUF2,NR(ST)
48875 NN = CVI(MID$(LE$,1,2))
48880 IF NN <> 0 THEN KK(ST)=-1: ST=ST+1: NR(ST) = NN: GOTO 48850
48940 '
48950 '------- found "greatest lower" leaf page -----
48960 '
49000 NUMBER=CVI(MID$(LE$,3,2)): N1$=REC$
49010 NUMBER=NUMBER-1
49090 '------- change node -------------
49100 MID$(RR$,1+T*K,T0)=MID$(REC$,1+T*NUMBER, T0)
49200 LSET REC$=RR$: LSET LE$=LR$: PUT BUF2, RR
49290 '------- change leaf --------------
49300 B$=MID$( N1$,1,T*NUMBER )
49350 LSET REC$ = B$
49375 LSET LE$ = MKI$(0) + MKI$(NUMBER)
49400 PUT BUF2,NR(ST)
49500 IF NUMBER > = ORDER THEN PRINT "** DELETED **":GOTO 49600 ELSE 33400
49510 '===========================================================
49512 '               search routine
49514 '===========================================================
49520 IF count = 0 THEN PRINT "File is empty": GOTO 50000
49525 ST = 0
49530 NR = root
49540 ' -------- search page NR for the word, W$ ----------
49545 GET BUF2, NR
49550 NUMBER = CVI(MID$(LE$,3,2)): NN=CVI(MID$(LE$,1,2))
49555 FOR K=0 TO NUMBER-1
49560 FF$ = MID$(REC$, 1 + T*K, T1)
49565 IF W$ = FF$ THEN 49577
49570 IF W$<FF$ THEN IF NN<>0 THEN NR=CVI(MID$(REC$,T2+T*K,2)): GOTO 49545 ELSE 49575
49572 NEXT
49574 IF NN <> 0 THEN NR = NN: GOTO 49545 ELSE PRINT "Not found": GOTO 50200
49575 PRINT:PRINT "Not found": GOTO 50200
49576 '----------- found W$ in tree; retrieve from storage -----------
49577 STORE = CVI(MID$(REC$, T3 + T*K, 2))
49579 GET BUF1, STORE
49580 PRINT:PRINT "Storage file contents and number of times entered:": PRINT WD$,
CVI(LEFT$(MN$,2))
49582 GOTO 50200
49585 '===========================================================
49587 '               input routine
49588 '===========================================================
49590 '---------- deletions ------------------
49600 GOSUB 65320: PRINT "To delete any existing keyword, type keyword now;"
49605 PRINT"or use any * command to do other functions";
```

```
49610 INPUT WWW$: IF LEFT$(WWW$,1) = "*" THEN 49650
49612 K$ = STRING$(T1," ")
49614 MID$(K$,1) = WWW$
49616 GOTO 30110
49640 '---------- deal with commands --------------
49650 IF MID$(WWW$,2,2) = "lc" THEN 18800 'lexical listing
49655 IF MID$(WWW$,2,2)="at" THEN PRINT "Record number":GOTO 64000 'see tree allocation
list
49657 IF MID$(WWW$,2,2)="as" THEN PRINT "Record number":GOTO 65000 'see word file
allocation list
49660 IF MID$(WWW$,2,2) = "lr" THEN 60000 'list in reverse order
49675 IF MID$(WWW$,2,2) = "ut" THEN 22250 'see tree structure
49685 IF MID$(WWW$,2,2) = "in" THEN 50000 'install word
49688 IF MID$(WWW$,2,2) = "de" THEN 49600 'delete word
49690 IF MID$(WWW$,2,2) = "se" THEN 50200 'search for word
49695 IF MID$(WWW$,2,2) = "qu" THEN GOSUB 53000: PRINT "bye bye"
49698 END
49700 PRINT "Invalid command": GOTO 49600
49722 '---------- installation ----------------
50000 GOSUB 65320: PRINT "To install any keyword, type keyword now;"
50001 PRINT"or use any * command to do other functions";
50002 INPUT WWW$
50005 IF LEFT$(WWW$,1) = "*" THEN 49650
50010 word$ = STRING$(T1," ")
50020 MID$(word$,1) = WWW$
50100 GOTO 3100
50190 ' ---------- search procedure ----------------------
50200 GOSUB 65320: PRINT "To search for any keyword, type keyword now;"
50205 PRINT"or use any * command to do other functions";
50210 INPUT WWW$
50220 IF LEFT$(WWW$,1) = "*" THEN 49650
50230 W$ = STRING$(T1," ")
50240 MID$(W$,1) = WWW$
50250 GOTO 49520
50251 '
52990 '============================================================
52994 '           up date control record
52998 '============================================================
53000 LSET REC$ = MKI$(root) + MKI$(count)
53010 LSET LE$ = MKI$(TALLOC) + MKI$(SALLOC)
53050 PUT BUF2,1
53060 RETURN
53061 '
59990 '============================================================
59994 '           reverse transversal of btree (right to left)
59998 '============================================================
60000 IF count=0 THEN PRINT "No words in file": GOTO 49600
60010 PRINT "Total words in file: "; count
60012 PRINT "order";TAB(14) "storage word and number of times entered"
60090 '
60100 STACK=0: E=0
60140 NR(STACK)=root
60150 '---------- search down to leaf page ----------------------
61000 GET BUF2, NR(STACK)
61005 NO(STACK)=CVI(MID$(LE$,3,2)):NR(STACK+1)=CVI(MID$(LE$,1,2)):TV(STACK)=NO(STACK)-1
```

```
61010 IF NR(STACK+1)<>0 THEN STACK=STACK+1: GOTO 61000
61015 '
61017 '----------------- read leaf page ------------------------------
61020 FOR I=NO(STACK)-1 TO 0 STEP -1
61030 TRANSVERSE = I: GOSUB 21800
61035 NEXT I
61037 IF NR(STACK)=root THEN PRINT "DONE": GOTO 49600
61038 '
61040 '------------- ascend from leaf page -----------------------
61045 STACK=STACK-1
61055 GET BUF2, NR(STACK)
61065 IF TV(STACK)=-1 THEN IF STACK<>0 GOTO 61200 ELSE PRINT "DONE": GOTO 49600
61070 TRANSVERSE = TV(STACK): GOSUB 21800
61095 TV(STACK)=TV(STACK)-1
61105 STACK=STACK+1: NR(STACK)=CVI(MID$(REC$, T2 + T*(TV(STACK-1)+1), 2))
61110 GET BUF2, NR(STACK): NO(STACK)=CVI(MID$(LE$,3,2)): GOTO 61020
61195 '
61197 ' ----------- ascend from node page --------------------------
61200 STACK=STACK-1
61210 GET BUF2, NR(STACK)
61220 IF TV(STACK)=-1 THEN IF STACK<>0 THEN 61200 ELSE PRINT "DONE": GOTO 49600
61230 TRANSVERSE = TV(STACK): GOSUB 21800
61240 TV(STACK)=TV(STACK)-1
61250 STACK=STACK+1
61255 NR(STACK)=CVI(MID$(REC$,T2+T*(TV(STACK-1)+1),2)): GOTO 61000
63990 '============================================================
63992 ' print the record numbers of the tree allocation list
63994 '============================================================
64000 IF TALLOC=-1 THEN PRINT "tree reallocation list empty": GOTO 50000
64050 TAM=TALLOC 'save TALLOC, use TAM for this routine
64070 GET BUF2, TAM
64100 PRINT TAM
64200 TAM=CVI(MID$(LE$,1,2))
64300 IF TAM=-1 THEN 50000 ELSE 64070
64990 '============================================================
64995 ' print the record numbers of the word allocation list
64997 '============================================================
65000 IF SALLOC=-1 THEN PRINT "word reallocation list empty": GOTO 50000
65050 TAM=SALLOC
65070 GET BUF1, TAM
65100 PRINT TAM
65200 TAM=CVI(MID$(WD$,1,2))
65300 IF TAM=-1 THEN 50000 ELSE 65070
65310 '=============================================================
65320 ' print main menu for user
65330 ' ============================================================
65350 PRINT
65360 PRINT "************** COMMANDS *************************"
65370 PRINT "***********************************************"
65380 PRINT " *in = Install (add) keyword to B-tree."
65390 PRINT " *de = Delete a keyword from B-tree."
65395 PRINT " *se = Search for keyword."
65400 PRINT " *lc = List storage in order (lexical listing)."
65420 PRINT " *lr = List storage in reverse order"
65422 PRINT " *ut = Utility to show B-tree structure."
```

```
65424 PRINT " *as = Show storage file allocation list."
65426 PRINT " *at = Show B-tree allocation list."
65430 PRINT " *qu = Save pointers and quit program."
65440 PRINT "**************************************************"
65450 PRINT "***** Number of database entries:";count;" **************"
65455 PRINT
65460 RETURN
```

APPENDIX D

Generating a Table of B-tree Page Lengths to Control Waste

As we discussed in the book, some people might be very concerned about waste (Waste is the amount of blank characters at the end of a B-tree page when the page is full of elements). In order to deal with waste, you need a program that calculates it for you. The program in this chapter does that.

On the next page is a program that will generate a table that tells you how much wasted space you have in a full B-tree page for a given sized keyword. You can, of course, adapt this program to do pages that are not 512 bytes long.

```
10 ' Appendix D - Program for finding waste
20 ' This is waste.bas
30 ' The purpose of this program is to take a keyword length given by
the user
40 ' and calculate the amount of waste in a 512 byte page and several
50 ' multiples of 512 bytes (we set the program to go up to 10 multiples
60 ' of 512 bytes for a 5,120 byte page length. You can easily change
it.
70 CLS
80 PRINT "*******************************************"
85 PRINT "******* Calculating waste in a B-tree page *******"
90 PRINT "*******************************************"
100 PRINT:PRINT "What is the length of your keyword";:INPUT key
112 PRINT:PRINT "Here is your waste:"
114 PRINT:PRINT " Page
length";TAB(20)"elements";TAB(34)"waste";TAB(45)"% of page wasted"
110 element = key +4 :' ** there is a 2 byte element pointer and a 2
byte storage file pointer.
120 page = 512 : ' This is the length of our desired page
130 FOR x=1 TO 10
140 thispage = (page * x)-4: ' *** We need to subtract the page pointer
and element counter at end of page
150 times = INT(thispage/element)
160 waste=thispage-(times*element)
170 Pwaste=(waste/(thispage+4))*100
180 PRINT USING "###########,";thispage+4;times; waste;:PRINT USING
"##########,.##%";Pwaste
200 NEXT x
210 PRINT:PRINT "Would you like to try another keyword (Y) or (N)
";:LINE INPUT Y$
215 IF Y$="Y" OR Y$="y" THEN 70 ELSE IF Y$="N" OR Y$="n" THEN END
220 GOTO 210
```

APPENDIX E

License and Disclaimer

The "TeachBase" program printed in this book in Appendix C is licensed by Baldar for your use only on the terms and conditions set forth below. Use of the program indicates your acceptance of these terms and conditions. If you do not agree with them, return the program and your money will be refunded.

1. **License.** Baldar hereby grants you a non-exclusive, non-transferable license for the "TeachBase" program ("the program"), subject to all of the following terms and conditions, but only:

   a. To use the program on any computer in your possession, but on no more than one computer at any time;

   b. To make one copy of the program for back-up purposes only;

   c. To modify the program or merge the program into another computer program for your own internal use (any such merged portion of the program to continue to be subject to the terms and conditions of this agreement);

   d. To modify the program by incorporating the program into other computer programs or by adding code to the program to create application programs;

   e. To compile the human-readable version of the program as incorporated in an application program into machine-readable form; and

   f. To copy the machine-readable version of the program as incorporated in an application program and to license or otherwise distribute machine-readable versions of application programs without the payment of a royalty hereunder. "Application programs" are programs which incorporate all or any portion of the program but which contain significant added functionality over that of the program such that the primary reason a person wishes to use the application program is other than to use the program.

2. **Limitations on license.**

   a. Baldar owns the program and its associated documentation and all copyrights therein. you may not use, copy, modify or transfer the program, its associated documentation, or any copy, modification or merged portion thereof, in whole or in part, except as expressly provided in this agreement. you must reproduce and include Baldar's copyright notices on any copy or modification, or any portion thereof, of the program and its associated documentation.

b. The program may be used only in connection with a single computer. you may physically transfer the program from one computer to another, provided that the program is used in connection with only one computer at any given time. you may not transfer the program electronically from one computer to another over a network. you may not distribute copies of the program except as expressly provided for in this license. if you transfer possession of any copy, modification or merged portion of the program to another party, except as expressly provided for in this license, your license shall be automatically terminated.

3. **No warranty of performance.** The program is licensed "as is" without warranty as to its performance, merchantability or fitness for any particular purpose. the entire risk as to the results and performance of the program is assumed by you. should the program prove defective, you (and not Baldar or its dealer) assume the entire cost of all necessary servicing, repair or correction.

4. **Limitation of liability.** Neither Baldar nor any other person who has been involved in the creation, production or delivery of the program shall be liable to you or to any other person for any direct, incidental or consequential damages, including but not limited to any lost data, re-run time, inaccurate input, work delays or lost profits, resulting from the use of the program or its associated documentation, even if Baldar has been advised of the possibility of such damages.

5. **Term.** The license granted hereunder is effective until terminated. you may terminate it at any time by destroying the program together with all copies, modifications and merged portions thereof in any form, with the exception of application programs. it will also terminate upon the conditions set forth elsewhere in this agreement or if you fail to comply with any term or condition of this agreement. you agree upon such termination to destroy the program and its associated documentation, together with all copies, modification and merged portions thereof in any form, with the exception of application programs.

6. **General.**

a. You may not sublicense the program or its associated documentation or assign or transfer this license except as expressly provided in this agreement. any attempt otherwise to sublicense, assign or transfer any of the rights, duties or obligations hereunder shall be void.

b. This agreement shall be governed by the laws of the state of California.

c. Should you have any questions concerning this agreement, you may write to: Baldar, P.O. Box 4340, Berkeley, California 94704, USA.

d. Your use of the program serves as an acknowledgment that you have read this agreement, and understand and agree to be bound by its terms and conditions. you further agree that this agreement is the complete and exclusive agreement between Baldar and you and supersedes any proposal or prior agreement, oral or written, and any other communications between you and Baldar relating to the subject matter of this agreement.

Glossary

A

Absorbing page: This resulting page in element pointer leaf absorption, containing both of the former pages and the pointing ancestor page element is called the absorbing page. The absorbing page is configured as follows: first, in their former order, are the elements of the too-small page; second, the pointing ancestor page element; and third, the elements of the right adjacent page, also in their former order.

Absorption: If the adjacent page is so small that you cannot borrow elements from it without it becoming unbalanced, then the too-small page can be absorbed into the adjacent page and this process is defined as absorption. In the case of branch pages we have to be aware of the pointers on the ancestor level; this is particularly true if the elements are absorbed into adjacent pages.

Ancestor branch: In database literature, and in this book, you will frequently find terms from the field of geneology used. Suppose you are looking at a family tree. Select any person on the tree. This person is obviously the child of the persons above them, their parents.You also can say that everyone above this child are the child's ancestors. Expect to see these terms child, parent and ancestor used in the literature. It is a direct analogy. The element pointer of one element points to that elements child, etc.

Appropriate adjacent page: The page we borrow from in the balancing process. If it is an element pointer, we check the adjacent page on the right; if it is a page pointer, we check the adjacent page to the left. If the appropriate adjacent page contains N+1 or more elements, we borrow one or more elements from it.

Ascend from a branch: Ascending from a leaf is no longer possible when we have just read a leaf pointed to by a page pointer. In the case where the root page is above our branch page, we go to the root page and read the number until t we have read all the keywords below and including the number . We then move over to the next keyword and, following the element pointers we drop to the lowest keyword on the leaf page. Then we repeat the keyword reading procedure until all the keywords are read.

Ascend from a leaf: Readout all the keywords on this smallest leaf in sequential order and ascend to the page above it to readout the keyword that pointed to our leaf. Then follow the element pointer of the next keyword on the page to the leaf it points to. After reading that leaf, again ascend, and this time there are no more elements. So we follow the page pointer. We repeat this process until we have read all the keywords in the leaf page pointed to by the page pointer.

B

B-tree: A random access file with a record number, called a pointer, in each record that tells you what record to go to next in order to list all the records in the file in order.

B trees*: This is a variation on B-trees put forth by Knuth [1973]. The idea is that if you are doing redistribution upon addition, then your pages are pretty full most of the time. Therefore, when it comes time to split a page, instead of splitting one record to get two records, each of which are about half-full, why not take the adjacent page to the page you are about to split, which should also be fairly full, and use it in the splitting process, causing a 2 to 3 split instead of a 1 to

2 split? The result will be pages that are 2/3 full instead of only half-full. This, of course, will require a rewrite of the procedures for deletion and redistribution.

Balancing: Trying to equalize the number of elements on the pages to give the B-tree a more balanced structure by borrowing element(s). When we say balance we mean that we want to finish the borrowing procedure with an equal number of elements on the two pages involved in the borrowing.

Branch level: In any tree, the levels between the root level and the leaf level are called branch levels, and the pages on these levels are called branch pages (also sometimes called "node" pages). Like the root page (unless the root page is the only page on the tree), branch pages are created with element pointers and page pointers, which point to pages on the level below.

Buffering of pages: Holding the root page in memory, because you will always be asking for it and it saves making a lot of disk accesses. It is possible, of course, to hold other pages in memory as well. The most called-for pages are usually the pages close to the root, and you can select the first few levels to put in memory.

C

Child branch: (See *Ancestor* definition)

D

Deletion element: When you decide that you want to delete a non-leaf element, we define this as the deletion element.

E

Element: This is defined as our keyword plus any "pointers" associated with the keyword.

Element pointer: This points to a page on the next lower level; all the elements on the page pointed to are less than the element that pointed to that page. The pointer associated with each element, by definition, is called an element pointer. Each element has only one element pointer.

Element-pointer balancing: When the too-small page is pointed to by an element pointer, we add the pointing element on the ancestor page to the end of it. Then, we remove the first element in the right adjacent page and put it in the place formerly occupied by that ancestor element. If another element will be borrowed, we repeat this process until all the borrowing has been completed.

Element-pointer leaf-absorption: The too-small page is absorbed into its right adjacent page. During this process, the element on the ancestor page that pointed to the too-small page is also absorbed into the right adjacent page.

I

Immediate predecessor element: The element that immediately precedes the element under discussion in value.

K

Keyword: a block of data which is the same length for every entry because we are using a random access file, and random access file records have a fixed length.

L

Leaf: The bottom level in any tree.

Lexical listing: In this sequence, numbers come first, then capital letters and then small letters, etc. ; our B-tree is kept in this order. You will note that everything is in numerical and alphabetical order with the exception that the entire alphabet in lowercase characters comes after the uppercase characters. You need to be aware of this because you would otherwise wonder why the keyword "Xapple" came before the keyword "apple".

Lifted: When the addition of a new element forces page splitting, the middle element of the old page is "lifted" to form a new root page.

Listing: Reading a B-tree's elements in ascending order. We accomplish this task by a simple algorithm.

LRU replacement: An arrangement where the pages held in memory are the pages that are called for the most frequently. For example, we could hold in memory the pages visited during insertion, so we don't have to get them if splitting is required. The pages visited during descent to a leaf during transversal should also be kept, because we will use them again.

M

Maximum tree: A B-tree whose pages all contain twice the order, which will grow to the least height and give the best performance. We can also call this tree *maximally loaded.*

Minimum tree: A B-tree, whose pages all contain order number of elements, with the root page containing a single element, which will grow to the greatest height and give the worst-case performance. We also call such a tree *minimally loaded*.

MKI$ format: BASIC's short integer format which converts all positive integers from 0 to 32,000 into a two-character expression.

N

NO(ST): The number of elements in page NR(ST).

NR(ST): The page number at level ST that you passed through on your way down; there can only be one page number at level ST that you pass through on your way down.

O

Order: The order of a B-tree can be any number greater than 1. It is the minimum number of elements any non-root page must contain. Also, the maximum number of elements any page may contain is defined as twice the order. The root page is the only exception to this rule, since it may contain as little as one element.

Order class: The order class refers to the whole range of orders searchable with a particular number of comparisons. For example, pages of orders 16 through 31 which can be searched in five comparisons, $\log_2 16 + 1$, are in Order Class 16; similarly Order Class 32 comprises pages of orders 32 through 63 that can be searched in six comparisons $\log_2 32 + 1$, and so forth.

Oversized pages: pages of lengths greater than 512 bytes.

P

Page: Each record in a B-tree file is a page.

Page pointer. The pointer on the end of each branch page is defined as the page pointer for that page, pointing to a page on the next level, all of whose elements are greater than any element on the page with the pointer. Each branch page has only one page pointer.

Page pointer borrowing: When the too-small page is pointed to by a page pointer, we take the last element on the ancestor page and place it at the beginning of the too-small page. We then remove the last element of the left adjacent page and write it onto the place formerly occupied by that ancestor element. Then, if another element is to be borrowed, we repeat the process until all the borrowing has been completed.

Page-pointer leaf-absorption: The too-small page is pointed to by the page pointer on its ancestor page. In this case, the too-small page absorbs the left adjacent page, which is always the page pointed to by the last element on the ancestor page. This last element on the ancestor page is also absorbed into the too-small page. Thus, the left adjacent page is completely wiped out, and the too-small page becomes configured as follows: first, there are all the elements of the left-adjacent page; second is the last element on the pointing ancestor page; and third, all the elements of the too-small page. Once the absorbing page is finally configured, we must remove the pointing element from the ancestor page.

Parent: See *Ancestor* definition.

Pointer: A pointer is defined as either a record number or the file name of a foreign file. In short, the pointer is used to tell you where to go to next.

Processing time: The time involved in processing pages consisting of a multiple of sectors, as opposed to pages consisting of a single sector.

R

Real time: This term means the list is instantly sorted as soon as you enter an item ("in real time"): you never have to stop and sort the file into order.

recsize: The size of a sector.

Redistribution upon addition: This is a routine that can be added to the B-tree to inspect and balance the pages as a keyword is entered.

Root: The top level of a B-tree, or root, consists of a single page, the root page.

S

Search tree: A numerically, alphabetically or otherwise ordered B-tree, which can be in either ascending or descending order.

Sectors: The hard disc's operating system employs a grid by creating concentric electronic bands, called tracks, that start from the center and emanate out (much like the rings in a tree). Each of these tracks are then segmented into 512-byte sections, called sectors.

Seek time: The average amount of time (actually, statistical mean time) that it takes a hard disk to find a random sector. (also see transfer time definition).

Simple leaf deletion: When you can delete an element without having fewer elements than the order of the tree afterward. This, is the simplest of all possible cases of tree deletion. We can simply remove the element from the page and be done with the deletion of that element; the B-tree requires no further modification. We refer to this type of deletion as simple leaf deletion.

Splitting:When the page is full, the addition of another element forces the splitting of this root page to form another page as well as a new root page.

ST: Stacking variable; it indicates the level under discussion.

T

Too-small page: If the order of the B-tree is N and the deletion of an element from a page leaves N-1 elements on the page, we will call this the too-small page; the B-tree is said to be unbalanced and does not conform to B-tree rules.

Storage file: A random access file that is separate from our B-tree file; every time you enter a keyword into the B-tree system, the keyword not only goes into the B-tree file, but we will make a copy of the keyword and stick it in the storage file as well. Then a short integer (MKI$) pointer is attached to your keyword to keep track of it in the storage file. So our storage file will consist of records that are just a few bytes longer than our keyword (the extra few bytes will be explained shortly) and each keyword on the B-tree will have a unique record in the storage file which will be pointed to by a "storage pointer" that comes after the keyword.

Transfer time: Once a sector has been located and the read head mechanically positioned at the start of a sector of data, there is some time needed to transfer the data to memory. The time required to transfer one sector of data to memory we define as transfer time and it is much faster than the seek time.

TV(ST): The next element to be read in page NR(ST).

U

Unbalanced: If the order of the B-tree is N and the deletion of an element from a page leaves N-1 elements on the page, we will call this the too-small page; the B-tree is said to be unbalanced and does not conform to B-tree rules.

Index

T

U

V

W

*Symbols-page 76

Notes

Notes

Notes

TeachBase Software

Order your copy of "TeachBase Software". Here are the items you will receive:

1) **TeachBase Programs** - The TeachBase program itself and all the other programs in the book - this saves you typing errors.

2) **Data Generator Program** - This program will generate a "Data File" with as many records as you like.

3) **Data Editor Program** - Editor for file made by the file generator. This allows you to go into the file created above and change any record or read what has been input.

4) **Input B-tree Program** - This program is the same as the TeachBase program except it has been modified to automatically read in all the contents of a foreign file (such as the one created with your file generator).

All of the above programs are in interpreted BASIC and easy to edit if you wish. With them you can create a file of whatever size records and whatever file length you want, edit the file, and then have it automatically read into your TeachBase B-tree system. The TeachBase program can then be called to work with the newly created database.

Cost: $45.00
Major credit cards & phone orders accepted.

Contact:
BALDAR
P.O. Box 4340
Berkeley, California
94704 USA

Telephone (800) 367-0930 or (510) 841-2474
FAX (510) 841-2695

www.ingramcontent.com/pod-product-compliance
Lightning Source LLC
Chambersburg PA
CBHW060537060326
40690CB00017B/3516

* 9 7 8 0 8 9 4 9 6 0 0 8 6 *